Measuring computer performance

A practitioner's guide

Measuring computer performance sets out the fundamental techniques used in analyzing and understanding the performance of computer systems. Throughout the book, the emphasis is on practical methods of measurement, simulation and analytical modeling.

The author discusses performance metrics and provides detailed coverage of the strategies used in benchmark programs. He gives intuitive explanations of the key statistical tools needed to interpret measured performance data. He also describes the general 'design of experiments' technique, and shows how the maximum amount of information can be obtained for the minimum effort. The book closes with a chapter on the technique of queueing analysis.

Appendices listing common probability distributions and statistical tables are included, along with a glossary of important technical terms. This practically oriented book will be of great interest to anyone who wants a detailed, yet intuitive, understanding of computer systems performance analysis.

Measuring
computer performance

A practitioner's guide

David J. Lilja

Department of Electrical and Computer Engineering
University of Minnesota, Minneapolis

CAMBRIDGE
UNIVERSITY PRESS

PUBLISHED BY THE PRESS SYNDICATE OF THE UNIVERSITY OF CAMBRIDGE
The Pitt Building, Trumpington Street, Cambridge, United Kingdom

CAMBRIDGE UNIVERSITY PRESS
The Edinburgh Building, Cambridge CB2 2RU, UK http://www.cup.cam.ac.uk
40 West 20th Street, New York, NY 10011-4211, USA http://www.cup.org
10 Stamford Road, Oakleigh, Melbourne, 3166, Australia
Ruiz de Alarcón 13, 28014 Madrid, Spain

First published 2000

Printed in the United Kingdom at the University Press, Cambridge

Typeface Times 10.5/14pt by Keyword Typesetting Services Ltd, Wallington, Surrey

A catalogue record for this book is available from the British Library

Library of Congress Cataloguing in Publication data

Lilja, David J.
Measuring computer performance: a practitioner's guide / David J. Lilja.
p.   cm
ISBN 0 521 64105 5
1. Electronic digital computers – Evaluation – Congresses.   I. Title.
QA76.9.E94 L54   2000
004.2′4–dc21   99-057225 CIP

#NJG,244

ISBN 0 521 64105 5 hardback

To Sarah
for her unwavering love, support,
and encouragement; and to Andrew,
for helping me to remember what's really important.

Contents

11   Queueing analysis

Preface

"Education is not to reform students or amuse them or to make them expert technicians. It is to unsettle their minds, widen their horizons, inflame their intellects, teach them to think straight, if possible."

Robert M. Hutchins

Goals

Most fields of science and engineering have well-defined tools and techniques for measuring and comparing phenomena of interest and for precisely communicating results. In the field of computer science and engineering, however, there is surprisingly little agreement on how to measure something as fundamental as the performance of a computer system. For example, the speed of an automobile can be readily measured in some standard units, such as meters traveled per second. The use of these standard units then allows the direct comparison of the speed of the automobile with that of an airplane, for instance. Comparing the performance of different computer systems has proven to be not so straightforward, however.

The problems begin with a lack of agreement in the field on even the seemingly simplest of ideas, such as the most appropriate metric to use to measure performance. Should this metric be MIPS, MFLOPS, QUIPS, or seconds, for instance? The problems then continue with many researchers obtaining and reporting results using questionable and even, in many cases, incorrect methodologies. Part of this lack of rigor in measuring and reporting performance results is due to the fact that tremendous advances have been made in the performance of computers in the past several decades using an *ad hoc* 'seat-of-the-pants' approach. Thus, there was little incentive for researchers to report results in a scientifically defensible way. Consequently, these researchers never taught their students sound scientific methodologies to use when conducting their own experiments.

One of the primary goals of this text is to teach the fundamental concepts behind the tools and techniques used in computer-systems performance analysis.

While specific programs or tools are sometimes mentioned as example implementations of the concepts presented, the goal is to teach the basic ideas, not the details of specific implementations. It is purposefully not a goal to make you an expert in using a specific software tool or system instrumentation package. My belief is that, if you understand the fundamental ideas behind these tools and techniques, including the basic assumptions inherent in the tool and in any statistical methods used to interpret the measured data, you can easily figure out how to use a specific tool or technique. True proficiency with individual tools can come only when you deeply understand the concepts on the basis of which they are developed.

So, if you want to learn how to use the latest and greatest version of the hottest simulation package, for instance, go buy its user's manual. If you want to develop a deeper understanding of the field of performance analysis, however, keep reading. When you then decide to use that exciting new software package, you will understand how to interpret its results in a meaningful way. Also you will, I hope, have developed some insight into the potential benefits and hazards that it may present.

Philosophy

The question of which topics to include in a text, and, perhaps more importantly, which topics to omit, has as many different answers as there are potential authors. So does the related question of how to treat each topic. Some authors would prefer to take a more mathematically rigorous approach to the topics than I have used in this text, perhaps, or they may choose to emphasize different aspects of the selected topics. Many, perhaps even most, texts on computer-systems performance analysis tend to focus on analytical modeling techniques from a rather mathematical point of view. While this is an important topic with an extensive body of literature, I chose in this text to instead emphasize practical tools and techniques that I have found to be useful in analyzing and evaluating the performance of a variety of different types of computer systems.

Furthermore, standard statistical tools, such as the analysis-of-variance (ANOVA) tests and the design-of-experiments concepts, have not found their way into the fabric of the computer-systems research community. This lack of statistical rigor has been a major weakness in the field of computer-systems performance-analysis. Consequently, I have chosen to present many practical statistical tools and techniques that are not commonly taught in a performance analysis course. While many of these ideas are presented in introductory probability and statistics courses, I have found that a surprisingly large number of computer engineering and computer science students never really learned these tools and techniques. Many, in fact, have never even been exposed to the ideas.

Instead of providing detailed mathematical derivations of these tools and techniques, though, I prefer to provide a more intuitive sense of why we might choose a certain type of statistical analysis, for instance. I want you to learn how to apply the appropriate tools and techniques so that you will become more thorough and careful in the experiments and analyses you perform. There are many other textbooks available if you then want to continue your studies into the deeper mathematical underpinnings of these tools and techniques.

Organization

The first chapter begins with an introduction to the basic ideas of measurement, simulation, and analytical modeling. It also describes some of the common goals of computer-systems performance analysis. The problem of choosing an appropriate metric of performance is discussed in Chapter 2, along with some basic definitions of speedup and relative change.

The next three chapters provide an intuitive development of several important statistical tools and techniques. Chapter 3 presents standard methods for quantifying average performance and variability. It also introduces the controversy surrounding the problem of deciding which of several definitions of the mean value is most appropriate for summarizing a set of measured values. The model of measurement errors developed in Chapter 4 is used to motivate the need for statistical confidence intervals. The ideas of accuracy, precision, and resolution of measurement tools are also presented in this chapter. Techniques for comparing various system alternatives in a statistically valid way are described in Chapter 5. This presentation includes an introduction to the analysis of variance (ANOVA), which is one of the fundamental statistical analysis techniques used in subsequent chapters.

While Chapters 3–5 focus on the use and interpretation of measured data, the next two chapters emphasize tools and techniques for actually obtaining these data. Chapter 6 begins with a discussion of the concept of events. It also describes several different types of measurement tools and techniques, including interval timers, basic block counting, execution-time sampling, and indirect measurement. The underlying ideas behind the development of benchmark programs are presented in Chapter 7, along with a brief description of several standard benchmark suites.

Chapter 8 uses a discussion of linear regression modeling to introduce the idea of developing a mathematical model of a system from measured data. Chapter 9 presents techniques for designing experiments to maximize the amount of information obtained while minimizing the amount of effort required to obtain this information.

Up to this point, the text has focused on gathering and analyzing measurements of existing computer systems. The fundamental problems involved in simulating systems are discussed in Chapter 10. The standard simulation strategies are presented along with a description of how the sequences of random numbers that are often needed to drive simulations can be generated. Finally, Chapter 11 concludes the text with a presentation of the fundamental analytical modeling techniques derived from queuing theory.

A glossary of some of the more important terms used in the text is presented in Appendix A. Several common probability distributions that are frequently used in simulation modeling are described in Appendix B. Appendix C tabulates critical values used in many of the statistical tests described in the earlier chapters.

While suggestions for further reading are provided at the end of each chapter, they by no means comprise an exhaustive bibliography of the field of computer-systems performance analysis. Rather, they are intended to guide the curious reader towards additional information that I have found to be both useful and interesting in my own research, in teaching my performance-analysis course, and in preparing this text.

Some exercises are provided at the end of each chapter to help the reader focus on some interesting aspects of the chapter's topic that are not covered in detail within the text. They also should help provide instructors using this book within a course with some ideas for further homework and project assignments.

Suggestions for using this text

This book is intended to be used as the primary text in a one-semester course for advanced undergraduate and beginning graduate students in computer science and engineering who need to understand how to rigorously measure the performance of computer systems. It should also prove useful as a supplemental text for students in other computer science and engineering courses who need to understand performance. It would make a good supplement for a course on high-performance computer architecture or high-speed computer networking, for instance.

This text will also be useful as a reference text for professional engineers and scientists who use computers in their daily work, or who design systems that incorporate computers as their primary control elements. Application experts from any discipline should also find this book useful in helping to understand how to analyze the performance of their systems and applications.

Acknowledgements

"The reason universities have students is so they can teach the professors."
John Wheeler, "No Ordinary Genius," p. 44.

I have had the pleasure of teaching a course on computer-systems performance analysis many times over the past several years. One of the advantages of this teaching has been the opportunity to practice many of the concepts and ideas presented in this text on (mostly) willing subjects. With that in mind, I would like to thank all of the students who have enrolled in this course over the years. Their insightful comments and feedback, both direct and indirect, helped me test out many of the following explanations and derivations. I especially would like to thank the students who enrolled in EE/CS 5863 in Spring quarter 1999. They gamefully waded their way through an early draft of this text as they tried to keep up with the course itself. Their comments and feedback on what did and did not work in the text are very much appreciated. Any remaining lack of clarity and errors are entirely my fault, however.

I also would like to thank Philip Meyler of Cambridge University Press for his comments on an early draft and for his efforts in helping transform the manuscript into an actual textbook; Steven Holt for his thorough and careful copyediting; and all of the other individuals at the Press for their efforts in shepherding this book through the entire publication process.

1   Introduction

'Performance can be bad, but can it ever be wrong?'

Jim Kohn, SGI/Cray Research, Inc.

1.1   Measuring performance

If the automobile industry had followed the same development cycles as the computer industry, it has been speculated that a Rolls Royce car would cost less than $100 with an efficiency of more than 200 miles per gallon of gasoline. While we certainly get more car for our money now than we did twenty years ago, no other industry has ever changed at the incredible rate of the computer and electronics industry.

Computer systems have gone from being the exclusive domain of a few scientists and engineers who used them to speed up some esoteric computations, such as calculating the trajectory of artillery shells, for instance, to being so common that they go unnoticed. They have replaced many of the mechanical control systems in our cars, thereby reducing cost while improving efficiency, reliability, and performance. They have made possible such previously science-fiction-like devices as cellular phones. They have provided countless hours of entertainment for children ranging in age from one to one hundred. They have even brought sound to the common greeting card. One constant throughout this proliferation and change, however, has been the need for system developers and users to understand the *performance* of these computer-based devices.

While measuring the cost of a system is usually relatively straightforward (except for the confounding effects of manufacturers' discounts to special customers), determining the performance of a computer system can oftentimes seem like an exercise in futility. Surprisingly, one of the main difficulties in measuring performance is that reasonable people often disagree strongly on how performance should be measured or interpreted, and even on what 'performance' actually means.

Performance analysis as applied to experimental computer science and engineering should be thought of as a combination of *measurement, interpretation,* and *communication* of a computer system's 'speed' or 'size' (sometimes referred to as its 'capacity'). The terms speed and size are quoted in this context to emphasize that their actual definitions often depend on the specifics of the situation. Also, it is important to recognize that we need not necessarily be dealing with complete systems. Often it is necessary to analyze only a small portion of the system independent of the other components. For instance, we may be interested in studying the performance of a certain computer system's network interface independent of the size of its memory or the type of processor. Unfortunately, the components of a computer system can interact in incredibly complex, and frequently unpredictable, ways. One of the signs of an expert computer performance analyst is that he or she can tease apart these interactions to determine the performance effect due only to a particular component.

One of the most interesting tasks of the performance analyst can be figuring out how to measure the necessary data. A large dose of creativity may be needed to develop good measurement techniques that perturb the system as little as possible while providing accurate, reproducible results. After the necessary data have been gathered, the analyst must interpret the results using appropriate statistical techniques. Finally, even excellent measurements interpreted in a statistically appropriate fashion are of no practical use to anyone unless they are communicated in a clear and consistent manner.

1.2   Common goals of performance analysis

The goals of any analysis of the performance of a computer system, or one of its components, will depend on the specific situation and the skills, interests, and abilities of the analyst. However, we can identify several different typical goals of performance analysis that are useful both to computer-system designers and to users.

- **Compare alternatives.** When purchasing a new computer system, you may be confronted with several different systems from which to choose. Furthermore, you may have several different options within each system that may impact both cost and performance, such as the size of the main memory, the number of processors, the type of network interface, the size and number of disk drives, the type of system software (i.e., the operating system and compilers), and on and on. The goal of the performance analysis task in this case is to provide quantitative information about which configurations are best under specific conditions.

- **Determine the impact of a feature.** In designing new systems, or in upgrading existing systems, you often need to determine the impact of adding or removing a specific feature of the system. For instance, the designer of a new processor may want to understand whether it makes sense to add an additional floating-point execution unit to the microarchitecture, or whether the size of the on-chip cache should be increased instead. This type of analysis is often referred to as a *before-and-after* comparison since only one well-defined component of the system is changed.

- **System tuning.** The goal of performance analysis in system tuning is to find the set of parameter values that produces the best overall performance. In time-shared operating systems, for instance, it is possible to control the number of processes that are allowed to actively share the processor. The overall performance perceived by the system users can be substantially impacted both by this number, and by the time quantum allocated to each process. Many other system parameters, such as disk and network buffer sizes, for example, can also significantly impact the system performance. Since the performance impacts of these various parameters can be closely interconnected, finding the best set of parameter values can be a very difficult task.

- **Identify relative performance.** The performance of a computer system typically has meaning only in the context of its performance relative to something else, such as another system or another configuration of the same system. The goal in this situation may be to quantify the change in performance relative to history – that is, relative to previous generations of the system. Another goal may be to quantify the performance relative to a customer's expectations, or to a competitor's systems, for instance.

- **Performance debugging.** Debugging a program for correct execution is a fundamental prerequisite for any application program. Once the program is functionally correct, however, the performance analysis task becomes one of finding performance problems. That is, the program now produces the correct results, but it may be much slower than desired. The goal of the performance analyst at this point is to apply the appropriate tools and analysis techniques to determine why the program is not meeting performance expectations. Once the performance problems are identified, they can, it is to be hoped, be corrected.

- **Set expectations.** Users of computer systems may have some idea of what the capabilities of the next generation of a line of computer systems should be. The task of the performance analyst in this case is to set the appropriate expectations for what a system is actually capable of doing.

In all of these situations, the effort involved in the performance-analysis task should be proportional to the cost of making the wrong decision. For example, if you are comparing different manufacturers' systems to determine which best satisfies the requirements for a large purchasing decision, the financial cost of making the wrong decision could be quite substantial, both in terms of the cost of the system itself, and in terms of the subsequent impacts on the various parts of a large project or organization. In this case, you will probably want to perform a very detailed, thorough analysis. If, however, you are simply trying to choose a system for your own personal use, the cost of choosing the wrong one is minimal. Your performance analysis in this case may be correctly limited to reading a few reviews from a trade magazine.

1.3   Solution techniques

When one is confronted with a performance-analysis problem, there are three fundamental techniques that can be used to find the desired solution. These are *measurements* of existing systems, *simulation*, and *analytical modeling*. Actual measurements generally provide the best results since, given the necessary measurement tools, no simplifying assumptions need to be made. This characteristic also makes results based on measurements of an actual system the most believable when they are presented to others. Measurements of real systems are not very flexible, however, in that they provide information about only the specific system being measured. A common goal of performance analysis is to characterize how the performance of a system changes as certain parameters are varied. In an actual system, though, it may be very difficult, if not impossible, to change some of these parameters. Evaluating the performance impact of varying the speed of the main memory system, for instance, is simply not possible in most real systems. Furthermore, measuring some aspects of performance on an actual system can be very time-consuming and difficult. Thus, while measurements of real systems may provide the most compelling results, their inherent difficulties and limitations produce a need for other solution techniques.

A simulation of a computer system is a program written to model important features of the system being analyzed. Since the simulator is nothing more than a program, it can be easily modified to study the impact of changes made to almost any of the simulated components. The cost of a simulation includes both the time and effort required to write and debug the simulation program, and the time required to execute the necessary simulations. Depending on the complexity of the system being simulated, and the level of detail at which it is modeled, these costs can be relatively low to moderate compared with the cost of purchasing a real machine on which to perform the corresponding experiments.

The primary limitation of a simulation-based performance analysis is that it is impossible to model every small detail of the system being studied. Consequently, simplifying assumptions are required in order to make it possible to write the simulation program itself, and to allow it to execute in a reasonable amount of time. These simplifying assumptions then limit the accuracy of the results by lowering the fidelity of the model compared with how an actual system would perform. Nevertheless, simulation enjoys tremendous popularity for computer-systems analysis due to its high degree of flexibility and its relative ease of implementation.

The third technique in the performance analyst's toolbox is analytical modeling. An analytical model is a mathematical description of the system. Compared with a simulation or a measurement of a real machine, the results of an analytical model tend to be much less believable and much less accurate. A simple analytical model, however, can provide some quick insights into the overall behavior of the system, or one of its components. This insight can then be used to help focus a more detailed measurement or simulation experiment. Analytical models are also useful in that they provide at least a coarse level of validation of a simulation or measurement. That is, an analytical model can help confirm whether the results produced by a simulator, or the values measured on a real system, appear to be reasonable.

Example. The delay observed by an application program when accessing memory can have a significant impact on its overall execution time. Direct measurements of this time on a real machine can be quite difficult, however, since the detailed steps involved in the operation of a complex memory hierarchy structure are typically not observable from a user's application program. A sophisticated user may be able to write simple application programs that exercise specific portions of the memory hierarchy to thereby *infer* important memory-system parameters. For instance, the execution time of a simple program that repeatedly references the same variable can be used to estimate the time required to access the first-level cache. Similarly, a program that always forces a cache miss can be used to indirectly measure the main memory access time. Unfortunately, the impact of these system parameters on the execution time of a complete application program is very dependent on the precise memory-referencing characteristics of the program, which can be difficult to determine.

Simulation, on the other hand, is a powerful technique for studying memory-system behavior due to its high degree of flexibility. Any parameter of the memory, including the cache associativity, the relative cache and memory delays, the sizes of the cache and memory, and so forth, can be easily changed to study its impact on performance. It can be challenging, however, to accurately model in a simulator the overlap of memory delays and the execution of other instructions in contemporary processors that incorporate such performance-enhancing features as out-of-order instruction issuing, branch prediction, and nonblocking caches. Even with the necessary simplifying assumptions, the results of a detailed simulation can still provide useful insights into the effect of the memory system on the performance of a specific application program.

Finally, a simple analytical model of the memory system can be developed as follows. Let t_c be the time delay observed by a memory reference if the memory location being referenced is in the cache. Also, let t_m be the corresponding delay if the referenced location is not in the cache. The cache *hit ratio*, denoted h, is the fraction of all memory references issued by the processor that are satisfied by the cache. The fraction of references that *miss* in the cache and so must also access the memory is $1 - h$. Thus, the average time required for all cache hits is ht_c while the average time required for all cache misses is $(1 - h)t_m$. A simple model of the overall average memory-access time observed by an executing program then is

$$t_{avg} = ht_c + (1 - h)t_m. \tag{1.1}$$

To apply this simple model to a specific application program, we would need to know the hit ratio, h, for the program, and the values of t_c and t_m for the system. These memory-access-time parameters, t_c and t_m, may often be found in the manufacturer's specifications of the system. Or, they may be inferred through a measurement, as described above and as explored further in the exercises in Chapter 6. The hit ratio, h, for an application program is typically more difficult to obtain. It is often found through a simulation of the application, though. Although this model will provide only a very coarse estimate of the average memory-access time observed by a program, it can provide us with some insights into the relative effects of increasing the hit ratio, or changing the memory-timing parameters, for instance. ◇

The key differences among these solution techniques are summarized in Table 1.1. The *flexibility* of a technique is an indication of how easy it is to change the system to study different configurations. The *cost* corresponds to the time, effort, and money necessary to perform the appropriate experiments using each technique. The *believability* of a technique is high if a knowledgeable individual has a high degree of confidence that the result produced using that technique is likely to be correct in practice. It is much easier for someone to believe that the execution time of a given application program will be within a certain range when you can demonstrate it on an actual machine, for instance, than when relying on a mere simulation. Similarly, most people are more likely to believe the results of a simulation study than one that relies entirely on an analytical model. Finally, the *accuracy* of a solution technique indicates how closely results obtained when using that technique correspond to the results that would have been obtained on a real system.

The choice of a specific solution technique depends on the problem being solved. One of the skills that must be developed by a computer-systems performance analyst is determining which technique is the most appropriate for the

Table 1.1. A comparison of the performance-analysis solution techniques

	Solution technique		
Characteristic	Analytical modeling	Simulation	Measurement
Flexibility	High	High	Low
Cost	Low	Medium	High
Believability	Low	Medium	High
Accuracy	Low	Medium	High

given situation. The following chapters are designed to help you develop precisely this skill.

1.4 Summary

Computer-systems performance analysis often feels more like an art than a science. Indeed, different individuals can sometimes reach apparently contradictory conclusions when analyzing the same system or set of systems. While this type of ambiguity can be quite frustrating, it is often due to misunderstandings of what was actually being measured, or disagreements about how the data should be analyzed or interpreted. These differences further emphasize the need to clearly communicate all results and to completely specify the tools, techniques, and system parameters used to collect and understand the data. As you study the following chapters, my hope is that you will begin to develop an appreciation for this art of measurement, interpretation, and communication in addition to developing a deeper understanding of its mathematical and scientific underpinnings.

1.5 Exercises

1. Respond to the question quoted at the beginning of this chapter, 'Performance can be bad, but can it ever be wrong?'
2. Performance analysis should be thought of as a decision-making process. Section 1.2 lists several common goals of a performance-analysis experiment. List other possible goals of the performance-analysis decision-making process. Who are the beneficiaries of each of these possible goals?

3. Table 1.1 compares the three main performance-analysis solution techniques across several criteria. What additional criteria could be used to compare these techniques?

4. Identify the most appropriate solution technique for each of the following situations.

    (a) Estimating the performance benefit of a new feature that an engineer is considering adding to a computer system currently being designed.

    (b) Determining when it is time for a large insurance company to upgrade to a new system.

    (c) Deciding the best vendor from which to purchase new computers for an expansion to an academic computer lab.

    (d) Determining the minimum performance necessary for a computer system to be used on a deep-space probe with very limited available electrical power.

2 Metrics of performance

'Time is a great teacher, but unfortunately it kills all its pupils.'

Hector Berlioz

2.1 What is a performance metric?

Before we can begin to understand any aspect of a computer system's performance, we must determine what things are interesting and useful to measure. The basic characteristics of a computer system that we typically need to measure are:

- a *count* of how many times an event occurs,
- the *duration* of some time interval, and
- the *size* of some parameter.

For instance, we may need to count how many times a processor initiates an input/output request. We may also be interested in how long each of these requests takes. Finally, it is probably also useful to determine the number of bits transmitted and stored.

From these types of measured values, we can derive the actual value that we wish to use to describe the performance of the system. This value is called a *performance metric*.

If we are interested specifically in the time, count, or size value measured, we can use that value directly as our performance metric. Often, however, we are interested in normalizing event counts to a common time basis to provide a speed metric such as operations executed per second. This type of metric is called a *rate metric* or *throughput* and is calculated by dividing the count of the number of events that occur in a given interval by the time interval over which the events occur. Since a rate metric is normalized to a common time basis, such as seconds, it is useful for comparing different measurements made over different time intervals.

Choosing an appropriate performance metric depends on the goals for the specific situation and the cost of gathering the necessary information. For example, suppose that you need to choose between two different computer systems to use for a short period of time for one specific task, such as choosing between two systems to do some word processing for an afternoon. Since the penalty for being wrong in this case, that is, choosing the slower of the two machines, is very small, you may decide to use the processors' clock frequencies as the performance metric. Then you simply choose the system with the fastest clock. However, since the clock frequency is not a reliable performance metric (see Section 2.3.1), you would want to choose a better metric if you are trying to decide which system to buy when you expect to purchase hundreds of systems for your company. Since the consequences of being wrong are much larger in this case (you could lose your job, for instance!), you should take the time to perform a rigorous comparison using a better performance metric. This situation then begs the question of what constitutes a good performance metric.

2.2   Characteristics of a good performance metric

There are many different metrics that have been used to describe a computer system's performance. Some of these metrics are commonly used throughout the field, such as MIPS and MFLOPS (which are defined later in this chapter), whereas others are invented for new situations as they are needed. Experience has shown that not all of these metrics are 'good' in the sense that sometimes using a particular metric can lead to erroneous or misleading conclusions. Consequently, it is useful to understand the characteristics of a 'good' performance metric. This understanding will help when deciding which of the existing performance metrics to use for a particular situation, and when developing a new performance metric.

A performance metric that satisfies all of the following requirements is generally useful to a performance analyst in allowing accurate and detailed comparisons of different measurements. These criteria have been developed by observing the results of numerous performance analyses over many years. While they should not be considered absolute requirements of a performance metric, it has been observed that using a metric that does not satisfy these requirements can often lead the analyst to make erroneous conclusions.

1. **Linearity.** Since humans intuitively tend to think in linear terms, the value of the metric should be linearly proportional to the actual performance of the machine. That is, if the value of the metric changes by a certain ratio, the actual performance of the machine should change by the same ratio. This proportionality characteristic makes the metric intuitively appealing to most people. For example, suppose that you are upgrading your system to a system

whose speed metric (i.e. execution-rate metric) is twice as large as the same metric on your current system. You then would expect the new system to be able to run your application programs in half the time taken by your old system. Similarly, if the metric for the new system were three times larger than that of your current system, you would expect to see the execution times reduced to one-third of the original values.

Not all types of metrics satisfy this proportionally requirement. Logarithmic metrics, such as the dB scale used to describe the intensity of sound, for example, are nonlinear metrics in which an increase of one in the value of the metric corresponds to a factor of ten increase in the magnitude of the observed phenomenon. There is nothing inherently wrong with these types of nonlinear metrics, it is just that linear metrics tend to be more intuitively appealing when interpreting the performance of computer systems.

2. **Reliability.** A performance metric is considered to be *reliable* if system A always outperforms system B when the corresponding values of the metric for both systems indicate that system A should outperform system B. For example, suppose that we have developed a new performance metric called WIPS that we have designed to compare the performance of computer systems when running the class of word-processing application programs. We measure system A and find that it has a WIPS rating of 128, while system B has a WIPS rating of 97. We then can say that WIPS is a reliable performance metric for word-processing application programs if system A always outperforms system B when executing these types of applications.

While this requirement would seem to be so obvious as to be unnecessary to state explicitly, several commonly used performance metrics do not in fact satisfy this requirement. The MIPS metric, for instance, which is described further in Section 2.3.2, is notoriously unreliable. Specifically, it is not unusual for one processor to have a higher MIPS rating than another processor while the second processor actually executes a specific program in less time than does the processor with the higher value of the metric. Such a metric is essentially useless for summarizing performance, and we say that it is unreliable.

3. **Repeatability.** A performance metric is *repeatable* if the same value of the metric is measured each time the same experiment is performed. Note that this also implies that a good metric is deterministic.

4. **Easiness of measurement.** If a metric is not easy to measure, it is unlikely that anyone will actually use it. Furthermore, the more difficult a metric is to measure directly, or to derive from other measured values, the more likely

it is that the metric will be determined incorrectly. The only thing worse than a bad metric is a metric whose value is measured incorrectly.

5. **Consistency.** A *consistent* performance metric is one for which the units of the metric and its precise definition are the same across different systems and different configurations of the same system. If the units of a metric are not consistent, it is impossible to use the metric to compare the performances of the different systems. While the necessity for this characteristic would also seem obvious, it is not satisfied by many popular metrics, such as MIPS (Section 2.3.2) and MFLOPS (Section 2.3.3).

6. **Independence.** Many purchasers of computer systems decide which system to buy by comparing the values of some commonly used performance metric. As a result, there is a great deal of pressure on manufacturers to design their machines to optimize the value obtained for that particular metric, and to influence the composition of the metric to their benefit. To prevent corruption of its meaning, a good metric should be *independent* of such outside influences.

2.3   Processor and system performance metrics

A wide variety of performance metrics has been proposed and used in the computer field. Unfortunately, many of these metrics are not good in the sense defined above, or they are often used and interpreted incorrectly. The following subsections describe many of these common metrics and evaluate them against the above characteristics of a good performance metric.

2.3.1   The clock rate

In many advertisements for computer systems, the most prominent indication of performance is often the frequency of the processor's central clock. The implication to the buyer is that a 250 MHz system must always be faster at solving the user's problem than a 200 MHz system, for instance. However, this performance metric completely ignores how much computation is actually accomplished in each clock cycle, it ignores the complex interactions of the processor with the memory subsystem and the input/output subsystem, and it ignores the not at all unlikely fact that the processor may not be the performance bottleneck.

Evaluating the clock rate against the characteristics for a good performance metric, we find that it is very repeatable (characteristic 3) since it is a constant for a given system, it is easy to measure (characteristic 4) since it is most likely stamped on the box, the value of MHz is precisely defined across all systems so that it is consistent (characteristic 5), and it is independent of any sort of manufacturers' games (characteristic 6). However, the unavoidable shortcomings of using this value as a performance metric are that it is nonlinear (characteristic 1), and unreliable (characteristic 2). As many owners of personal computer systems can attest, buying a system with a faster clock in no way assures that their programs will run correspondingly faster. Thus, we conclude that the processor's clock rate is not a good metric of performance.

2.3.2   MIPS

A *throughput* or *execution-rate* performance metric is a measure of the amount of computation performed per unit time. Since rate metrics are normalized to a common basis, such as seconds, they are very useful for comparing relative speeds. For instance, a vehicle that travels at 50 m s^{-1} will obviously traverse more ground in a fixed time interval than will a vehicle traveling at 35 m s^{-1}.

The MIPS metric is an attempt to develop a rate metric for computer systems that allows a direct comparison of their speeds. While in the physical world speed is measured as the distance traveled per unit time, MIPS defines the computer system's unit of 'distance' as the execution of an instruction. Thus, MIPS, which is an acronym for *millions of instructions executed per second*, is defined to be

$$MIPS = \frac{n}{t_e \times 10^6} \tag{2.1}$$

where t_e is the time required to execute n total instructions.

Defining the unit of 'distance' in this way makes MIPS easy to measure (characteristic 4), repeatable (characteristic 3), and independent (characteristic 6). Unfortunately, it does not satisfy any of the other characteristics of a good performance metric. It is not linear since, like the clock rate, a doubling of the MIPS rate does not necessarily cause a doubling of the resulting performance. It also is neither reliable nor consistent since it really does not correlate well to performance at all.

The problem with MIPS as a performance metric is that different processors can do substantially different amounts of computation with a single instruction. For instance, one processor may have a branch instruction that branches after checking the state of a specified condition code bit. Another processor, on the other hand, may have a branch instruction that first decrements a specified count register, and then branches after comparing the resulting value in the register with zero. In the first case, a single instruction does one simple operation, whereas in the second case, one instruction actually performs several operations. The failing of the MIPS metric is that each instruction corresponds to one unit of 'distance,' even though in this example the second instruction actually performs more real computation. These differences in the amount of computation performed by an instruction are at the heart of the differences between RISC and CISC processors and render MIPS essentially useless as a performance metric. Another derisive explanation of the MIPS acronym is *meaningless indicator of performance* since it is really no better a measure of overall performance than is the processor's clock frequency.

2.3.3   MFLOPS

The MFLOPS performance metric tries to correct the primary shortcoming of the MIPS metric by more precisely defining the unit of 'distance' traveled by a computer system when executing a program. MFLOPS, which is an acronym for *millions of floating-point operations executed per second,* defines an arithmetic operation on two floating-point (i.e. fractional) quantities to be the basic unit of 'distance.' MFLOPS is thus calculated as

$$MFLOPS = \frac{f}{t_e \times 10^6} \tag{2.2}$$

where f is the number of floating-point operations executed in t_e seconds. The MFLOPS metric is a definite improvement over the MIPS metric since the results of a floating-point computation are more clearly comparable across computer systems than is the execution of a single instruction. An important problem with this metric, however, is that the MFLOPS rating for a system executing a program that performs no floating-point calculations is exactly zero. This program may actually be performing very useful operations, though, such as searching a database or sorting a large set of records.

A more subtle problem with MFLOPS is agreeing on exactly how to count the number of floating-point operations in a program. For instance, many of the Cray vector computer systems performed a floating-point division operation using successive approximations involving the reciprocal of the denominator and several multiplications. Similarly, some processors can calculate transcendental functions, such as sin, cos, and log, in a single instruction, while others require several multiplications, additions, and table look-ups. Should these operations be counted as a single floating-point operation or multiple floating-point operations? The first method would intuitively seem to make the most sense. The second method, however, would increase the value of f in the above calculation of the MFLOPS rating, thereby artificially inflating its value. This flexibility in counting the total number of floating-point operations causes MFLOPS to violate characteristic 6 of a good performance metric. It is also unreliable (characteristic 2) and inconsistent (characteristic 5).

2.3.4   SPEC

To standardize the definition of the actual result produced by a computer system in 'typical' usage, several computer manufacturers banded together to form the System Performance Evaluation Cooperative (SPEC). This group identified a set of integer and floating-point benchmark programs that was intended to reflect the way most workstation-class computer systems were actually used. Additionally, and, perhaps, most importantly, they also standardized the methodology for measuring and reporting the performance obtained when executing these programs.

The methodology defined consists of the following key steps.

1. Measure the time required to execute each program in the set on the system being tested.
2. Divide the time measured for each program in the first step by the time required to execute each program on a standard basis machine to normalize the execution times.
3. Average together all of these normalized values using the geometric mean (see Section 3.3.4) to produce a single-number performance metric.

While the SPEC methodology is certainly more rigorous than is using MIPS or MFLOPS as a measure of performance, it still produces a problematic performance metric. One shortcoming is that averaging together the individual normalized results with the geometric mean produces a metric that is not linearly related to a program's actual execution time. Thus, the SPEC metric is not intuitive (characteristic 1). Furthermore, and more importantly, it has been shown to be an unreliable metric (characteristic 2) in that a given program may execute faster on a system that has a lower SPEC rating than it does on a competing system with a higher rating.

Finally, although the defined methodology appears to make the metric independent of outside influences (characteristic 6), it is actually subject to a wide range of tinkering. For example, many compiler developers have used these benchmarks as practice programs, thereby tuning their optimizations to the characteristics of this collection of applications. As a result, the execution times of the collection of programs in the SPEC suite can be quite sensitive to the particular selection of optimization flags chosen when the program is compiled. Also, the selection of specific programs that comprise the SPEC suite is determined by a committee of representatives from the manufacturers within the cooperative. This committee is subject to numerous outside pressures since each manufacturer has a strong interest in advocating application programs that will perform well on their machines. Thus, while SPEC is a significant step in the right direction towards defining a good performance metric, it still falls short of the goal.

2.3.5 QUIPS

The QUIPS metric, which was developed in conjunction with the HINT benchmark program, is a fundamentally different type of performance metric. (The details of the HINT benchmark and the precise definition of QUIPS are given in Section 7.2.3). Instead of defining the *effort* expended to reach a certain result as the measure of what is accomplished, the QUIPS metric defines the *quality of the solution* as a more meaningful indication of a user's final goal. The quality is rigorously defined on the basis of mathematical characteristics of the problem being solved. Dividing this measure of solution quality by the time required to achieve that level of quality produces QUIPS, or *quality improvements per second*.

This new performance metric has several of the characteristics of a good performance metric. The mathematically precise definition of 'quality' for the defined problem makes this metric insensitive to outside influences (characteristic 6) and makes it entirely self-consistent when it is ported to different machines (characteristic 5). It is also easily repeatable (characteristic 3) and it is linear (characteristic 1) since, for the particular problem chosen for the HINT benchmark, the resulting measure of quality is linearly related to the time required to obtain the solution.

Given the positive aspects of this metric, it still does present a few potential difficulties when used as a general-purpose performance metric. The primary potential difficulty is that it need not always be a reliable metric (characteristic 2) due to its narrow focus on floating-point and memory system performance. It is generally a very good metric for predicting how a computer system will perform when executing numerical programs. However, it does not exercise some aspects of a system that are important when executing other types of application programs, such as the input/output subsystem, the instruction cache, and the operating system's ability to multiprogram, for instance. Furthermore, while the developers have done an excellent job of making the HINT benchmark easy to measure (characteristic 4) and portable to other machines, it is difficult to change the quality definition. A new problem must be developed to focus on other aspects of a system's performance since the definition of quality is tightly coupled to the problem being solved. Developing a new problem to more broadly exercise the system could be a difficult task since it must maintain all of the characteristics described above.

Despite these difficulties, QUIPS is an important new type of metric that rigorously defines interesting aspects of performance while providing enough flexibility to allow new and unusual system architectures to demonstrate their capabilities. While it is not a completely general-purpose metric, it should prove to be very useful in measuring a system's numerical processing capabilities.

It also should be a strong stimulus for greater rigor in defining future performance metrics.

2.3.6 Execution time

Since we are ultimately interested in how quickly a given program is executed, the fundamental performance metric of any computer system is the time required to execute a given application program. Quite simply, the system that produces the smallest total execution time for a given application program has the highest performance. We can compare times directly, or use them to derive appropriate rates. However, without a precise and accurate measure of time, it is impossible to analyze or compare most any system performance characteristics. Consequently, it is important to know how to measure the execution time of a program, or a portion of a program, and to understand the limitations of the measuring tool.

The basic technique for measuring time in a computer system is analogous to using a stopwatch to measure the time required to perform some event. Unlike a stopwatch that begins measuring time from 0, however, a computer system typically has an internal counter that simply counts the number of clock ticks that have occurred since the system was first turned on. (See also Section 6.2.) A time interval then is measured by reading the value of the counter at the start of the event to be timed and again at the end of the event. The elapsed time is the difference between the two count values multiplied by the period of the clock ticks.

As an example, consider the program example shown in Figure 2.1. In this example, the init_timer() function initializes the data structures used to access the system's timer. This timer is a simple counter that is incremented continuously by a clock with a period defined in the variable clock_cycle. Reading the address pointed to by the variable read_count returns the current count value of the timer.

To begin timing a portion of a program, the current value in the timer is read and stored in start_count. At the end of the portion of the program being timed, the timer value is again read and stored in end_count. The difference between these two values is the total number of clock ticks that occurred during the execution of the event being measured. The total time required to execute this event is this number of clock ticks multiplied by the period of each tick, which is stored in the constant clock_cycle.

This technique for measuring the elapsed execution time of any selected portion of a program is often referred to as the *wall clock* time since it measures the total time that a user would have to wait to obtain the results produced by the program. That is, the measurement includes the time spent waiting for input/

```
main()
{
    int i;
    float a;

    init_timer();

    /* Read the starting time. */
    start_count = read_count;

    /* Stuff to be measured */
    for (i=0;i< 1000;i++){
        a = i * a / 10;
    }

    /* Read the ending time. */
    end_count = read_count;

    elapsed_time = (end_count - start_count) * clock_cycle;
}
```

Figure 2.1. An example program showing how to measure the execution time of a portion of a program.

output operations to complete, memory paging, and other system operations performed on behalf of this application, all of which are integral components of the program's execution. However, when the system being measured is time-shared so that it is not dedicated to the execution of this one application program, this elapsed execution time also includes the time the application spends waiting while other users' applications execute.

Many researchers have argued that including this time-sharing overhead in the program's total execution time is unfair. Instead, they advocate measuring performance using the total time the processor actually spends executing the program, called the total *CPU time*. This time does not include the time the program is context switched-out while another application runs. Unfortunately, using only this CPU time as the performance metric ignores the waiting time that is inherent to the application as well as the time spent waiting on other programs. A better solution is to report both the CPU time and the total execution time so the reader can determine the significance of the time-sharing interference. The point is to be explicit about what information you are actually reporting to allow the reader to decide for themselves how believable your results are.

In addition to system-overhead effects, the measured execution time of an application program can vary significantly from one run to another since the program must contend with random events, such as the execution of background operating system tasks, different virtual-to-physical page mappings and cache mappings from explicitly random replacement policies, variable system load in a time-shared system, and so forth. As a result, a program's execution time is nondeterministic. It is important, then, to measure a program's total elapsed execution time several times and report at least the mean and variance of the times. Errors in measurements, along with appropriate statistical techniques to quantify them, are discussed in more detail in Chapter 4.

When it is measured as described above, the elapsed (wall clock) time measurement produces a performance metric that is intuitive, reliable, repeatable, easy to measure, consistent across systems, and independent of outside influences. Thus, since it satisfies all of the characteristics of a good performance metric, program execution time is one of the best metrics to use when analyzing computer system performance.

2.4   Other types of performance metrics

In addition to the processor-centric metrics described above, there are many other metrics that are commonly used in performance analysis. For instance, the system *response time* is the amount of time that elapses from when a user submits a request until the result is returned from the system. This metric is often used in analyzing the performance of online transaction-processing systems, for example. System *throughput* is a measure of the number of jobs or operations that are completed per unit time. The performance of a real-time video-processing system, for instance, may be measured in terms of the number of video frames that can be processed per second. The *bandwidth* of a communication network is a throughput measure that quantifies the number of bits that can be transmitted across the network per second. Many other *ad hoc* performance metrics are defined by performance analysts to suit the specific needs of the problem or system being studied.

2.5   Speedup and relative change

Speedup and *relative change* are useful metrics for comparing systems since they normalize performance to a common basis. Although these metrics are defined in terms of throughput or speed metrics, they are often calculated directly from execution times, as described below.

Speedup. The *speedup* of system 2 with respect to system 1 is defined to be a value $S_{2,1}$ such that $R_2 = S_{2,1}R_1$, where R_1 and R_2 are the 'speed' metrics being compared. Thus, we can say that system 2 is $S_{2,1}$ times faster than system 1. Since a speed metric is really a rate metric (i.e. throughput), $R_1 = D_1/T_1$, where D_1 is analogous to the 'distance traveled' in time T_1 by the application program when executing on system 1. Similarly, $R_2 = D_2/T_2$. Assuming that the 'distance traveled' by each system is the same, $D_1 = D_2 = D$, giving the following definition for speedup:

$$\textit{Speedup of system 2 w.r.t. system 1} = S_{2,1} = \frac{R_2}{R_1} = \frac{D/T_2}{D/T_1} = \frac{T_1}{T_2}. \tag{2.3}$$

If system 2 is faster than system 1, then $T_2 < T_1$ and the speedup ratio will be larger than 1. If system 2 is slower than system 1, however, the speedup ratio will be less than 1. This situation is often referred to as a *slowdown* instead of a speedup.

Relative change. Another technique for normalizing performance is to express the performance of a system as a percent change *relative* to the performance of another system. We again use the throughput metrics R_1 and R_2 as measures of the speeds of systems 1 and 2, respectively. The relative change of system 2 with respect to system 1, denoted $\Delta_{2,1}$, (that is, using system 1 as the basis) is then defined to be

$$\textit{Relative change of system 2 w.r.t. system 1} = \Delta_{2,1} = \frac{R_2 - R_1}{R_1}. \tag{2.4}$$

Again assuming that the execution time of each system is measured when executing the same program, the 'distance traveled' by each system is the same so that $R_1 = D/T_1$ and $R_2 = D/T_2$. Thus,

$$\Delta_{2,1} = \frac{R_2 - R_1}{R_1} = \frac{D/T_2 - D/T_1}{D/T_1} = \frac{T_1 - T_2}{T_2} = S_{2,1} - 1. \tag{2.5}$$

Typically, the value of $\Delta_{2,1}$ is multiplied by 100 to express the relative change as a percentage with respect to a given basis system. This definition of relative change will produce a positive value if system 2 is faster than system 1, whereas a negative value indicates that the basis system is faster.

Example. As an example of how to apply these two different normalization techniques, the speedup and relative change of the systems shown in Table 2.1 are found using system 1 as the basis. From the raw execution times, we can easily see that system 4 is the fastest, followed by systems 2, 1, and 3, in that order. However, the speedup values give us a more precise indication of exactly how much faster one system is than the others. For instance, system 2 has a

Table 2.1. An example of calculating speedup and relative change using system 1 as the basis

System x	Execution time T_x (s)	Speedup $S_{x,1}$	Relative change $\Delta_{x,1}$ (%)
1	480	1	0
2	360	1.33	+33
3	540	0.89	−11
4	210	2.29	+129

speedup of 1.33 compared with system 1 or, equivalently, it is 33% faster. System 4 has a speedup ratio of 2.29 compared with system 1 (or it is 129% faster). We also see that system 3 is actually 11% slower than system 1, giving it a slowdown factor of 0.89.   ◇

2.6   Means versus ends metrics

One of the most important characteristics of a performance metric is that it be reliable (characteristic 2). One of the problems with many of the metrics discussed above that makes them unreliable is that they measure what was done *whether or not it was useful.* What makes a performance metric reliable, however, is that it accurately and consistently measures *progress towards a goal.* Metrics that measure what was done, useful or not, have been called *means-based* metrics whereas *ends-based* metrics measure what is actually accomplished.

To obtain a feel for the difference between these two types of metrics, consider the vector dot-product routine shown in Figure 2.2. This program executes N floating-point addition and multiplication operations for a total of $2N$ floating-point operations. If the time required to execute one addition is t_+ cycles and one multiplication requires t_* cycles, the total time required to execute this program is $t_1 = N(t_+ + t_*)$ cycles. The resulting execution rate then is

```
s = 0;
for (i = 1; i < N; i++)
    s = s + x[i] * y[i];
```

Figure 2.2. A vector dot-product example program.

$$R_1 = \frac{2N}{N(t_+ + t_*)} = \frac{2}{t_+ + t_*} \text{FLOPS/cycle}. \tag{2.6}$$

Since there is no need to perform the addition or multiplication operations for elements whose value is zero, it may be possible to reduce the total execution time if many elements of the two vectors are zero. Figure 2.3 shows the example from Figure 2.2 modified to perform the floating-point operations only for those nonzero elements. If the conditional if statement requires t_{if} cycles to execute, the total time required to execute this program is $t_2 = N[t_{if} + f(t_+ + t_*)]$ cycles, where f is the fraction of N for which both x[i] and y[i] are nonzero. Since the total number of additions and multiplications executed in this case is $2Nf$, the execution rate for this program is

$$R_2 = \frac{2Nf}{N[t_{if} + f(t_+ + t_*)]} = \frac{2f}{t_{if} + f(t_+ + t_*)} \text{FLOPS/cycle}. \tag{2.7}$$

If t_{if} is four cycles, t_+ is five cycles, t_* is ten cycles, f is 10%, and the processor's clock rate is 250 MHz (i.e. one cycle is 4 ns), then $t_1 = 60N$ ns and $t_2 = N[4 + 0.1(5 + 10)] \times 4$ ns $= 22N$ ns. The speedup of program 2 relative to program 1 then is found to be $S_{2,1} = 60N/22N = 2.73$.

Calculating the execution rates realized by each program with these assumptions produces $R_1 = 2/(60 \text{ ns}) = 33$ MFLOPS and $R_2 = 2(0.1)/(22 \text{ ns}) = 9.09$ MFLOPS. Thus, even though we have reduced the total execution time from $t_1 = 60N$ ns to $t_2 = 22N$ ns, the means-based metric (MFLOPS) shows that program 2 is 72% slower than program 1. The ends-based metric (execution time), however, shows that program 2 is actually 173% faster than program 1. We reach completely different conclusions when using these two different types of metrics because the means-based metric unfairly gives program 1 credit for all of the useless operations of multiplying and adding zero. This example highlights the danger of using the wrong metric to reach a conclusion about computer-system performance.

```
s = 0;
for (i = 1; i < N; i++)
      if (x[i] != 0 && y[i] != 0)
          s = s + x[i] * y[i];
```

Figure 2.3. The vector dot-product example program of Figure 2.2 modified to calculate only nonzero elements.

2.7   Summary

Fundamental to measuring computer-systems performance is defining an appropriate metric. This chapter identified several characteristics or criteria that are important for a 'good' metric of performance. Several common performance metrics were then introduced and analyzed in the context of these criteria. The definitions of speedup and relative change were also introduced. Finally, the concepts of ends-based versus means-based metrics were presented to clarify what actually causes a metric to be useful in capturing the actual performance of a computer system.

2.8   For further reading

• The following paper argues strongly for total execution time as the best measure of performance:

James E. Smith, 'Characterizing Computer Performance with a Single Number,' *Communications of the ACM*, October 1988, pp. 1202–1206.

• The QUIPS metric is described in detail in the following paper, which also introduced the idea of means-based versus ends-based metrics:

J. L. Gustafson and Q. O. Snell, 'HINT: A New Way to Measure Computer Performance,' *Hawaii International Conference on System Sciences,* 1995, pp. II:392–401.

• Some of the characteristics of the SPEC metric are discussed in the following papers:

Ran Giladi and Niv Ahituv, 'SPEC as a Performance Evaluation Measure,' *IEEE Computer,* Vol. 28, No. 8, August 1995, pp. 33–42.

Nikki Mirghafori, Margret Jacoby, and David Patterson, 'Truth in SPEC Benchmarks,' *ACM Computer Architecture News,* Vol. 23, No. 5, December 1995, pp. 34–42.

• Parallel computing systems are becoming more common. They present some interesting performance measurement problems, though, as discussed in

Lawrence A. Crowl, 'How to Measure, Present, and Compare Parallel Performance,' *IEEE Parallel and Distributed Technology,* Spring 1994, pp. 9–25.

2.9   Exercises

1. (a) Write a simple benchmark program to estimate the maximum effective MIPS rating of a computer system. Use your program to rank the performance of three different, but roughly comparable, computer systems.
   (b) Repeat part (a) using the maximum effective MFLOPS rating as the metric of performance.
   (c) Compare the rankings obtained in parts (a) and (b) with the ranking obtained by comparing the clock frequencies of the different systems.
   (d) Finally, compare your rankings with those published by authors using some standard benchmark programs, such as those available on the SPEC website.

2. What makes a performance metric 'reliable?'

3. Classify each of the following metrics as being either means-based or ends-based; MIPS, MFLOPS, execution time, bytes of available memory, quality of a final answer, arithmetic precision, system cost, speedup, and reliability of an answer.

4. Devise an experiment to determine the following performance metrics for a computer system.
   (a) The effective memory bandwidth between the processor and the data cache if all memory references are cache hits.
   (b) The effective memory bandwidth if all memory references are cache misses.

5. What are the key differences between 'wall clock time' and 'CPU time?' Under what conditions should each one be used? Is it possible for these two different times to be the same?

6. The execution time required to read the current time from an interval counter is a minimum of at least one memory-read operation to obtain the current time value and one memory-write operation to store the value for later use. In some cases, it may additionally include a subroutine call and return operation. How does this timer 'overhead' affect the time measured when using such an interval timer to determine the duration of some event, such as the total execution time of a program?

7. Calculate the speedup and relative change of the four systems shown in Table 2.1 when using System 4 as the basis. How do your newly calculated values affect the relative rankings of the four systems?

Average performance and variability

'The continued fantasy that there is, will be, or should be a single computer architecture for all problem spaces (or a single yardstick to measure such things) continues to fascinate me. Why should computing be different from everything else in Human experience?'

Keith Bierman, in comp.benchmarks

3.1 Why mean values?

The performance of a computer system is truly multidimensional. As a result, it can be very misleading to try to summarize the overall performance of a computer system with a single number. For instance, a computer system may be optimized to execute some types of programs very well. However, this specialization may cause it to perform very poorly when executing a different class of applications. Since the measured execution times of the different classes of applications running on this system will have a very wide range, trying to summarize the performance of this system over all classes of applications using a single mean value can result in very misleading conclusions.

Nevertheless, human nature being what it is, people continue to want a simple way to compare different computer systems. As a result, there continues to be a very strong demand to reduce the performance of a computer system to a single number. The hope is that this single number will somehow capture the essential performance of the system so that comparing performance can be reduced to simply comparing a single mean value for each system. While this is an impossible goal, mean values can be useful for performing coarse comparisons. Furthermore, the performance analyst may be pressured to calculate mean values, and will certainly see others use mean values to justify some result or conclusion. Consequently, it is important to understand how to correctly calculate an appropriate mean value, and how to recognize when a mean has been calculated incorrectly or is being used inappropriately.

As you read this chapter, keep in mind that the computer industry is very competitive, with considerable amounts of money at stake. Each manufacturer wants their system to have a better performance than their competitors' systems, so they invest a great deal of time and effort in comparing the performances of their system with those of their competitors'. This intense competition pressures them to put the best possible 'spin' on their performance numbers. The seemingly simple question of choosing the correct mean to use, which you would probably assume should be made on purely mathematical grounds, is a good example of the controversy that can develop as a result of these competitive pressures. The discussion of benchmark programs in Chapter 7 will further highlight the pressures performance analysts face to put results in the most favorable light possible.

3.2   Indices of central tendency

The previous chapter pointed out the importance of making several measurements of a program's execution time since the execution time is subject to a variety of nondeterministic effects. The problem then is to summarize all of these measurements into a single number that somehow specifies the center of the distribution of these values. In addition, you may wish to summarize the performance of a system using a single value that is somehow representative of the execution times of several different benchmark programs running on that system. There are three different *indices of central tendency* that are commonly used to summarize multiple measurements: the mean, the median, and the mode.

3.2.1   The sample mean

The *sample arithmetic mean*, or *average*, is the most commonly used measure of central tendency. If the possible values that could be measured are thought of as a random process on the discrete random variable X, the *expected value* of X, denoted $E[X]$, is defined to be

$$E[X] = \sum_{i=1}^{n} x_i p_i \tag{3.1}$$

where p_i is the probability that the value of the random variable X is x_i, and there are n total values. This value is also referred to as the *first moment* of the random variable X.

Using the term 'sample' when discussing the mean value emphasizes the fact that the values used to calculate the mean are but one possible sample of values that could have been measured from the experimental process. This sample mean, denoted $\bar{x}$, is our approximation of the true mean of the underlying random variable X. This true mean is typically denoted μ. Its true value cannot actually be known since determining this value would require an infinite number of measurements. The best we can do is approximate the true mean with the sample mean. In Chapter 4 we discuss techniques for quantifying how close the sample mean is to the true mean. When there is no chance of confusing whether we mean sample mean or true mean, we simply use the more convenient term 'mean.'

Given n different measurements that we wish to average together, we typically assume that the probabilities of obtaining any of the n values are all equally likely. Thus, our estimate of the sample mean, commonly referred to as the *arithmetic mean*, is

$$\bar{x}_A = \frac{1}{n} \sum_{i=1}^{n} x_i. \tag{3.2}$$

As an example of how to calculate a mean, consider the five measurements shown in Table 3.1. The average value is simply the sum of the $n = 5$ measurements divided by n, giving $\bar{x}_A = 15.8$.

3.2.2   The sample median

By design, one of the properties of the sample mean is that it gives equal weight to all measurements. As a result, one value that is significantly different from the other values, called an *outlier*, can have a large influence on the computed value of the resulting mean. For example, if we add a sixth measurement with the value 200 to the five measurements in Table 3.1, the new value for the mean is $\bar{x}_A = 46.5$. This value is substantially higher than most of the measurements and does not seem to capture our 'sense' of the central tendency of the six measurements.

The *median* is an index of central tendency that reduces the skewing effect of outliers on the value of the index. It is found by first ordering all of the n measurements. The middle value is then defined to be the median of the set of measurements. If n is even, the median is defined to be the mean of the middle two values. Using this definition, the median of the five values in Table 3.1 is 16. If the sixth measurement of 200 is also included in this set of measurements, the median becomes the mean of x_4 and x_5 which is 17. So, while adding the sixth value to the set of measurements increases the mean from 15.8 to 46.5, the median increases only from 16 to 17. Thus, given the large outlier in these measurements, the median appears to more intuitively capture a sense of the central tendency of these data than does the mean.

Table 3.1. Sample execution-time measurements used to demonstrate the calculation of the mean and median

Measurement	Execution time
x_1	10
x_2	20
x_3	15
x_4	18
x_5	16

3.2.3   The sample mode

The *mode* is simply the value that occurs most frequently. Note that the mode need not always exist for a given set of sample data. In the example data of Table 3.1, no one value occurs more than once, so there is no mode. Furthermore, the mode need not be unique. If there are several x_i samples that all have the same value, for instance, there would be several modes, specifically each of those x_i sample values.

3.2.4   Selecting among the mean, median, and mode

One nice property of the arithmetic mean is that it gives equal weight to all of the measured values. As a result, it incorporates information from the entire sample of data into the final value. However, this property also makes the mean more sensitive to a few outlier values that do not cluster around the rest of the samples. The median and mode, on the other hand, do not efficiently use all of the available information, but, as a result, they are less sensitive to outliers. So the question becomes that of which index of central tendency is most appropriate for a given situation. The answer to this question lies in the type of data being analyzed, and in its general characteristics.

Categorical data are those that can be grouped into distinct types or categories. For example, the number of different computers in a organization manufactured by different companies would be categorical data. The mode would be the appropriate index to use in this case to summarize the most common type of computer the organization owns. The mean and median really do not make sense in this context.

If the sum of all measurements is a meaningful and interesting value, then the arithmetic mean is an appropriate index. The sum of all of the values shown in Table 3.1 is the total time required to execute all five of the programs tested, which is an interesting and meaningful value. Thus, the mean of these measurements is also meaningful. However, the sum of the MFLOPS ratings that could be calculated using these execution times is not a meaningful value. Consequently, it is inappropriate to calculate an arithmetic mean for MFLOPS (this issue is discussed further in Section 3.3.2).

Finally, if the sample data contain a few values that are not clustered together with the others, the median may give a more meaningful or intuitive indication of the central tendency of the data than does the mean. As an example, assume that we wish to determine how much memory is installed in the workstations in our laboratory. We investigate and find that 25 machines contain 16 MBytes of memory, 38 machines contain 32 Mbytes, four machines contain 64 Mbytes, and one machine contains 1024 Mbytes. The sum of these values is the total amount of memory in all of the machines, which is calculated to be 2,896 Mbytes. Since this sum is a meaningful value by itself, the mean value of 42.6 Mbytes per machine is also a meaningful value. However, 63 of the 68 machines have 32 Mbytes of memory or less, making the mean value somewhat misleading. Instead, the median value of 32 Mbytes gives a value that is more indicative of the 'typical' machine.

3.3   Other types of means

To complicate matters further, once we have decided that the mean is the appropriate index of central tendency to use for the current situation, we must decide which *type* of mean to use! So far we have discussed the arithmetic mean, but, in fact, there are two other means that are commonly used to summarize computer-systems performance – the harmonic mean and the geometric mean. Unfortunately, these means are sometimes used incorrectly, which can lead to erroneous conclusions.

3.3.1   Characteristics of a good mean

It is possible to apply the formulas described below to calculate a mean value from any set of measured values. However, depending on the physical meaning of these measured values, the resulting mean value calculated need not make any sense. In particular, as discussed in Chapter 2, there are several characteristics that are important for a good performance metric. Since a mean value is calculated directly from the more basic performance metrics described in Chapter 2, any such mean value should also satisfy all of those characteristics.

For instance, if time values are to be averaged together, then the resulting mean value should be *directly proportional* to the total weighted time. Thus, if the total execution time were to double, so would the value of the corresponding mean, as desired. Conversely, since a rate metric is calculated by dividing the number of operations executed by the total execution time, a mean value calculated with rates should be *inversely* proportional to the total weighted time. That is, if the total execution time were to double, the value of the corresponding mean of the rates should be reduced to one-half of its initial value. Given these basic assumptions, we can now determine whether the arithmetic mean, geometric mean, and harmonic mean produce values that correctly summarize both execution times and rates.

Throughout the following discussion, we assume that we have measured the execution times of n benchmark programs[1] on the same system. Call these times T_i, $1 \leq i \leq n$. Furthermore, we assume that the total work performed by each of the n benchmark programs is constant. Specifically, we assume that each benchmark executes F floating-point operations. This workload then produces an execution rate for benchmark program i of $M_i = F/T_i$ floating-point operations executed per second. We relax this constant-work assumption in Section 3.3.5 when we discuss how to calculate weighted means.

3.3.2 The arithmetic mean

As discussed above, the arithmetic mean is defined to be

$$\bar{x}_A = \frac{1}{n} \sum_{i=1}^{n} x_i. \tag{3.3}$$

where the x_i values are the individual measurements being averaged together. In our current situation, $x_i = T_i$ so that the mean execution time is

$$\bar{T}_A = \frac{1}{n} \sum_{i=1}^{n} T_i. \tag{3.4}$$

This equation produces a value for $\bar{T}_A$ that is directly proportional to the total execution time. Thus, the arithmetic mean is the correct mean to summarize execution times.

If we use the arithmetic mean to summarize the execution rates, we find

$$\overline{M}_A = \frac{1}{n} \sum_{i=1}^{n} M_i = \sum_{i=1}^{n} \frac{F/T_i}{n} = \frac{F}{n} \sum_{i=1}^{n} \frac{1}{T_i}. \tag{3.5}$$

---

[1] A *benchmark program* is any program that is used to measure the performance of a computer system. Certain programs are sometimes defined as a standard reference that can be used for comparing performance results. See Chapter 7 for more details.

This equation produces a result that is directly proportional to the sum of the inverse of the execution times. However, in terms of the characteristics described in Section 3.3.1, we need a value that is inversely proportional to the sum of the times. We conclude, then, that the arithmetic mean is inappropriate for summarizing rates.

3.3.3   The harmonic mean

The second type of mean that is commonly used by performance analysts is the *harmonic mean*. It is defined to be

$$\bar{x}_{\mathrm{H}} = \frac{n}{\sum_{i=1}^{n} 1/x_i} \tag{3.6}$$

where, as before, the x_i values represent the n separate values that are being averaged together.

If we use the harmonic mean to summarize execution-time values, then $x_i = T_i$ and we obtain the following expression:

$$\bar{T}_{\mathrm{H}} = \frac{n}{\sum_{i=1}^{n} 1/T_i}. \tag{3.7}$$

This value is obviously not directly proportional to the total execution time, as required in terms of the properties of a good mean in Section 3.3.1. Thus, we conclude that the harmonic mean is inappropriate for summarizing execution-time measurements.

We find that the harmonic mean is the appropriate mean to use for summarizing rates, however. In this case, $x_i = M_i = F/T_i$, giving

$$\bar{M}_{\mathrm{H}} = \frac{n}{\sum_{i=1}^{n} 1/M_i} = \frac{n}{\sum_{i=1}^{n} T_i/F} = \frac{Fn}{\sum_{i=1}^{n} T_i}. \tag{3.8}$$

This value, which is simply the total number of operations executed by all of the programs measured divided by the sum of all of the execution times, is obviously inversely proportional to the total execution time. Thus, the harmonic mean is appropriate for summarizing rate measurements.

Example. Consider the measurements shown in Table 3.2. The arithmetic mean of the execution times is easily calculated using the sum of the total times. The execution rates are calculated by dividing the total number of floating-point operations executed in each program by its corresponding execution time. The harmonic mean of these rates is then found by calculating the value $\bar{M}_{\mathrm{H}} = 5/(\frac{1}{405} + \frac{1}{367} + \frac{1}{405} + \frac{1}{419} + \frac{1}{388})$. Notice that this value is the same as that obtained by taking the ratio of the total number of floating-point operations executed by all of the programs to the sum of their execution times (within the error due to rounding off). ◇

Table 3.2. An example of calculating the harmonic mean

Measurement (i)	T_i (s)	F (10^9 FLOP)	M_i (MFLOPS)
1	321	130	405
2	436	160	367
3	284	115	405
4	601	252	419
5	482	187	388
$\sum_{i=1}^{5} x_i$	2124	844	
$\overline{T}_A$	425		
$\overline{M}_H$			396

3.3.4   The geometric mean

Some performance analysts have advocated the geometric mean as the appro-priate mean to use when summarizing normalized numbers. In fact, it is the mean that is used to summarize the normalized execution times measured in the SPEC benchmark (see Section 2.3.4). It also has been suggested that it is the most appropriate mean to use when summarizing measurements with a wide range of values since a single value has less influence on the geometric mean than it would on the value of the arithmetic mean.

The geometric mean is defined to be the nth root of the product of the n individual x_i values. That is,

$$\bar{x}_G = \sqrt[n]{x_1 x_2 \cdots x_i \cdots x_n} = \left(\prod_{i=1}^{n} x_i \right)^{1/n}. \tag{3.9}$$

Unfortunately, as we will see below, the geometric mean is not an appropriate mean to summarize either times or rates, irrespective of whether they are normal-ized.

Proponents of the geometric mean say that one of its key advantages is that it maintains consistent relationships when comparing normalized values regardless of the basis system used to normalize the measurements. To test this assertion, we compare the performance of three different computer systems when executing five different benchmark programs. The programs are run on the different sys-tems, producing the execution-time measurements shown in Table 3.3. Using the geometric mean of these measurements to compare these systems shows that S_3 performs the best, followed by S_2 and S_1, in that order. Normalizing the mea-surements using S_1 as the basis produces the same rank ordering of systems, as

Table 3.3. Execution times of five benchmark programs executed on three different systems

Program	S_1	S_2	S_3
1	417	244	134
2	83	70	70
3	66	153	135
4	39,449	33,527	66,000
5	772	368	369
Geometric mean	587	503	499
Rank	3	2	1

shown in Table 3.4. Similarly, Table 3.5 shows that the same ordering is again preserved when all of the measurements are normalized relative to system S_2.

Unfortunately, although the geometric mean produces a consistent ordering of the systems being compared, it is the wrong ordering. Table 3.6 shows the sums of the execution times of the benchmark programs for each system along with the arithmetic means of these execution times. When these times are used to rank the performances of the three different systems, we see that S_2 performs the best; that is, it produces the shortest execution time, followed by S_1 and then S_3. Since the execution time is the measure of performance in which we are ultimately most interested, it is apparent that the geometric mean produced the wrong ordering. We conclude that, although the geometric mean is consistent regardless of the normalization basis, it is consistently wrong.

It is easy to see why the geometric mean produces the wrong ordering when it is used to average together execution times. In this case, $x_i = T_i$, and

$$\overline{T}_G = \left(\prod_{i=1}^{n} T_i \right)^{1/n}. \tag{3.10}$$

This value is obviously not directly proportional to the total execution time. Similarly, averaging together execution rates with the geometric mean produces

$$\overline{M}_G = \left(\prod_{i=1}^{n} M_i \right)^{1/n} = \left(\prod_{i=1}^{n} \frac{F}{T_i} \right)^{1/n} \tag{3.11}$$

which is not inversely proportional to the total execution time. Both $\overline{T}_G$ and $\overline{M}_G$ violate the characteristics of a good mean value, forcing the conclusion that the geometric mean is inappropriate for summarizing both execution times and rates, irrespective of whether they are normalized.

Table 3.4. The execution times of the benchmark programs in Table 3.3 normalized with respect to that of S_1

Program	S_1	S_2	S_3
1	1.0	0.59	0.32
2	1.0	0.84	0.85
3	1.0	2.32	2.05
4	1.0	0.85	1.67
5	1.0	0.48	0.45
Geometric mean	1.0	0.86	0.84
Rank	3	2	1

Table 3.5. The execution times of the benchmark programs in Table 3.3 normalized with respect to that of S_2

Program	S_1	S_2	S_3
1	1.71	1.00	0.55
2	1.19	1.00	1.00
3	0.43	1.00	0.88
4	1.18	1.00	1.97
5	2.10	1.00	1.00
Geometric mean	1.17	1.00	0.99
Rank	3	2	1

Table 3.6. The total and average execution times of the benchmark programs in Table 3.3.

Program	S_1	S_2	S_3
1	417	244	134
2	83	70	70
3	66	153	135
4	39,449	33,527	66,000
5	772	368	369
Total time	40,787	34,362	66,798
Arithmetic mean	8157	6872	13,342
Rank	2	1	3

3.3.5   Weighted means

The above definitions for the arithmetic and harmonic means implicitly assume that each of the n individual measurements being averaged together is equally important in calculating the mean. In many situations, however, this assumption need not be true. For instance, you may know that half of the time you use your computer system you are running program 1, with the remaining time split evenly between four other application programs. In this case, then, you would like the mean value you calculate to reflect this mix of application-program usage.

This type of *weighted mean* can easily be calculated by assigning an appropriate fraction, or *weight*, to the measurement associated with each program. That is, a value w_i is assigned to program i such that w_i is a fraction representing the relative importance of program i in calculating the mean value, and

$$\sum_{i=1}^{n} w_i = 1. \tag{3.12}$$

In the situation mentioned above, program 1 is used half of the time, so $w_i = 0.5$. The other four programs are used equally in the remaining half of the time, giving $w_2 = w_3 = w_4 = w_5 = 0.125$. Given these weights, the formula for calculating the arithmetic mean becomes

$$\bar{x}_{A,w} = \sum_{i=1}^{n} w_i x_i \tag{3.13}$$

and the harmonic mean becomes

$$\bar{x}_{H,w} = \frac{1}{\sum_{i=1}^{n} w_i / x_i}. \tag{3.14}$$

We ignore the geometric mean in this discussion since it is not an appropriate mean for summarizing either execution times or rates.

3.4   Quantifying variability

While mean values are useful for summarizing large amounts of data into a single number, they unfortunately hide the details of how these data are actually distributed. It is often the case, however, that this distribution, or the *variability* in the data, is of more interest than the mean value.

A *histogram* is a useful device for displaying the distribution of a set of measured values. To generate a histogram, first find the minimum and maximum values of the measurements. Then divide this range into b subranges. Each of these subranges is called a histogram *cell* or *bucket*. Next, count the number of measurements that fall into each cell. A plot of these counts on the vertical axis with the cells on the horizontal axis in a bar-chart format is the histogram. It is also possible to normalize the histogram by dividing the count in each cell by the total number of measurements. The vertical axis then represents the fraction of all measurements that falls into that cell.

One difficulty in constructing a histogram is determining the appropriate size for each cell. There is no hard and fast rule about the range of values that should be grouped into a single cell, but a good rule of thumb is that the width of the cells should be adjusted so that each cell contains a minimum of four or five measurements. (This rule of thumb comes indirectly from our typical assumptions about the distribution of measurement errors, which is discussed in Chapter 4.)

Example. Consider an experiment in which the performance analyst measures the sizes of messages sent on two different computer networks. The average message size for network A was calculated to be 14.9 kbytes, while the average for network B was found to be 14.7 kbytes. On the sole basis of these mean values, the analyst may conclude that the characteristics of the message traffic carried on each network are roughly similar. To verify this conclusion, the message-size measurements are grouped into histogram cells, each with a width of 5 kbytes, as shown in Table 3.7. That is, the first cell is the number of messages within the range 0–5 kbytes, the second cell counts the number of messages within the range 5–10 kbytes, and so forth. As shown in the plots of these two histograms in Figures 3.1 and 3.2, the messages on the two networks have completely different distributions, even though they have almost identical means.   ◇

This example demonstrates the problem with relying on a single value to characterize a group of measurements. It also shows how the additional detail in a histogram can provide further insights into the underlying system behavior. However, while the two histograms in this example are obviously substantially different, visually comparing two histograms can be imprecise. Furthermore, histograms can often provide too much detail, making it difficult to quantitatively compare the spread of the measurements around the mean value. What is needed, then, is a single number that somehow captures how 'spread out' the measurements are. In conjunction with the mean value, this *index of dispersion* provides a more precise metric with which to summarize the characteristics of a group of measurements. The question then becomes one of choosing an appropriate metric to quantify this dispersion.

Perhaps the simplest metric for an index of dispersion is the *range*. The range is found by taking the difference of the maximum and minimum of the measured values:

Table 3.7. The number of messages of the indicated sizes sent on two different networks

Message size (kbytes)	Network A	Network B
$0 < x_i \leq 5$	11	39
$5 < x_i \leq 10$	27	25
$10 < x_i \leq 15$	41	18
$15 < x_i \leq 20$	32	5
$20 < x_i \leq 25$	21	19
$25 < x_i \leq 30$	12	42
$30 < x_i \leq 35$	4	0

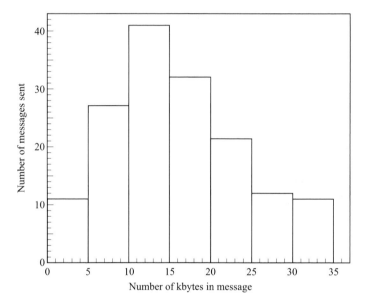

Figure 3.1 A histogram plot of the data for network A from Table 3.7.

$$R_{max} = \max_{\forall i} x_i - \min_{\forall i} x_i. \tag{3.15}$$

Although it is simple to calculate, the range does not use all of the available information in summarizing the dispersion. Thus, it is very sensitive to a few extreme values that need not be representative of the overall set of measurements. A slight improvement is to find the maximum of the absolute values of the difference of each measurement from the mean value:

$$\Delta_{max} = \max_{\forall i} |x_i - \bar{x}|. \tag{3.16}$$

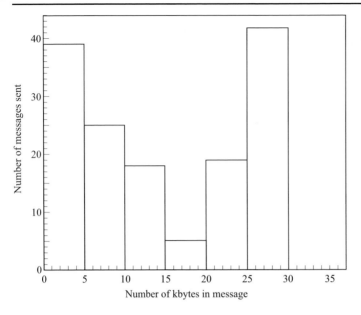

Figure 3.2 A histogram plot of the data for network B from Table 3.7.

Again, however, this value does not efficiently take advantage of all of the available information, and is overly sensitive to extreme values.

A better, and perhaps the most commonly accepted, index of dispersion is the variance. The *sample variance* is our calculated estimate of the actual variance of the underlying distribution from which our measurements are taken. It incorporates all of the information available about the difference of each measurement from the mean value. It is defined to be

$$s^2 = \frac{\sum_{i=1}^{n}(x_i - \bar{x})^2}{n - 1} \tag{3.17}$$

where the x_i are the n independent measurements, and $\bar{x}$ is the corresponding arithmetic mean. Notice in this equation that only $n - 1$ of the differences $x_i - \bar{x}$ are independent. That is, the nth difference, $x_n - \bar{x}$, could be computed given the other $n - 1$ differences. Thus, the number of *degrees of freedom* in this equation, which is the number of independent terms in the sum, is $n - 1$. As a result, the sum of the squared differences in this equation is divided by $n - 1$ instead of n.

This equation defines the sample variance, but it is not particularly useful for calculating the variance given a set of measurements. Furthermore, this definition requires our knowing the mean value, $\bar{x}$, before calculating the variance. This implies that two passes must be made through the data, once to calculate the mean and a second pass to find the variance. This requirement makes it difficult to calculate the variance 'on the fly' as the data are being generated, for instance. To facilitate calculating the variance, we can expand Equation (3.17) to give

$$s^2 = \frac{\sum_{i=1}^n (x_i - \bar{x})^2}{n-1} = \frac{1}{n-1} \sum_{i=1}^n (x_i^2 - 2\bar{x}x_i + \bar{x}^2)$$

$$= \frac{n \sum_{i=1}^n x_i^2 - (\sum_{i=1}^n x_i)^2}{n(n-1)}.$$

(3.18)

This equation shows that, to calculate the variance, we need to make only a single pass through the data to find the sum of the x_i values and the sum of the x_i^2 values. We can then use these sums to calculate both the mean and the variance.

One of the problems in using the variance to obtain an indication of how large the dispersion of data is relative to the mean is that the units of the variance are the square of the units of the values actually measured. In the above example, for instance, the units of the individual measurements, and so, therefore, of the mean, are bytes. The units of the variance, however, are bytes squared. This squared relationship of the units of the variance to those of the mean makes it difficult to compare the magnitude of the variance directly with the magnitude of the mean.

A more useful metric for this type of comparison is the *standard deviation*, which is defined as the positive square root of the variance. That is, the sample standard deviation is

$$s = \sqrt{s^2} = \sqrt{\frac{\sum_{i=1}^n (x_i - \bar{x})^2}{n-1}}.$$

(3.19)

With this definition, the mean and standard deviation have the same units, making comparisons easier. Finally, use of the *coefficient of variation* (COV) eliminates the problem of specific units by normalizing the standard deviation with respect to the mean. The coefficient of variation is defined to be

$$COV = s/\bar{x}$$

(3.20)

and so provides a dimensionless value that compares the relative size of the variation in the measurements with the mean value of those measurements.

3.5   Summary

Several different types of means can be used to summarize a collection of measurements with a single number. Although this summarization hides much of the information provided by the n different measurements, human nature persists in wanting to reduce performance to a single number to simplify the task of making comparisons. Consequently, it is important for the performance analyst to understand the definitions of the different means, and how to use each appropriately. The following points summarize how to select an appropriate mean for a given situation.

- **The arithmetic mean.** The arithmetic mean is the appropriate choice whenever the sum of the raw results has some physical meaning and is an 'interesting' value. For example, the sum of execution times is a total execution time, which is both meaningful and interesting. Similarly, the total number of bytes sent by messages on a communications network has physical meaning and by itself is an interesting value. The arithmetic mean should *not* be used to summarize rates.
- **The harmonic mean.** The harmonic mean is the appropriate mean for summarizing rates since it reduces to the total number of operations executed by all of the test programs divided by the total time required to execute those operations, which is simply the definition of the total execution rate. It is not appropriate to use the harmonic mean to summarize measurements that should be summarized using the arithmetic mean, such as execution times.
- **The geometric mean.** Although it has been advocated as the best mean to use for summarizing normalized values, the geometric mean is not appropriate for summarizing either rates or times, irrespective of whether they are normalized.
- **Normalization.** Owing to the mathematical difficulties of averaging together normalized values, it is best to first calculate the appropriate mean and then perform the desired normalization.

In addition to these mean values, we introduced the median and the mode as other measures of central tendency. As the middle value in a collection of measurements, the median is useful when the measurements have a few outlying values that tend to distort the intuitive sense of the measurement's central tendency. The mode is useful for quantifying the most common value among a set of categorical measurements.

One of the problems with these single-value summaries of a collection of measurements is that they hide their variability. A histogram is a useful graphical representation for displaying this variability. The variance (or the standard deviation) is a statistic that can be used to summarize in a single number the variability shown in a histogram.

3.6   For further reading

- This paper describes the three types of means and argues for the use of the geometric mean for averaging normalized numbers:

P. J. Fleming and J. J. Wallace, 'How Not To Lie With Statistics: The Correct
Way To Summarize Benchmark Results,' *Communications of the ACM*,
Vol. 29, No. 3, March 1986, pp. 218–221.

- The following paper, however, argues against the use of the geometric mean.
  It also introduces several of the ideas of what constitutes a good mean that
  were presented in this chapter:

James E. Smith, 'Characterizing Computer Performance with a Single
Number,' *Communications of the ACM*, October 1988, pp. 1202–1206.

Taken together, these two papers provide an interesting glimpse into the
controversy that can arise among performance analysts over such fundamental concepts as selecting an appropriate mean with which to summarize a set
of measured values.

- Almost any introductory statistics text will provide a development of the basic
  types of means and the variance.

3.7   Exercises

1. What aspects of a computer system's performance is it reasonable to summarize with a single number?
2. It has been said (Smith, 1988) that the geometric mean is consistent, but it is
   consistently wrong. A mean is calculated according to a well-defined formula,
   so in what sense can it be wrong?
3. Which measure of central tendency, the mean, median, or mode, should be
   used to summarize the following types of data: size of messages in a communication network, number of cache hits and misses, execution time, MFLOPS,
   MIPS, bandwidth, latency, speedup, price, image resolution, and communication throughput? For those for which the mean is the best choice, which
   mean should be used (arithmetic, geometric, or harmonic)?
4. Table 3.8 shows the execution times measured for several different benchmark
   programs when they are executed on three different systems. The last column
   shows the number of instructions executed by each of the benchmark programs. Assuming that each benchmark should be equally weighted, calculate
   the following values:
   (a) the average execution time,
   (b) the average MIPS rate, and
   (c) the average speedup and relative change when using S_3 as the basis
       system.

Table 3.8. The times measured on several different systems for a few benchmark programs

Program	S_1	S_2	S_3	Number of instructions
1	33.4	28.8	28.3	1.45×10^{10}
2	19.9	22.1	25.3	7.97×10^{9}
3	6.5	5.3	4.7	3.11×10^{9}
4	84.3	75.8	80.1	3.77×10^{10}
5	101.1	99.4	70.2	4.56×10^{10}

(d) Are these average values reasonable summaries of the data presented? Why or why not?

5. Repeat the above problem when benchmark program 1 represents 40% of the expected workload, benchmark program 2 35%, benchmark program 3 15%, and benchmark programs 4 and 5 each 5%.

6. Determine the coefficient of variation of the execution times for each system shown in Table 3.8.

4 Errors in experimental measurements

'To free a man of error is to give, not to take away. Knowledge that a thing is false is a truth.'

Schopenhauer

4.1 Accuracy, precision, and resolution

In trying to measure and understand the performance of computer systems, we are constantly confronted by the nitty-gritty details of the real world. Unfortunately, these annoying details effectively introduce *uncertainty* into our measurements. We refer to these uncertainties in measurements as *errors* or *noise*. To determine how much uncertainty exists in our measurements, and, therefore, to determine what conclusions we can actually draw from them, we must use the tools and techniques of probability and statistics to quantify the errors.

We learned in previous chapters that time is a fundamental quantity that needs to be measured to determine almost any aspect of a computer system's performance. Any measurement tool, such as the interval timer, has three important characteristics that determine the overall quality of its measurements. The first is its *accuracy*. In the case of the timer, accuracy is an indication of the closeness of the timer's measurement to that of a standard measurement of time defined by a recognized standards organization, such as the United States National Institute of Standards and Technology. More generally, accuracy is the absolute difference between a measured value and the corresponding reference value. Note that the reference value is an agreed-upon standard, such as the duration of a second, the length of a meter, and so on, that is typically derived from some physical phenomenon.

The second important characteristic of a measurement tool is its *precision*. Precision relates to the repeatability of the measurements made with the tool. It is sometimes easier to think of precision in terms of its inverse. *Imprecision* is the amount of scatter in the measurements obtained by making multiple measurements of a particular characteristic of the system being tested. A histogram of these measurements shows the number of times each specific measurement occurred. The resulting distribution is an indication of the precision of the measuring process. Highly precise measurements would be very tightly clustered around a single measured value whereas imprecise measurements would tend to have a broader distribution.

Finally, the measuring tool's *resolution* is the smallest incremental change that can be detected and displayed. The finite resolution of a measuring tool introduces a quantization effect into the values it is used to measure. Most interval timers, for example, are implemented using a counter driven by a signal derived from the system clock. The resolution of this type of interval timer is the period between clock ticks. Thus, the resolution of the timer limits the accuracy of its measurements to be no better than plus or minus one clock period.

To obtain an intuitive view of the differences between accuracy and precision, Figure 4.1 shows a plot of several hypothetical measurements. The precision of these measurements is indicated by the spread of the measurements around the mean value. The accuracy, on the other hand, is the difference between the mean of the measured values and the (unknown) 'true' value. Note that an inaccurate measurement tool still may be very precise, as indicated by a very narrow spread of the measurements made with the tool.

In the final value obtained by any measuring device, it is difficult to separate the individual contributions to the error made by its accuracy, precision, and resolution. Typically, we use the variance of the measurements to quantify their precision. Quantifying the accuracy of measurements is much more difficult, however. For instance, quantifying the accuracy of an interval timer would

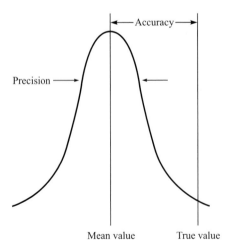

Figure 4.1 A plot of hypothetical measurements showing the differences between accuracy and precision.

require us to verify the calibration of the clock source with a standard measurement of time. Instead, we typically simply trust the accuracy of the clock source, but use a *confidence interval* for the mean value (described in Section 4.4.1) to quantify the precision of our measurements. For this specific technique to be applicable, however, the model of the sources of the errors in our experiments must correspond to the error distribution assumed in the derivation of the confidence-interval formula, as described in Section 4.4.4.

4.2   Sources of errors

Beyond the measurement errors introduced by the accuracy, precision, and resolution of our measuring device, there are many other sources of errors introduced into the measurement process that can affect the final values actually recorded. For instance, there is the time required to read and store the current time value. Furthermore, the program statements added to a program to access the timer change, or *perturb*, the program being measured. As a result, we are no longer measuring quite the thing we want to measure, which is, after all, the unmodified program.

Additional errors can be introduced into our measurements due to the unique characteristics of the computer system itself. The time-sharing of a system among multiple users and the processing of real-time events, such as interrupts to service network interfaces, time-of-day clocks, user interactions, and so forth, affect the program being measured. Additionally, other nondeterministic events, such as cache misses, system exceptions, memory page faults, and so on, also perturb the system. All of these factors interact in ways that can both increase and decrease the duration of the interval being measured. As a result, multiple measurements of the same event may all produce different measured values. From the performance analyst's point of view, these different measurements are all estimates of the true value of the duration of the event being measured. The differences in these measurements are unpredictable, however, and must be treated as 'noise' or errors in the measurements.

It is useful to classify all of the different sources of error into two different types, *systematic errors*, and *random errors*. Systematic errors are the result of some experimental 'mistake,' such as some change in the experimental environment or an incorrect procedure, that introduces a bias into the measurements. A change in the temperature, for instance, may cause the clock period to drift, or the experimenter may fail to restore the identical system state at the start of each experiment. Systematic errors tend to be constant across all measurements, or slowly varying with time. These errors affect the accuracy of the measurements. It is up to the skill of the experimenter to control and eliminate systematic errors.

Random errors, on the other hand, are completely unpredictable, nondeterministic, and need not be controllable. They are also unbiased in that a random error has an equal probability of either increasing or decreasing a measurement. Random errors may be the result of the measuring tool, the observer reading the output of the tool, or the random processes within the system being studied. As an example of a random error in a performance experiment, consider the resolution of the timer itself. Assume that the period of the timer is T, for instance, and that there are no other sources of error in the experiment. Then multiple measurements of the same event would be expected to vary by plus or minus T with equal probability since a continuous time interval is being quantized by the timer measurement. (Timer quantization is discussed further in Section 6.2.2.) Random errors affect the precision of the measurements and thereby determine the repeatability of the results.

4.3   A model of errors

By carefully controlling the experimental environment, the experimenter tries to minimize the impact of systematic errors on the accuracy of the measurements. When these sources of error cannot be eliminated or controlled, the experimenter should at least be able to understand how these systematic errors bias the results. Random errors, on the other hand, are, by definition, unpredictable. As a result, they have unpredictable effects on the outcomes of any measurements.

While it is impossible to predict the precise effect of specific sources of random errors, it is possible to develop a statistical model to describe their overall effect on the experimental results. This model can then help us to determine how to use appropriate statistical tools to quantify the precision of our measurements.

Experimental errors are typically assumed to be *Gaussian*. That is, if multiple measurements of the same value are made, these measurements will tend to follow a Gaussian (also called *normal*) distribution centered on the actual mean value x. We now develop a simple error model to obtain an intuitive feel for why this may be a reasonable assumption for the distribution of errors in a performance-measurement experiment.

First, assume that a single source of random error can change the value actually measured for x up or down by $+E$ or $-E$ with equal probability. That is, this random error source will cause us to measure $x + E$ half of the time and $x - E$ half of the time. If there are two sources of random errors, each of which has a 50% probability of shifting the value of x measured up or down by E, then there are four possible combinations of how these errors can affect the final value measured. As shown in Table 4.1, these four combinations result in three possible outcomes. If both errors shift the measured value in the same direction, either positively or negatively, the final value measured will be $x + 2E$ or $x - 2E$, respectively. Each of these two outcomes occurs once for the four possible combinations, so each outcome occurs, on average, 25% of the time. In the case in which the two error sources cancel each other out, the value actually measured is the true value x. Since these canceling errors occur in two of the four cases, we expect to measure the actual value x half of the time.

Extending this line of reasoning to include n sources of random error, we can construct a lattice diagram of the possible measurement outcomes, as shown in Figure 4.2. Any particular measurement can be thought of as the result of taking a path down through this diagram beginning at the true value, x, at the top. At each node in the lattice, there is a 50% chance of choosing either the left or the right branch, such that going left corresponds to subtracting E from the value at that node and going right corresponds to adding E. Since there are n sources of error, the potential range of values that could be measured is $[x - nE, x + nE]$ with a step of $2E$ between each of the $n + 1$ possible values.

Since some outcomes can be reached through several different paths, not all possible measurements are equally likely to occur. In fact, the probability of obtaining any particular measurement is proportional to the number of paths that lead to that measurement. It is straightforward to show that this configuration produces a binomial distribution for the possible measurement outcomes. Furthermore, as the number of error sources, n, becomes large, the binomial distribution approaches a Gaussian distribution. Consequently, this intuition, combined with our experience, leads to the conclusion that experimental errors can be reasonably modeled using a Gaussian distribution centered around the true value.

4.4   Quantifying errors

In general, it is very difficult to quantify the accuracy of our measurements since the accuracy is a function of the bias introduced into our measuring process due to systematic errors. To quantify this bias requires us to calibrate our measurement tools to some standard value, and to carefully control our experimental procedure. We can use the model of random errors described above, however, to quantify the precision, or repeatability, of our measurements using *confidence intervals*.

Table 4.1. Two sources of random error, each of which can shift a measurement with equal probability by $\pm$ E, can produce three possible measured values

Error 1	Error 2	Measured value	Probability
$-E$	$-E$	$x - 2E$	$\frac{1}{4}$
$-E$	$+E$	x	$\frac{1}{4}$
$+E$	$-E$	x	$\frac{1}{4}$
$+E$	$+E$	$x + 2E$	$\frac{1}{4}$

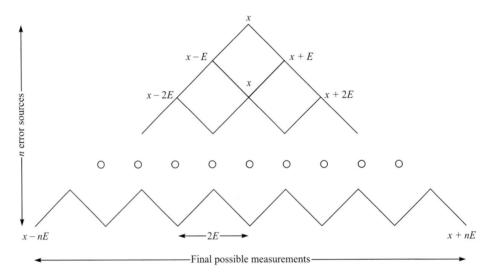

Figure 4.2 With n sources of error, the probability of obtaining any particular measurement for the true value x is proportional to the number of paths that lead to that measurement.

4.4.1   Confidence intervals for the mean

If the distribution of random errors in our measurements can be reasonably approximated by a Gaussian distribution, we can use the unique properties of this distribution to determine how well our estimate of the true value approximates the actual true value. Specifically, we use statistical *confidence intervals* to find a range of values that has a given probability of including the actual value.

4.4.1.1   Case 1: When the number of measurements is large ($n \geq 30$)

We use the sample mean of our n measurements, $\bar{x}$, as the best approximation of the true value x. If the $\{x_1, x_2, ..., x_n\}$ samples used to calculate $\bar{x}$ are all independent and come from the same population with mean μ and standard deviation σ, the central limit theorem then assures us that, for large values of n (typically assumed to mean $n \geq 30$), the sample mean $\bar{x}$ is approximately Gaussian distributed with mean μ and standard deviation $\sigma/\sqrt{n}$. In this case, we assume that the population mean, μ, is the true value x that we are trying to measure. Thus, the x_i values that we have measured occur with a probability that follows the Gaussian distribution shown in Figure 4.3.

To quantify the precision of these measurements, we want to find two values, c_1 and c_2, such that the probability of the mean value being between c_1 and c_2 is $1 - \alpha$. This probability is simply the area under the curve between c_1 and c_2. That is,

$$\Pr[c_1 \leq x \leq c_2] = 1 - \alpha. \tag{4.1}$$

Typically, we choose c_1 and c_2 to form a symmetric interval such that

$$\Pr[x < c_1] = \Pr[x > c_2] = \frac{\alpha}{2}. \tag{4.2}$$

The interval $[c_1, c_2]$ is called the *confidence interval* for the mean value $\bar{x}$, α is called the *significance level*, and $(1 - \alpha) \times 100$ is called the *confidence level*. The normalization

$$z = \frac{\bar{x} - x}{\sigma/\sqrt{n}} \tag{4.3}$$

transforms $\bar{x}$ to follow the standard unit normal distribution, which is simply a Gaussian distribution with mean $\mu = 0$ and variance $\sigma^2 = 1$. Applying the central-limit theorem, we find that

$$c_1 = \bar{x} - z_{1-\alpha/2} \frac{s}{\sqrt{n}} \tag{4.4}$$

$$c_2 = \bar{x} + z_{1-\alpha/2} \frac{s}{\sqrt{n}} \tag{4.5}$$

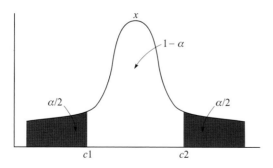

Figure 4.3 The probability that the actual value being measured, x, is within the confidence interval (c_1, c_2) is $1 - \alpha$.

where $\bar{x}$ is the sample mean, s is the sample standard deviation, n is the number of measurements, and $z_{1-\alpha/2}$ is the value of a standard unit normal distribution that has an area of $1 - \alpha/2$ to the left of $z_{1-\alpha/2}$. That is, for a random variable Z that is normally distributed with mean $\mu = 0$ and variance $\sigma^2 = 1$,

$$\Pr[Z \le z_{1-\alpha/2}] = 1 - \alpha/2. \tag{4.6}$$

The value $z_{1-\alpha/2}$ is typically obtained from a precomputed table, such as that in Appendix C.

4.4.1.2 Case 2: When the number of measurements is small ($n < 30$)

When the number of measurements is greater than approximately 30, the sample variance s^2 provides a good estimate of the actual variance σ^2 of the distribution. In particular, if the value of s^2 does not vary from one set of measurements to another, then the transformation $z = (\bar{x} - x)/(\sigma/\sqrt{n})$ closely approximates a standard normal distribution. As a result, the values from a standard normal table can be used for $z_{1-\alpha/2}$ when calculating a confidence interval for experiments with $n \ge 30$.

However, for a relatively small number of measurements, which is typically assumed to mean $n < 30$, the sample variances s^2 calculated for several different groups of measurements can vary significantly from group to group. In this case, it can be shown that the distribution of the transformed value $z = (\bar{x} - x)/(\sigma/\sqrt{n})$ actually follows what is known as the t distribution with $n - 1$ degrees of freedom. In determining a confidence interval for $\bar{x}$ when $n < 30$, then, we find c_1 and c_2 as follows:

$$c_1 = \bar{x} - t_{1-\alpha/2;n-1}\frac{s}{\sqrt{n}} \tag{4.7}$$

$$c_2 = \bar{x} + t_{1-\alpha/2;n-1}\frac{s}{\sqrt{n}} \tag{4.8}$$

where $\bar{x}$ is the sample mean, s is the sample standard deviation, n is the number of measurements, and $t_{1-\alpha/2;n-1}$ is the value from the t distribution that has an area of $1 - \alpha/2$ to the left of $t_{1-\alpha/2;n-1}$ with $n - 1$ degrees of freedom. As before the value $t_{1-\alpha/2;n-1}$ is typically obtained from a table (see Appendix C.1).

The t distribution is similar to the Gaussian distribution in that they are both bell-shaped and symmetric around a mean of zero. The t distribution tends to be more 'spread out' (i.e. its variance is greater), however, since it is dependent on two varying values, the sample mean and the sample standard deviation. In addition, the variance of the t distribution is always greater than unity and is dependent on the number of measurements, n. The t distribution becomes the same as the standard normal distribution as n becomes large.

Example. We want to determine, on the average, how long it takes to write a file of a particular size to a disk drive. Knowing that this time can vary due to random system effects that can change the specific values we measure, we make the following measurements of the time, in seconds, required to write this file to a disk eight different times: 8.0, 7.0, 5.0, 9.0, 9.5, 11.3, 5.2, and 8.5. We easily compute the mean value to be $\bar{x} = 7.94$ s. We also notice, though, that these times have a relatively large range. We thus want to calculate a confidence interval for this mean time to quantify the precision of our measurements for estimating the mean.

We sum all of the measurements to find

$$\sum x_i = 8 + 7 + \cdots + 8.5 = 63.5 \tag{4.9}$$

$$\bar{x} = \frac{\sum x_i}{n} = \frac{63.5}{8} = 7.94. \tag{4.10}$$

The sum of squares is then calculated to be

$$\sum x_i^2 = 8^2 + 7^2 + \cdots + 8.5^2 = 536.23. \tag{4.11}$$

The standard deviation is then

$$s = \sqrt{\frac{8(536.23) - 63.5^2}{8(7)}} = 2.14. \tag{4.12}$$

Choosing a 90% confidence interval will ensure that there is a 90% chance that the actual mean time, x, will be contained within the computed interval. A 90% confidence interval corresponds to $\alpha = 0.10$. Since there are $n = 8$ total measurements, we must use the t distribution with seven degrees of freedom. From the table of t distribution values we find

$$t_{1-\alpha/2;n-1} = t_{0.95;7} = 1.895. \tag{4.13}$$

On substituting these values for $\bar{x}$, s, and $t_{0.95;7}$ into Equations (4.7) and (4.8), we find

$$c_1 = 7.94 - \frac{1.895(2.14)}{\sqrt{8}} = 6.5 \tag{4.14}$$

$$c_2 = 7.94 + \frac{1.895(2.14)}{\sqrt{8}} = 9.4. \tag{4.15}$$

Similarly, we can calculate the 95% confidence interval for the mean time to be

$$c_1 = \bar{x} - t_{0.975;7} \frac{s}{\sqrt{n}} = 7.94 - \frac{2.365(2.14)}{\sqrt{8}} = 6.1 \tag{4.16}$$

$$c_2 = \bar{x} + t_{0.975;7}\frac{s}{\sqrt{n}} = 7.94 + \frac{2.365(2.14)}{\sqrt{8}} = 9.7. \tag{4.17}$$

Thus, we can say that there is a 90% chance that the actual mean time required to write this particular size file is in the range (6.5, 9.4) seconds. We can also say that there is a 95% chance that it is in the range (6.1, 9.7) seconds. Finally, by calculating a 99% confidence interval, we find that there is a 99% chance that the actual time is in the range (5.3,10.6) seconds.   ◇

The intuition behind the formula. This example highlights a potential source of confusion when trying to interpret what a confidence interval is actually telling us. With 90% confidence, we calculated that the actual mean value is in the interval (6.5, 9.4). When we increase our confidence to 95%, however, we find that the interval increases to (6.1, 9.7). That is, when we increase our confidence about the mean, we end up with a wider interval. However, this wider interval would then seem to imply that we now know less about the actual mean than when we used a lower confidence level. Increasing our confidence further to 99% widens the interval around the mean to (5.3, 10.6), which suggests that we now have even less precise knowledge about the actual mean. Thus, we seem to have a contradiction – the higher our confidence about the mean, the less precise is the information we seem to have.

The apparent contradiction here really comes from a misunderstanding about what a confidence interval actually tells us. A 90% confidence interval, for instance, means that there is a 90% chance that the actual mean is within that interval. Increasing the confidence level to 95% means that we are increasing the probability that the actual mean is in the resulting interval. Since we have not changed the data values that we measured, our information about the mean is no more precise for this interval than it is for the 90% interval. Thus, the only way to increase the probability of the mean being within the new interval is to increase its size. We must increase the size of the interval even further if we want to ensure that there is only a 1% chance that the mean is *not* in the interval. Consequently, the 99% confidence interval is even larger than the 90 or 95% intervals.

4.4.2   Determining the number of measurements needed

We can see from the confidence-interval formula that the size of the interval is inversely dependent on the square root of the number of measurements that we make. Since we typically would like to minimize the number of measurements, we can use this formula to determine how many measurements are necessary to produce a confidence interval of a specified width.

Suppose that we wish to determine a confidence interval for $\bar{x}$ so that there is a probability of $1 - \alpha$ that the actual value x is within the interval $(c_1, c_2) = ((1 - e)\bar{x}, (1 + e)\bar{x})$. Then we have

$$c_1 = (1 - e)\bar{x} = \bar{x} - z_{1-\alpha/2} \frac{s}{\sqrt{n}} \tag{4.18}$$

$$c_2 = (1 + e)\bar{x} = \bar{x} + z_{1-\alpha/2} \frac{s}{\sqrt{n}}. \tag{4.19}$$

Since c_1 and c_2 form a symmetric interval, we can use either equation to find

$$z_{1-\alpha/2} \frac{s}{\sqrt{n}} = \bar{x}e. \tag{4.20}$$

Solving for n gives

$$n = \left(\frac{z_{1-\alpha/2}s}{e\bar{x}}\right)^2. \tag{4.21}$$

Note that this equation for determining the number of measurements, n, requires an estimate of the standard deviation of the measurements, s. However, we cannot know anything about s until we make some measurements! Consequently, the procedure is to make a relatively small number of measurements to find an estimate for s. This estimate is then used in Equation (4.21) to determine approximately how many measurements must be made to obtain an interval of the desired size.

Example. In the example above, we found that the average time required to write a file was 7.94 s with a standard deviation of 2.14 s. Approximately how many measurements would be required if we wanted to be 90% confident that the mean value is within 7% of the actual value?

For a 90% confidence interval, we know that $\alpha = 0.10$, so that $1 - \alpha/2 = 0.95$. Additionally, to find the value within 7% of the actual value means that we are allowed an error of $\pm 3.5\%$. Thus, $e = 0.035$. Then, from Equation (4.21), we find

$$n = \left(\frac{z_{1-\alpha/2}s}{e\bar{x}}\right)^2 = \left(\frac{1.895(2.14)}{0.035(7.94)}\right)^2 = 212.95. \tag{4.22}$$

Thus, we need to make approximately 213 measurements to be assured that there is a 90% chance that the true value is within this $\pm 3.5\%$ interval.   ◇

4.4.3   Confidence intervals for proportions

Oftentimes in analyzing the performance of computer systems we are interested in discrete values, such as a count of the number of times several different events occur. We then may want to find the fraction of the time each event occurs. In this case, we need to determine a confidence interval for the proportion p, where p is the probability of success in each of n trials in a binomial experiment. We estimate the true proportion p using the sample proportion $\bar{p} = m/n$, where m is the number of times the desired outcome occurs out of the n total events recorded.

A binomial distribution with parameters p and n has a mean of p and a variance of $p(1 - p)/n$. If $np \geq 10$, we can approximate the binomial distribution with a Gaussian distribution with mean $\bar{p}$ and variance $\bar{p}(1 - \bar{p})/n$. Applying the same analysis as that in Section 4.4.1, we find the confidence interval for the proportion p to be

$$c_1 = \bar{p} - z_{1-\alpha/2}\sqrt{\frac{\bar{p}(1 - \bar{p})}{n}} \tag{4.23}$$

$$c_2 = \bar{p} + z_{1-\alpha/2}\sqrt{\frac{\bar{p}(1 - \bar{p})}{n}} \tag{4.24}$$

where $\bar{p} = m/n$, m is the number of outcomes of the type of interest, n is the total number of events, and $z_{1-\alpha/2}$ is the value of a standard unit normal distribution that has an area of $1 - \alpha/2$ to the left of $z_{1-\alpha/2}$.

Example. We have a multitasked computer system that alternates execution between several user programs and the operating system. We wish to determine how much time the processor spends executing the operating system compared with how much time it spends executing the users' application programs.

To make this measurement, we configure the system to interrupt the processor every 10 ms. The interrupt-service routine then maintains two counters. One counter, n, is incremented every time the interrupt-service routine is executed and thus counts how many times the interrupt occurs. The interrupt-service routine also checks the return-address value stored on the stack to determine whether the operating system was executing when the interrupt occurred. If it was, then the second counter, m, is incremented. Running this experiment for approximately 1 min results in $m = 658$ and $n = 6,000$.

With this experimental configuration, the ratio $\bar{p} = m/n = 0.1097$ approximates the fraction of the total time that the processor is executing the operating system. A 95% confidence interval for this ratio is found to be $(c_1, c_2) = (\bar{p} - z, \bar{p} + z)$, where

$$z = z_{1-\alpha/2}\sqrt{\frac{\bar{p}(1 - \bar{p})}{n}} = 1.96\sqrt{\frac{0.1097(1 - 0.1097)}{6000}} = 0.0079. \tag{4.25}$$

The confidence interval is then $(0.1018, 0.1176)$. Thus, with only a 5% chance of being wrong, we can say the the processor spends 10.2–11.8% of its time executing the operating system.   ◇

4.4.3.1 Determining the number of measurements needed

Using the same line of reasoning as in Section 4.4.2, we can determine how many measurements are needed to obtain a confidence interval of a desired size for a proportion. Similar to what we did with Equation (4.18), we extend Equation (4.23) to give

$$(1 - e)\bar{p} = \bar{p} - z_{1-\alpha/2}\sqrt{\frac{\bar{p}(1 - \bar{p})}{n}}. \tag{4.26}$$

Rearranging gives us

$$e\bar{p} = z_{1-\alpha/2}\sqrt{\frac{\bar{p}(1 - \bar{p})}{n}}. \tag{4.27}$$

Solving for n produces

$$n = \frac{z_{1-\alpha/2}^2 \bar{p}(1 - \bar{p})}{(\bar{p}e)^2}. \tag{4.28}$$

As before, this calculation of n requires taking a preliminary measurement to estimate the value of $\bar{p}$.

Example. How long must the experiment in the above example be run to know with 95% confidence the fraction of time the processor spends executing the operating system within a range of $\pm 0.5\%$?

An interval of $\pm 0.5\%$ gives $e = 0.005$. If we use the value of $\bar{p} = 0.1097$ measured in the previous example as an estimate of the actual value of p, we can use Equation (4.28) to find

$$n = \frac{z_{1-\alpha/2}^2 \bar{p}(1 - \bar{p})}{(e\bar{p})^2} = \frac{(1.960)^2(0.1097)(1 - 0.1097)}{[0.005(0.1097)]^2} = 1,247,102. \tag{4.29}$$

Since interrupts occur every 10 ms, $n = 1,247,102$ samples would require approximately 3.46 h.

When we actually run this experiment again for approximately 3.5 h, we obtain $m = 142,892$ and $n = 1,300,203$. This produces $\bar{p} = 0.1099$, which leads to a 95% confidence interval of (0.1094, 0.1104). Note that this interval is $\pm 0.46\%$ of the sample mean value of 0.1099.   ◇

4.4.4 Normalizing data for confidence intervals

The techniques described above produce confidence intervals for the *mean of the population* from which the measurements are made. This mean is not necessarily the 'true value' of x being sought, however. The mean value will be the same as the desired true value only if the measuring process used to gather the samples is unbiased. It is important to remember that the confidence interval is an indication only of the precision of the measuring process, not its accuracy.

Furthermore, these confidence intervals assume that the errors in the measurements are randomly distributed with the probability of obtaining specific measurements following a normal (or Gaussian) distribution. If the measuring process itself cannot ensure that the underlying error distribution is Gaussian, then the data must be *normalized*. This normalization can be accomplished by finding the arithmetic mean of four or more randomly selected measurements. The central-limit theorem then assures us that these averaged values follow a Gaussian distribution, so that the confidence intervals apply to the overall mean of these average values.

Similarly, if it is impossible to measure the event of interest directly, then you can measure the mean of the event several times and calculate a confidence interval for the overall mean. For example, the duration of an event may be too short to measure directly. Instead, you can measure the duration of m_j repetitions of the event to calculate the average time for one event as $\overline{x}_j = T_j/m_j$, where T_j is the time required to repeat the event m_j times in succession. If this measurement process is repeated n times, we end up with the sequence of values $\overline{x}_1, \overline{x}_2, ..., \overline{x}_n$. We can then apply the confidence interval formula to these n mean values to calculate a confidence-interval for the mean of these means.

It is important to realize that, by analyzing the mean values (i.e. the $\overline{x}_j$ values), we *confound* the data so that we can no longer calculate a confidence interval for the isolated event. Instead, since we have aggregated the data, any questions being asked regarding the population from which the measurements were taken must now be asked in terms of the average values. That is, we can obtain a confidence interval for the average values, but not the individual values themselves.

While this normalization allows us to apply these standard statistical techniques to measurements with any arbitrary underlying error distribution, the normalization does exact a penalty. Specifically, the cost of this normalization is a reduction in the number of measurements available for analysis. This reduction results in a loss of information about the system being measured. For instance, after aggregating the m_j short-duration events above into a single long-duration event, we can provide confidence intervals only for the mean value of the aggregated events, not for the individual events themselves. The normalization process also tends to smooth out the variance that would have been seen in the measurements of the individual events. Thus, the variance calculated for the aggregated values tends to be smaller than the actual variance of the individual events themselves.

4.5   Summary

Errors are inherent in our measurements of real computer systems. Systematic errors tend to introduce a constant or slowly varying bias into our measurements. Since these types of errors are due to experimental 'mistakes,' they must be controlled and eliminated through the skills of the experimenter. Random errors, in contrast, are completely unpredicatable and cause unbiased changes to the measured values. We typically model these random errors using a Gaussian (normal) distribution. Alternatively, we can normalize our measurements by adding together subsets of the raw data. The central-limit theorem then assures us that the errors in these normalized values will follow a Gaussian distribution. This Gaussian error model then allows us to use confidence intervals for the mean to quantify the precision of our set of measurements.

4.6   For further reading

- In his book

    N. C. Barford, *Experimental Measurements: Precision, Error, and Truth* (Second Edition), John Wiley and Sons, New York, 1985,

    provides a good intuitive explanation of why random errors in physical systems can reasonably be modeled using a Gaussian (or normal) distribution. This explanation is the basis of the error model presented in Section 4.3. Although errors in computer systems do not always correspond to the physical intuition used by Barford, the central-limit theorem still allows us to model our experimental errors with a Gaussian distribution. This result is important since many common statistical techniques, including use of the confidence intervals studied in this chapter, require the underlying error model to be Gaussian.

- The statistical techniques discussed in this chapter have been commonly used for many years. Two sources that do a nice job describing these techniques, and interpretation of experimental data in general, are

    John Mandel, *The Statistical Analysis of Experimental Data,* Interscience Publishers, a division of John Wiley and Sons, New York, 1964,

    Mary Gibbons Natrella, *Experimental Statistics,* National Bureau of Standards Handbook 91, October 1966.

4.7   Exercises

1. As the confidence level used in estimating the mean is increased (i.e. a smaller value of α is used), the size of the resulting confidence interval increases. A larger confidence interval, however, would seem to imply that we know less about the mean value, so that the confidence should actually be decreasing. Explain this apparent contradiction.

2. How do we know what confidence level to choose?

3. Why is it unreasonable to always choose a 99% confidence level?

4. Describe the differences among accuracy, resolution, and precision for a tool used to measure distances, such as a tape measure.

5. What is the single most important difference between a systematic error and a random error?

6. Consider an experiment in which we randomly toss a dart onto a line that is one unit long and is subdivided into 1000 intervals. Assume that we are perfect dart throwers so that the dart always hits the line between the end-points at 0 and 1. The outcome of a single throw is the value at that point on the line, such as 0.250, 0.654, and so on. If we throw the dart $n = 100$ times, we will obtain 100 values that are uniformly distributed in the range [0, 1]. We can then calculate a 90% confidence interval for the mean of these n values. We now repeat this experiment $k = 2,000$ times. When we are done, we will have calculated k different confidence intervals for the mean value.

   (a) How many of the k confidence intervals do we expect will include the true mean of 0.5? (How do we know that 0.5 is the true mean? Notice that, in a real experimental measurement, we do not actually know the true mean. In fact, this mean is exactly what we are trying to determine!)

   (b) How many of the k confidence intervals do we expect will include the true mean of 0.5 if we repeat the experiment using a 99% confidence interval?

   (c) How many of the k confidence intervals do we expect will include the true mean of 0.5 if we repeat the experiment using a 60% confidence interval?

   (It is interesting to try this experiment using a random-number generator to simulate the throwing of the darts. See Section 10.3 for more information about random number generation.)

7. Many compilers have several different levels of optimization that can be selected to improve performance. Using some appropriate benchmark program, determine whether these different optimization levels actually

make a statistically significant difference in the overall execution time of this program. Run the program $n = 4$ times for each of the different optimizations. Use a 90% and a 99% confidence level to determine whether each of the optimizations actually improves the performance. Explain your results.

8. Using the following two techniques, measure the overhead of the interval timer that you have available on your computer system to measure execution time.

   (a) Measure the timer overhead time directly:

```
for i = 1 to n1
        start timer
        read timer
        stop timer
    end
```

   (b) Measure the timer overhead time in a loop:

```
    for j = 1 to k
        start timer
        for i = 1 to n2
                read timer
        end
        stop timer
    end
```

For (a), generate a histogram of the times required to read the timer, and determine a 90% confidence interval for the mean time, for n1 = 10, 1,000, and 100,000.

For (b), choose a reasonable value for n2 on the basis of your results from part (a). Then generate a histogram of the average times required to read the timer, and determine a 90% confidence interval for the mean time, for k = 10, 1,000, and 100,000.

Explain the differences you see between the results of (a) and (b). For instance, consider what you are actually measuring with approach (b) compared with approach (a).

9. The use of a confidence interval for a mean value requires the distribution of the errors in the measured samples to be normally (i.e. Gaussian) distributed. However, in the problem above, your histograms probably did not look very normal. How then can we justify using confidence intervals in this situation?

10. In the example in Section 4.4.3, an interrupt-driven technique was used to determine how much time a processor spent executing in the operating-system code. What would happen to the confidence interval in this example if the interrupt period were reduced to one-half its original value, that is, if the interrupts occurred twice as often?

11. How long would the program have to be run to reduce the size of the confidence interval by a factor of q?

5 Comparing alternatives

"Measurements are not to provide numbers but insights."

Ingrid Bucher

In Chapter 4 we learned that the measurements we make of a computer system are subject to error and, thus, are said to be "noisy." We also learned that, if the errors in the measurements can reasonably be modeled with a Gaussian distribution, we can use confidence intervals to quantify the precision of the measurements. Alternatively, if the errors in our measurements are not Gaussian, we can *normalize* the set of measurements by computing the averages of groups of four or more randomly selected measurements. We can then use confidence intervals to characterize the variability of these average values.

While these confidence intervals tell us something about how much noise there is in our measurements, we ultimately want to use these measurements to make a decision about some aspect of the performance of one or more computer systems. For instance, we may want to compare the performance of some component of two different systems, or we may want to determine how some change to a system, such as installing a new operating system or enhancing a communications protocol, affects its performance. Since there is noise in any of the measurements we make, however, we need a technique for determining whether any changes we see are due to random fluctuations in the measurements or whether they are actually significant in a statistical sense.

At this point, many statistics textbooks would introduce the concept of *hypothesis testing*, which is a statistical technique for making decisions. With this technique, mutually exclusive hypotheses are proposed as statements or assumptions about the *population* or *process* that is being measured. One of these hypotheses is called the *null hypothesis*. The goal of this hypothesis testing is to determine whether it is likely that the null hypothesis is false, and, consequently, that we have no evidence on the basis of which to reject the alternative hypothesis.

Whether these hypotheses are true or not cannot be known for certain without making all possible measurements of the system being tested. Clearly, this exhaustive measurement is impossible in most situations. Instead, we must be satisfied with a random sample of measurements. Since it is randomly selected, this sample is assumed to represent the behavior of the whole. We then calculate some appropriate *statistic* as a function of the measurements. If the error distribution underlying the process we measured is of the type assumed by the statistic, we can ensure that the calculated statistic will be distributed according to a known function. Many functions that have been found to be useful for hypothesis testing have been tabulated previously. Given our desired level of significance, α, we can find the *critical value* of this statistic from the tabulated distribution. Finally, we compare our calculated statistic with the critical value. From this comparison, we can conclude whether the results of our measurements are most likely due to random fluctuations (noise) or whether they are *statistically significant* so that we can reject the null hypothesis.

This type of hypothesis testing is very general. Furthermore, a creative experimenter can cleverly phrase the hypotheses to reduce the likelihood of being wrong. However, one important criticism of hypothesis testing is that it provides only a binary *accept/reject* result with no indication of how close the decision may have been. In analyzing the performance of computer systems, however, we often want to know not only whether the differences between two configurations are statistically significant, but also the magnitude of that difference. As a result, instead of using only the hypothesis-testing technique, this chapter describes how to apply confidence intervals to compare two alternatives. This approach not only allows us to determine whether there is a statistically significant difference between the two alternatives, but also provides an indication of how large the difference is. This type of information is often more intuitive and easier to understand and explain to someone else than is the result of a hypothesis-testing experiment.

This chapter also introduces a general statistical analysis technique called analysis of variance (ANOVA). ANOVA partitions the total variation observed in a set of measurements into several meaningful components. In Section 5.2, we show how to use ANOVA to compare more than two alternatives. We extend the ANOVA technique to more complex situations in Chapter 9.

5.1   Comparing two alternatives

The simplest approach to using confidence intervals to compare alternatives is to determine whether the confidence intervals for the two sets of measurements being compared overlap. If they do, then it is impossible to say that any differences seen in the mean value are not due to random (chance) fluctuations. If they do not overlap, however, we conclude that there is no evidence to suggest that there is not a statistically significant difference.

Note that careful phrasing of the second conclusion. When the confidence intervals do not overlap, we cannot say with complete assurance that there actually is a real difference between the alternatives. We can only say that there is no reason to believe that there is not a difference. There is still the probability α, however, that the differences we see are due simply to random fluctuations in our measurements. Although this type of ambiguous conclusion is often not very satisfying, it is unfortunately the best we can do given the statistical nature of our measurements.

There are more powerful statistical tools for comparing two or more alternatives, such as the analysis of variance (ANOVA) technique discussed in Section 5.2.1. Nevertheless, the confidence-interval approach for comparing two alternatives is quick, simple, and intuitively satisfying. Additionally, and, perhaps, more importantly, comparison tests using confidence intervals are easy to explain to someone else, such as your boss!

We examine three different cases in this subsection – a *before-and-after* comparison in which there is an obvious pairing to the measurements made before and after some change, a comparison of *noncorresponding* or *unpaired* measurements, and a comparison involving *proportions*.

5.1.1   Before-and-after comparisons

Before-and-after comparisons are commonly used to determine whether some change made to a system has a statistically significant impact on its performance. For example, we may be interested in determining whether adding a faster disk drive to a system improves its performance on a set of application programs. Or we may want to determine whether it is worthwhile to upgrade the system with the latest version of its operating system. Or we may want to compare the execution times of a set of application programs on two different systems to determine whether one system is generally faster than the other.

In all of these types of situations, the before-and-after measurements are not independent and the variances of these two sets of measurements are not necessarily equal. In fact, measurements from each set are related and so form an obvious corresponding pair. To determine whether there is a statistically significant difference between the means of the two sets of measurements, we must find a confidence interval for the *mean of the differences* of the paired observations. If this interval includes zero, we conclude that the measured differences are not statistically significant.

Let $b_1, b_2, \ldots, b_n$ be the set of n *before* measurements and $a_1, a_2, \cdots, a_n$ be the set of corresponding *after* measurements. Then we simply need to find a confidence interval for the n difference values, $d_1 = a_1 - b_1, d_2 = a_2 - b_2, \ldots, d_n = a_n - b_n$. Using the same derivation as in Section 4.4.1, the confidence interval (c_1, c_2) for the mean of the differences when $n \geq 30$ is given by

$$c_1 = \overline{d} - z_{1-\alpha/2} \frac{s_d}{\sqrt{n}} \tag{5.1}$$

$$c_2 = \overline{d} + z_{1-\alpha/2} \frac{s_d}{\sqrt{n}} \tag{5.2}$$

where $\overline{d}$ is the arithmetic mean of the d_i values and s_d is the corresponding standard deviation. As before, if the number of measurements is less than 30, the $z_{1-\alpha/2}$ value should be replaced by the $t_{1-\alpha/2;n-1}$ value, which is a t distribution with $n - 1$ degrees of freedom.

Example. We want to compare the performance of a new, supposedly improved, network communication protocol with that of the existing protocol. We begin the comparison by measuring the time required to send $n = 6$ differently sized messages, first with the original protocol, and then with the new protocol. Since we send the same size of message once with the original protocol and once with the new protocol, there is an obvious correspondence between pairs of measurements. These times and their corresponding differences are shown in Table 5.1

On calculating the mean of the six differences, $d_i = b_i - a_i$, we find $\overline{d} = -1$. The standard deviation of these differences is found to be $s_d = 4.15$. Since there are fewer than 30 total measurements, we must use the t distribution. For a 95% confidence level, we find $t_{1-\alpha/2;n-1} = t_{0.975;5} = 2.571$. We then calculate the confidence interval for the mean difference to be $(-5.36, 3.36)$.

By looking only at the mean difference of $\overline{d} = -1$, we might guess that the new protocol is slightly worse than the original protocol. However, since the confidence interval for the mean difference includes 0, we can say with 95% confidence that the differences we measured in the two cases are due to random measurement errors. Thus, we conclude with 95% confidence that there is no significant difference between these two communication protocols.   ◇

5.1.2 Noncorresponding measurements

In many situations, there is no direct correspondence between pairs of measurements. In fact, the number of measurements made to compare two different systems need not even be the same. In this case, we say that the measurements

Table 5.1. The measured times required to send differently sized messages with two different communication protocols

Measurement number (i)	Original protocol (b_i)	New protocol (a_i)	Difference $(d_i = b_i - a_i)$
1	85	86	−1
2	83	88	−5
3	94	90	4
4	90	95	−5
5	88	91	−3
6	87	83	4

are *noncorresponding* or *unpaired*. As before, there are two cases to consider. The first case is when the numbers of measurements made for both systems are sufficiently large (i.e. greater than or equal to 30) so that the underlying distributions may be assumed to be normal. If there are fewer than 30 values in at least one set of measurements, however, the normal approximation no longer applies. Instead, a t distribution must be used, with an appropriate number of degrees of freedom.

To compare two different systems, we first make n_1 measurements of the first system and n_2 measurements of the second system. Now, however, we cannot simply apply the same calculation as that used when there is a direct correspondence between the before and after measurements. Since the measurements can be directly paired in the before-and-after situation, we could first calculate the differences of each of the pairs of measurements. We then found the mean and standard deviation of these differences.

In this current situation, however, there is no correspondence or pairing between the measurements. As a result, we must first find the means, $\bar{x}_1$ and $\bar{x}_2$, and the standard deviations, s_1 and s_2, for each set of measurements separately. Then we calculate the *difference of the means* to be $\bar{x} = \bar{x}_1 - \bar{x}_2$. It can then be shown that the standard deviation of this difference of mean values is the sum of the standard deviations of each set of measurements, appropriately weighted by the total number of measurements in each set. That is, the standard deviation of the difference of the means is

$$s_x = \sqrt{\frac{s_1^2}{n_1} + \frac{s_2^2}{n_2}}. \tag{5.3}$$

This calculation of the standard deviation of the difference of the means makes intuitive sense if you recall that both mean values, $\bar{x}_1$ and $\bar{x}_2$, are calculated from measurements with random errors. Thus, their difference would be expected to have even more error. Since the standard deviation is an indication of the error in the measurements, the error in the difference of the means should be the sum of the error in each set of measurements, weighted appropriately by the total number of measurements in each set.

Now that we have an estimate of the difference of the mean values of each set of measurements, $\bar{x}$, and an estimate of its standard deviation, s_x, we can apply the same derivation as before to find the confidence interval, (c_1, c_2) for the difference of the means to be given by

$$c_1 = \bar{x} - z_{1-\alpha/2}s_x \tag{5.4}$$

$$c_2 = \bar{x} + z_{1-\alpha/2}s_x \tag{5.5}$$

where $\bar{x}$ and s_x are as defined above. If the resulting confidence interval includes 0, we can conclude that, at the confidence level chosen, there is no significant difference between the two sets of measurements.

Recall that the above formula applies only when at least approximately 30 measurements have been made for each system, that is both $n_1 \geq 30$ and $n_2 \geq 30$. In the case when either $n_1 < 30$ or $n_2 < 30$ so that the normal approximation does not apply, we can again simply substitute $t_{1-\alpha/2;n_{df}}$ for $z_{1-\alpha/2}$ in Equations (5.4) and (5.5) for (c_1, c_2). The only change in this case is that the number of degrees of freedom to use in the t distribution, n_{df} is *not* simply $n_1 + n_2 - 2$, as might have been expected. Instead, it has been shown that the number of degrees of freedom in this case is approximately

$$n_{df} = \frac{\left(\dfrac{s_1^2}{n_1} + \dfrac{s_2^2}{n_2}\right)^2}{\dfrac{(s_1^2/n_1)^2}{(n_1-1)} + \dfrac{(s_2^2/n_2)^2}{(n_2-1)}}. \tag{5.6}$$

This value most likely will not be a whole number. Consequently, it should be rounded to the nearest whole number.

Example. You are asked to compare the performance of two different computer-system installations using a standard benchmark program. These are large, complex systems that require a significant amount of time and effort on your part to make the benchmark program run. By the time you have the benchmark running on both systems, you have time to make only $n_1 = 8$ measurements on the first system and $n_2 = 5$ measurements on the second system. Your measurements, and the resulting means and standard deviations for each set, are shown in Table 5.2.

Table 5.2. The times measured when running a standard benchmark program on two different computer-system installations, along with the corresponding means and standard deviations

Measurement number	Time (s)	
	System 1	System 2
1	1,011	894
2	998	963
3	1,113	1,098
4	1,008	982
5	1,100	1,046
6	1,039	
7	1,003	
8	1,098	
n_i	8	5
$\bar{x_i}$	1,046.25	996.6
s_i	49.25	78.41

At first glance, it appears that system 2 is slightly faster than system 1. However, the standard deviation of the measurements is relatively large compared with the mean values. Furthermore, the standard deviation of system 2 is larger than that of system 1. As a result, the difference between the mean values may be due to measurement error, rather than to any real differences between the systems themselves. To characterize this difference, you decide to construct a 90% confidence interval for the difference of the mean execution times.

First, you calculate the effective number of degrees of freedom, n_{df}, for this difference using Equation (5.6):

$$n_{df} = \frac{\left(\frac{49.25^2}{8} + \frac{78.41^2}{5} \right)^2}{\frac{(49.25^2/8)^2}{(8-1)} + \frac{(78.41^2/5)^2}{(5-1)}} = 6.01 \tag{5.7}$$

which is rounded to $n_{df} = 6$. You then find the required value from the t distribution table to be $t_{0.95;6} = 1.943$.

The difference of the means is simply

$$\bar{x} = 1046.25 - 996.60 = 49.65. \tag{5.8}$$

The corresponding standard deviation is determined to be

$$s_x = \sqrt{\frac{49.25^2}{8} + \frac{78.41^2}{5}} = 39.15. \tag{5.9}$$

The confidence-interval values then can be calculated, giving

$$c_1 = 49.65 - 1.943(39.15) = -26.42 \tag{5.10}$$

$$c_2 = 49.65 + 1.943(39.15) = 125.7. \tag{5.11}$$

Since this confidence interval includes 0, we conclude that there is not a statistically significant difference between the two systems.   ◇

A special case. When only a small number of measurements have been made (i.e. $n_1 < 30$ or $n_2 < 30$), but it is known that the errors in the measurements are normally distributed and that the variances in both sets of measurements are equal, then a slight variation of Equations (5.4) and (5.5) can be applied. This special case also applies even if the variances are known or suspected to be different so long as the errors in both sets of measurements are normal and the number of measurements in each set is the same, that is, $n_1 = n_2$. The resulting confidence interval for this special case is

$$c_1 = \overline{x} - t_{1-\alpha/2;n_{df}} s_p \sqrt{\frac{1}{n_1} + \frac{1}{n_2}} \tag{5.12}$$

$$c_2 = \overline{x} + t_{1-\alpha/2;n_{df}} s_p \sqrt{\frac{1}{n_1} + \frac{1}{n_2}} \tag{5.13}$$

where the number of the degrees of freedom for the t distribution is $n_{df} = n_1 + n_2 - 2$ and the standard deviations of the individual sets of measurements are pooled together as follows:

$$s_p = \sqrt{\frac{s_1^2(n_1 - 1) + s_2^2(n_2 - 1)}{n_1 + n_2 - 2}}. \tag{5.14}$$

The advantage of using this special-case formula is that it typically results in a tighter confidence interval than that in the more general case.

Example. A few weeks after performing the comparison in the above example, you are provided with some additional time to complete your measurements on the second system. You measure three more values for the second system obtaining values of 1,002, 989, and 994 s. Since now $n_1 = n_2$, you can apply the special case formula above.

With these three additional values, the mean and standard deviation of the measurements for system 2 are found to be $\overline{x}_2 = 996.0$ and $s_2 = 59.38$. The difference of the means is now $\overline{x} = 1046.25 - 996.0 = 50.25$ and the pooled standard deviation value is

$$s_p = \sqrt{\frac{49.25^2(8-1) + 59.38^2(8-1)}{(8+8-2)}} = 54.55. \qquad (5.15)$$

Since the effective number of degrees of freedom in this case is $n_{df} = n_1 + n_2 - 2 = 8 + 8 - 2 = 14$, the t value appropriate for a 90% confidence interval is $t_{0.95;14} = 1.761$. The confidence interval is then found to be

$$c_1 = 50.25 - (1.761)(54.55)\sqrt{\frac{1}{8} + \frac{1}{8}} = 2.22 \qquad (5.16)$$

$$c_2 = 50.25 + (1.761)(54.55)\sqrt{\frac{1}{8} + \frac{1}{8}} = 98.3. \qquad (5.17)$$

Thus, with these additional measurements, you can conclude, with 90% confidence, that there is a slight, but statistically significant, difference between the two systems. ◇

5.1.3   Comparing proportions

In determining whether the difference between two proportions is statistically significant, we exploit the fact that measurements of proportions follow a binomial distribution. In particular, let m_1 be the number of times that the event in which we are interested occurs in system 1 out of a total of n_1 events measured in the system. Then the ratio $p_1 = m_1/n_1$ is the proportion of all events measured in system 1 that are of interest to us. Similarly, let the corresponding values for the second system be m_2 and n_2, giving $p_2 = m_2/n_2$. From the characteristics of a binomial distribution, we know that the estimate of the mean for system i is simply p_i with a variance of $p_i(1 - p_i)/n_i$.

If both m_1 and m_2 are larger than about 10, we can approximate the distribution of these proportions using a normal distribution with mean p_i and variance of $p_i(1 - p_i)/n_i$. This approximation allows us to use the same approach for developing a confidence interval for the difference of the mean values p_1 and p_2 as that we used for noncorresponding measurements described in Section 5.1.2. The confidence interval for the difference of the mean values then is

$$c_1 = p - z_{1-\alpha/2}s_p \qquad (5.18)$$

$$c_2 = p + z_{1-\alpha/2}s_p \qquad (5.19)$$

where $p = (p_1 - p_2)$ and s_p is the standard deviation of this difference. Specifically, s_p is again the weighted sum of the individual standard deviations:

$$s_p = \sqrt{\frac{p_1(1 - p_1)}{n_1} + \frac{p_2(1 - p_2)}{n_2}}. \qquad (5.20)$$

Example. In the example in Section 4.4.3 we used a sampling technique to estimate the fraction of the time an application program spends executing in the operating system. In particular, we assumed that the application program was interrupted every 10 ms. Two different counters were maintained, one to count the total number of interrupts, and another to count the number of times operating-system code was executing when the interrupt occurred.

After running the test for approximately 3.5 h, we found the count of the total number of interrupts to be $n_1 = 1,300,203$ and the count of the total number of interrupts that occurred when the operating system was executing to be $m_1 = 142,892$. The ratio of these two values, $p_1 = m_1/n_1 = 0.1099$, is then our estimate of the fraction of the total time spent in the operating system when executing this application.

We now have received an upgrade of the operating system that has been installed on the system. We want to use the technique of comparing proportions to determine whether this new operating system is more efficient than the old one. After running the same application with the new operating system for approximately 2 h 45 min, we find $m_2 = 84,876$ and $n_2 = 999,382$. Thus, $p_2 = m_2/n_2 = 0.0849$, indicating that, with the new operating system, the application spends approximately 8.5% of its time executing in the operating system.

The difference of these two proportions gives $p = p_1 = p_2 = 0.0250$, with a corresponding standard deviation of

$$s_p = \sqrt{\frac{0.1099(1 - 0.1099)}{1300203} + \frac{0.0849(1 - 0.0849)}{999382}} = 3.911 \times 10^{-4}. \qquad (5.21)$$

The 90% confidence interval for the difference of these two proportions then is given by

$$c_1 = 0.0250 - 1.960(3.911 \times 10^{-4}) = 0.0242 \qquad (5.22)$$

$$c_2 = 0.0250 + 1.960(3.911 \times 10^{-4}) = 0.0257. \qquad (5.23)$$

Since this interval does not include zero, we can conclude, with 90% confidence, that there is no evidence to suggest that there is not a statistically significant difference between the performances of the two operating systems when executing this application program. $\diamond$

Note the careful phrasing of this conclusion when the confidence interval does not include zero. As mentioned at the beginning of this chapter, we cannot unambiguously state that there is a real difference between the alternatives. Rather, due to the effects of random fluctuations, we can only state that we have no reason to believe otherwise.

5.2   Comparing more than two alternatives

The confidence-interval approach for comparing two alternatives described in the previous section is simple to understand and, as a result, is intuitively appealing. It also is easy to explain the results of this type of comparison to someone else. It is considered by statisticians to be a relatively weak method of comparison, however. A more robust approach is the general technique called *analysis of variance (ANOVA)*. ANOVA separates the total variation in a set of measurements into a component due to random fluctuations and a component due to actual differences among the alternatives. Using ANOVA for comparing several different alternatives is called a *one-way classification* or an analysis of a *one-factor experiment*.

5.2.1   Analysis of variance (ANOVA)

Analysis of variance is a very general technique for dividing the total variation observed in a collection of measurements into meaningful components. This analysis assumes that the errors in the measurements for the different alternatives are independent with a normal (Gaussian) distribution. It further assumes that the variance in the measurement errors is the same for all of the alternatives. The ANOVA procedure then separates the total variation observed in all of the measurements into (i) the variation observed *within* each system, which is assumed to be caused only by measurement error, and (ii) the variation *between* systems. This second component of variation can be due both to actual differences between the systems and to measurement error. The goal then is to determine whether the magnitude of component (ii) of the variation is significantly larger in some appropriate statistical sense than the magnitude of component (i). That is, are the differences among the mean values observed for the alternatives due to real differences among the alternatives, or are they simply due to measurement errors?

To answer this question, we make n measurements on each of k alternatives. It is convenient to organize all kn of these measurements as shown in Table 5.3, where y_{ij} is the ith measurement made on the jth alternative. The column means in this table, $\bar{y}_{.1}, \bar{y}_{.2}, \ldots, \bar{y}_{.j}, \ldots, \bar{y}_{.k}$, are the average values of all of the measurements made within a single alternative. That is,

$$\bar{y}_{.j} = \frac{\sum_{i=1}^{n} y_{ij}}{n}. \tag{5.24}$$

The overall mean, $\bar{y}_{..}$, is the average of all measurements made on all alternatives:

Table 5.3. Entry y_{ij} in this table is the ith measurement from the jth alternative when using the ANOVA technique to compare k distinct alternatives

| Measurements | Alternatives | | | | | | Overall mean |
	1	2	$\cdots$	j	$\cdots$	k	
1	y_{11}	y_{12}	$\cdots$	y_{1j}	$\cdots$	y_{1k}	
2	y_{21}	y_{22}	$\cdots$	y_{2j}	$\cdots$	y_{2k}	
$\vdots$	$\vdots$	$\vdots$		$\vdots$		$\vdots$	
i	y_{i1}	y_{i2}	$\cdots$	y_{ij}	$\cdots$	y_{ik}	
$\vdots$	$\vdots$	$\vdots$		$\vdots$		$\vdots$	
n	y_{n1}	y_{n2}	$\cdots$	y_{nj}	$\cdots$	y_{kn}	
Column means	$\bar{y}_{.1}$	$\bar{y}_{.2}$	$\cdots$	$\bar{y}_{.j}$	$\cdots$	$\bar{y}_{.k}$	$\bar{y}_{..}$
Effects	α_1	α_2	$\cdots$	α_j	$\cdots$	α_k	

$$\bar{y}_{..} = \frac{\sum_{j=1}^{n} \sum_{i=1}^{n} y_{ij}}{kn}. \tag{5.25}$$

It is then useful to write each measurement, y_{ij}, as the sum of the mean of all of the measurements made of alternative j, $\bar{y}_{.j}$, and a value e_{ij} that represents the deviation of measurement y_{ij} from the mean. That is, we can write

$$y_{ij} = \bar{y}_{.j} + e_{ij}. \tag{5.26}$$

Furthermore, we can extend this idea to represent each column mean as the sum of the overall mean, $\bar{y}_{..}$, and the deviation of the column mean from this overall mean, α_j, giving

$$\bar{y}_{.j} = \bar{y}_{..} + \alpha_j. \tag{5.27}$$

Substituting Equation (5.27) into Equation (5.26) then gives

$$y_{ij} = \bar{y}_{..} + \alpha_j + e_{ij}. \tag{5.28}$$

Intuitively, you can think of this expression as showing how far away each measured value (y_{ij}) is from the overall mean value as we move horizontally across alternatives in Table 5.3, represented by α_j, and as we move vertically among measurements within one alternative, represented by e_{ij}.

The α_j value for each alternative is commonly called the *effect* of that alternative. The α_j values must satisfy the property

$$\sum_{j=1}^{k} \alpha_j = 0. \tag{5.29}$$

Expressing the individual measurements in this fashion now allows us to split the total variation in all of the measurements into two separate components: (1) the variation due to the effects of the alternatives, and (2) the variation due to the errors. The *variation due to the effects* of the alternatives, which should not be confused with the *variance*, is defined to be the sum of the squares of the differences between the mean of the measurements for each alternative (i.e. the column means) and the overall mean, times the number of measurements made for each alternative. More precisely, this variation, which is denoted SSA, is

$$SSA = n \sum_{j=1}^{k} (\bar{y}_j - \bar{y}_{..})^2. \tag{5.30}$$

Similarly, the variation due to errors, denoted SSE, is the sum of the squares of the differences between the individual measurements and their corresponding column means. Thus, we have

$$SSE = \sum_{j=1}^{k} \sum_{i=1}^{n} (y_{ij} - \bar{y}_j)^2. \tag{5.31}$$

Finally, the sum-of-squares total, denoted SST, is defined to be

$$SST = \sum_{j=1}^{k} \sum_{i=1}^{n} (y_{ij} - \bar{y}_{..})^2. \tag{5.32}$$

Thus, SST is the sum of the squares of the differences between each measurement and the overall mean.

It can be shown that

$$SST = SSA + SSE. \tag{5.33}$$

This expression shows that the total variation in all of the measured values can in fact be split into the SSA and SSE components. Proving this relationship is done by expanding the SST expression (Equation (5.32)) and noting that, due to the constraint in Equation (5.29), the cross-product terms reduce to zero.

It is now helpful to pause and recall our overall goal in this analysis. At this point, we have made n measurements on each of k alternatives. There is some variation in the n measurements made for each alternative due to fluctuations (i.e. random errors) inherent in these types of measurements. Similarly, we see some differences among the mean values calculated for each alternative due to these errors and, possibly, due to real differences among the alternatives. Our goal, then, is to determine whether any of the observed differences among the mean values of each alternative are due to real differences among the alternatives, or whether they are simply due to measurement errors.

To answer this question, we split the total variation in all of the measurements with respect to the overall mean value into two separate components. The first, *SSA*, is the variation of the mean value of each alternative compared with the overall mean. It can be thought of as the variation across the 'column means' compared with the 'overall mean' in Table 5.3. The second component, *SSE*, is the variation of each measurement for one alternative relative to the mean of all of the measurements taken of that alternative. It can be thought of as the variation down the rows within a single column in Table 5.3. If the differences among alternatives are due not simply to measurement error but rather to some real difference among the alternatives, we would expect the variation across alternatives (which includes measurement errors), *SSA*, to be 'larger' in some statistical sense than the variation due only to errors within each alternative, *SSE*. To make this type of determination, we need some appropriate statistical test.

One of the simplest comparisons we can make is to find the ratios of each of the components of variation, *SSA* and *SSE*, to the total variation, *SST*. Thus, *SSA/SST* is the fraction of the total variation explained by the differences among alternatives. Similarly, *SSE/SST* is the fraction of the total variation that is due to experimental error. However, the question of whether the fraction of total variation explained by the alternatives is statistically significant still remains.

The statistical test that has been shown to be appropriate for this comparison is called the *F-test*. This test, which is based on the *F* distribution (see Appendix C.2), is used to test whether two variances are significantly different. Since the *F* statistic is computed as the ratio of two variances, values close to 1 will indicate that no significant difference likely exists.

In our current situation, we compute the ratio of the variance across alternatives (i.e. corresponding to *SSA*) to the variance due to experimental error (i.e. corresponding to *SSE*). If this ratio is greater than the critical value obtained from the *F* distribution at a given significance level, we conclude that the difference in the variances is statistically significant. Thus, we can conclude that there is a statistically significant difference among the alternatives beyond the differences due to experimental error.

Estimates of the variances of *SSA* and *SSE* are found by calculating their corresponding *mean-square* values. The mean-square value is simply the total variation for the component divided by the number of degrees of freedom for that component. Since there are k alternatives being compared, there are $k - 1$ degrees of freedom in the *SSA* term. Thus, the estimate of the variance for this term is

$$s_a^2 = \frac{SSA}{k - 1}. \tag{5.34}$$

Similarly, the *mean-square error* is found by dividing the SSE term by the total number of degrees of freedom for this component. Since each of the alternatives had n total measurements, each alternative has $n - 1$ degrees of freedom. Thus, the total number of degrees of freedom for SSE is $k(n - 1)$, since there are k alternatives. The estimate of the variance in the error then is

$$s_e^2 = \frac{SSE}{k(n - 1)}. \tag{5.35}$$

It is worthwhile to note that the total number of degrees of freedom for SST is $kn - 1$ since there are kn total measurements. Furthermore, notice that the number of degrees of freedom for SSA, which is $k - 1$, plus the number of degrees of freedom for SSE, which is $k(n - 1)$, equals $kn - 1$. Thus,

$$df(SST) = df(SSA) + df(SSE) \tag{5.36}$$

where $df(\cdot)$ is the number of degrees of freedom of the corresponding argument. This relationship provides a good check to ensure that the proper numbers of degrees of freedom are used with both SSA and SSE.

Finally, the F statistic for this test is calculated as

$$F = \frac{s_a^2}{s_e^2}. \tag{5.37}$$

Since this F statistic is the ratio of two variances, it actually requires two values for the degrees of freedom, one from the numerator and one from the denominator. If this computed F value is larger than the value $F_{[1-\alpha;(k-1),k(n-1)]}$ obtained from the table of critical F values, we can say that the variation due to actual differences among the alternatives, SSA, is significantly higher than the variation due to errors, SSE, at the α level of significance, or, equivalently, with a confidence level of $1 - \alpha$.

For purposes of calculation, it is useful to rewrite the expressions for SST, SSA, and SSE as follows:

$$SST = \sum_{j=1}^{k} \sum_{i=1}^{n} y_{ij}^2 - \frac{y_{..}^2}{kn} \tag{5.38}$$

$$SSA = \frac{\sum_{j=1}^{k} \left(\sum_{i=1}^{n} y_{ij} \right)^2}{n} - \frac{y_{..}^2}{kn} \tag{5.39}$$

$$SSE = SST - SSA \tag{5.40}$$

where

$$y_{..} = \sum_{j=1}^{k} \sum_{i=1}^{n} y_{ij}.$$ (5.41)

The components of an ANOVA test are typically summarized in the format shown in Table 5.4.

Example. As one aspect of comparing the performance of $k = 3$ different computer systems, we have measured the time required for each system to perform a subroutine `call` and `return` operation. We decide to use the ANOVA technique to compare the systems, so we organize the $n = 5$ measurements for each system as shown in Table 5.5.

The first step in this analysis is to compute the sum of squares as follows:

$$SST = [(0.0972^2 + 0.0971^2 + \cdots + 0.5298^2) - \frac{(0.0972 + 0.0971 + \cdots + 0.5298)^2}{3(5)}$$

$$= 0.8270$$

(5.42)

$$SSA = [(0.0972 + \cdots + 0.0974)^2 + (0.1382 + \cdots + 0.1383)^2 + (0.7966 +$$

$$\cdots + 0.5298)^2]/5 - \frac{(0.0972 + 0.0971 + \cdots + 0.5298)^2}{3(5)}$$

(5.43)

$$= 0.7585$$

$$SSE = SST - SSA = 0.8270 - 0.7585 = 0.0685.$$ (5.44)

We can then compute the fractions of the total variation explained by each component to be

$$\frac{SSA}{SST} = \frac{0.7585}{0.8270} = 0.917$$ (5.45)

$$\frac{SSE}{SST} = \frac{0.0685}{0.8270} = 0.083.$$ (5.46)

Thus, we can say that 91.7% of the total variation in the measurements is due to differences among the systems, while 8.3% of the total variation is due to noise in the measurements.

While this allocation of variation certainly suggests that there is a significant difference among the systems, we next perform an *F-test* to determine whether this difference is statistically significant. The computations for this test are summarized in Table 5.6. We find the computed F value to be larger than the F value obtained from the table so we can conclude that, at the 0.05 level of significance, the differences among the systems are statistically significant.   ◇

Table 5.4. A summary of using an analysis of variance (ANOVA) test for comparing several alternatives: if the computed F value is larger than the F value obtained from the table, the variation due to actual differences among the alternatives, SSA, can be considered statistically significant at the α level of significance

Source of variation	Alternatives	Error	Total
Sum of squares	SSA	SSE	SST
Degrees of freedom	$k-1$	$k(n-1)$	$kn-1$
Mean square	$s_a^2 = SSA/(k-1)$	$s_e^2 = SSE/[k(n-1)]$	
Computed F value	s_a^2/s_e^2		
F value from table	$F_{[1-\alpha;(k-1),k(n-1)]}$		

Table 5.5. Measurements of the time (in microseconds) required to perform a subroutine call and return on three different systems

Measurements	Alternatives			Overall mean
	1	2	3	
1	0.0972	0.1382	0.7966	
2	0.0971	0.1432	0.5300	
3	0.0969	0.1382	0.5152	
4	0.1954	0.1730	0.6675	
5	0.0974	0.1383	0.5298	
Column means	0.1168	0.1462	0.6078	0.2903
Effects	−0.1735	−0.1441	0.3175	

Table 5.6. The calculations for the ANOVA F-test for the data from Table 5.5, the F value from the table was determined by interpolating the values shown in Appendix C.2

Source of variation	Alternatives	Error	Total
Sum of squares	$SSA = 0.7585$	$SSE = 0.0685$	$SST = 0.8270$
Degrees of freedom	$k-1 = 2$	$k(n-1) = 12$	$kn-1 = 14$
Mean square	$s_a^2 = 0.7585/2 = 0.3793$	$s_e^2 = 0.0685/12 = 0.0057$	
Computed F value	$0.3793/0.0057 = 66.4$		
F value from table	$F_{[0.05;2,12]} = 3.89$		

5.2.2   Contrasts

After completing an ANOVA test, we may find that there is a statistically significant difference among the various alternatives. That is, by applying the *F-test* we may find that the differences we see in measurements across the alternatives are due to actual differences among the alternatives rather than to random fluctuations in the measurements. However, this test does not tell us *where* the differences occur.

For example, from the *effects* calculated in Table 5.5, we see that system 1 is, on the average, 0.1735 µs below the overall average, system 2 is 0.1441 µs below, and system 3 is 0.3175 µs above. The corresponding *F-test* in Table 5.6 confirms that these deviations from the overall mean are significant for $\alpha = 0.05$. However, from this test alone we cannot determine whether system 1 is actually faster than system 2, or whether this difference is due to measurement errors.

To make these more detailed comparisons between individual alternatives, we can use the method of contrasts. A *contrast*, *c*, is a linear combination of the effects, α_j, of the alternatives. Thus,

$$c = \sum_{j=1}^{k} w_j \alpha_j. \tag{5.47}$$

The weights in this linear combination must be chosen such that

$$\sum_{j=1}^{k} w_j = 0. \tag{5.48}$$

These contrasts can be used to compare the effects of any subset of the alternatives. For example, if there are $k = 3$ alternatives in an experiment, choosing $w_1 = 1$, $w_2 = -1$, and $w_3 = 0$ gives $c = (1)\alpha_1 + (-1)\alpha_2 + (0)\alpha_3 = \alpha_1 - \alpha_2$. Note that $w_1 + w_2 + w_3 = 0$. Constructing an appropriate confidence interval for this contrast then indicates whether the effect of alternative 1 is statistically different than the effect of alternative 2.

Note that the weights, w_j, can be chosen to be any values that satisfy Equation (5.48). In practice, however, it typical to choose $w_k = 1$ and $w_l = -1$, when we wish to compare alternatives k and l. The remaining weights are all set to zero.

The confidence interval for the contrast $c = \sum_{j=1}^{k} w_j \alpha_j$ is found using the same procedure as that we have used previously. Specifically, we need an estimate of the standard deviation (or variance) of c and an appropriate value from the t table or from a normal distribution.

Although we do not present a formal derivation of this variance, intuitively this variance is determined by assuming that the variation due to measurement errors is equally distributed among all of the kn total measurements. Then, recall from introductory statistics that, for any random variable X and some arbitrary constant a, $\text{Var}[aX] = a^2\text{Var}[X]$. Furthermore, if the random variables X_1 and X_2 are independent, then $\text{Var}[X_1 + X_2] = \text{Var}[X_1] + \text{Var}[X_2]$. Thus, since the contrast $c = \sum_{j=1}^{k} w_j \alpha_j$, the variance of c is

$$s_c^2 = \frac{\sum_{j=1}^{k}(w_j^2 s_e^2)}{kn} \tag{5.49}$$

where $s_e^2 = SSE/k(n-1)$ is the mean-square error. The number of degrees of freedom for s_c^2 is the same as the number of degrees of freedom for s_e^2, namely $k(n-1)$.

The confidence interval, (c_1, c_2) for the contrast c is then given simply by

$$c_1 = c - t_{[1-\alpha/2;k(n-1)]}s_c \tag{5.50}$$

$$c_2 = c + t_{[1-\alpha/2;k(n-1)]}s_c. \tag{5.51}$$

Just like in previous situations, values from the normal distribution with $\mu = 0$ and $\sigma^2 = 1$ can substituted for the $t_{[1-\alpha/2;k(n-1)]}$ distribution when the number of degrees of freedom, $k(n-1)$, is greater than about 30.

Note that it is possible to use the *F-test* to determine whether the value of a contrast is statistically significant. Constructing a confidence interval for a contrast typically provides a more intuitive feel for the measured data, however, and is usually all that is needed to obtain a good understanding of the results of an experiment.

Example. From the data in Table 5.5, we found the *effects* of the three systems to be $\alpha_1 = -0.1735$, $\alpha_2 = -0.1441$, and $\alpha_3 = 0.3175$ µs. Using the weights $w_1 = 1$, $w_2 = -1$, and $w_3 = 0$ gives us a contrast for the difference between the effects of systems 1 and 2, where $c_{[1-2]} = -0.1735 - (-0.1441) = -0.0294$. The standard deviation for all contrasts using this set of measurements is

$$s_c = \sqrt{\frac{\sum_{j=1}^{k}(w_j^2 s_e^2)}{kn}} = s_e \sqrt{\frac{\sum_{j=1}^{3}(1^2 + (-1)^2 + 0^2)}{3(5)}} = 0.0754(0.3651) = 0.0275. \tag{5.52}$$

For a 90% confidence interval we find $t_{[1-\alpha/2;k(n-1)]} = 1.782$, giving the confidence interval $[-0.0294 \mp (1.782)(0.0275)] = [-0.0784, 0.0196]$. Since this confidence interval includes zero, we conclude that there is no statistically significant difference between the times required to perform a subroutine `call` and `return` pair with systems 1 and 2.

In the same fashion, we can construct a contrast for the difference between the effects of systems 1 and 3 by using $w_1 = 1$, $w_2 = 0$, and $w_3 = -1$, giving $c_{[1-3]} = -0.4910$ µs. The corresponding 90% confidence interval for this contrast is found to be $[-0.4910 \mp (1.782)(0.0275)] = [-0.540, -0.442]$ µs. Since this interval does *not* include zero, we thus conclude that we cannot say that there is no statistically significant difference between these two systems.   ◇

5.3   Summary

The need to compare several different alternatives is common in computer-systems performance analysis. For instance, we may need to choose the best computer system out of several different possibilities. The difficulty is that, due to the errors that are inherent in our measurements, we cannot simply compare the means of the measurements made of the various systems being compared. For *before-and-after* comparisons in which there is an obvious direct correspondence between measurements made on two different alternatives, we can construct a confidence interval for the mean of the individual differences. If this interval includes zero, we conclude that there is no statistically significant difference between the two alternatives. In the case when there is no direct correspondence between pairs of measurements, we construct a confidence interval for the difference of the mean values of each set of measurements. As before, we conclude that there is no statistically significant difference between the two alternatives if this interval includes zero. We exploited the characteristics of the binomial distribution to construct a confidence interval for the difference between two proportions. Finally, we introduced the general ANOVA technique for partitioning the total variation observed in a set of measurements into meaningful components. This ANOVA technique is found to be useful when comparing more than two alternatives.

5.4   For further reading

- Determining whether there is a statistically significant difference between means is a concept that is covered well in most introductory statistics textbooks. One example is

  Ronald E. Walpole and Raymond H. Myers, *Probability and Statistics for Engineers and Scientists* (Second Edition), Macmillan Publishing, New York, 1978.

- Also, the following text provides a good intuitive summary of one-factor experimental design, as well as some good examples of comparing alternatives:

  Raj Jain, *The Art of Computer Systems Performance Analysis,* John Wiley and Sons, Inc., 1991.

5.5   Exercises

1. Using the "before-and-after" comparison technique with both a 90% and a 99% confidence level, determine whether turning a specific compiler optimization on makes a statistically significant difference. Repeat your analysis using an ANOVA test with $k = 2$ alternatives. Explain your results.

2. A certain computer network rejects messages that any program attempts to send on the network whenever the network runs out of buffer space to temporarily store the outgoing messages. This occurs when the network temporarily becomes very busy. Your measurements over the course of several days showed that, out of 5,456,876 message requests, 4,342 of them were rejected by the network. You are considering whether it is worthwhile to purchase additional buffer memory to reduce the number of messages rejected. With 90% confidence, what message-rejection rate (measured as messages rejected per 1,000,000 attempts) can be tolerated by the upgraded network while showing a statistically significant improvement in performance?

3. Prove that $SST = SSA + SSE$ in the ANOVA derivation.

4. Use an ANOVA test to compare the performances of three different, but roughly comparable, computer systems measured in terms of the execution time of an appropriate benchmark program. The ANOVA test shows only whether there is a statistically significant difference among the systems, not how large the difference really is. Use appropriate contrasts to compare the differences between all possible pairs of the systems. Explain and interpret your results.

6 Measurement tools and techniques

'When the only tool you have is a hammer, every problem begins to resemble a nail.'

Abraham Maslow

The previous chapters have discussed what performance metrics may be useful for the performance analyst, how to summarize measured data, and how to understand and quantify the systematic and random errors that affect our measurements. Now that we know what to do with our measured values, this chapter presents several tools and techniques for actually measuring the values we desire.

The focus of this chapter is on fundamental measurement concepts. The goal is not to teach you how to use specific measurement tools, but, rather, to help you understand the strengths and limitations of the various measurement techniques. By the end of this chapter, you should be able to select an appropriate measurement technique to determine the value of a desired performance metric. You also should have developed some understanding of the trade-offs involved in using the various types of tools and techniques.

6.1   Events and measurement strategies

There are many different types of performance metrics that we may wish to measure. The different strategies for measuring the values of these metrics are typically based around the idea of an *event*, where an event is some predefined change in the system state. The precise definition of a specific event is up to the performance analyst and depends on the metric being measured. For instance, an event may be defined to be a memory reference, a disk access, a network communication operation, a change in a processor's internal state, or some pattern or combination of other subevents.

6.1.1   Events-type classification

The different types of metrics that a performance analyst may wish to measure can be classified into the following categories based on the type of event or events that comprise the metric.

1. **Event-count metrics.** Metrics that fall into this category are those that are simple counts of the number of times a specific event occurs. Examples of event-count metrics include the number of page faults in a system with virtual memory, and the number of disk input/output requests made by a program.

2. **Secondary-event metrics.** These types of metrics record the values of some secondary parameters whenever a given event occurs. For instance, to determine the average number of messages queued in the send buffer of a communication port, we would need to record the number of messages in the queue each time a message was added to, or removed from, the queue. Thus, the triggering event is a message-enqueue or -dequeue operation, and the metrics being recorded are the number of messages in the queue and the total number of queue operations. We may also wish to record the size (e.g. the number of bytes) of each message sent to later determine the average message size.

3. **Profiles.** A profile is an aggregate metric used to characterize the overall behavior of an application program or of an entire system. Typically, it is used to identify where the program or system is spending its execution time.

6.1.2   Measurement strategies

The above event-type classification can be useful in helping the performance analyst decide on a specific strategy for measuring the desired metric, since different types of measurement tools are appropriate for measuring different types of events. These different measurement tools can be categorized on the basis of the fundamental strategy used to determine the actual values of the metrics being measured. One important concern with any measurement strategy is how much it *perturbs* the system being measured. This aspect of performance measurement is discussed further in Section 6.6.

1. **Event-driven.** An event-driven measurement strategy records the information necessary to calculate the performance metric whenever the preselected event or events occur. The simplest type of event-driven measurement tool uses a simple counter to directly count the number of occurrences of a specific event. For example, the desired metric may be the number of page faults that occur during the execution of an application program. To find this value, the performance analyst most likely would have to modify the page-fault-handling

routine in the operating system to increment a counter whenever the routine is entered. At the termination of the program's execution, an additional mechanism must be provided to dump the contents of the counter.

One of the advantages of an event-driven strategy is that the system overhead required to record the necessary information is incurred only when the event of interest actually occurs. If the event never occurs, or occurs only infrequently, the perturbation to the system will be relatively small. This characteristic can also be a disadvantage, however, when the events being monitored occur very frequently.

When recording high-frequency events, a great deal of overhead may be introduced into a program's execution, which can significantly alter the program's execution behavior compared with its uninstrumented execution. As a result, what the measurement tool measures need not reflect the typical or average behavior of the system. Furthermore, the time between measurements depends entirely on when the measured events occur so that the inter-event time can be highly variable and completely unpredictable. This can increase the difficulty of determining how much the measurement tool actually perturbs the executing program. Event-driven measurement tools are usually considered most appropriate for low-frequency events.

2. **Tracing.** A tracing strategy is similar to an event-driven strategy, except that, rather than simply recording that fact that the event has occurred, some portion of the system state is recorded to uniquely identify the event. For example, instead of simply counting the number of page faults, a tracing strategy may record the addresses that caused each of the page faults. This strategy obviously requires significantly more storage than would a simple count of events. Additionally, the time required to save the desired state, either by storing it within the system's memory or by writing to a disk, for instance, can significantly alter the execution of the program being measured.

3. **Sampling.** In contrast to an event-driven measurement strategy, a sampling strategy records at fixed time intervals the portion of the system state necessary to determine the metric of interest. As a result, the overhead due to this strategy is independent of the number of times a specific event occurs. It is instead a function of the sampling frequency, which is determined by the resolution necessary to capture the events of interest.

The sampling of the state of the system occurs at fixed time intervals that are independent of the occurrence of specific events. Thus, not every occurrence of the events of interest will be recorded. Rather, a sampling strategy produces a statistical summary of the overall behavior of the system. Consequently, events that occur infrequently may be completely missed by this statistical approach. Furthermore, each run of a sampling-based experiment is likely to produce a different result since the samples occur asynchronously with respect to a program's execution. Nevertheless, while the exact behavior may differ, the statistical behavior should remain approximately the same.

4. **Indirect.** An indirect measurement strategy must be used when the metric that is to be determined is not directly accessible. In this case, you must find another metric that can be measured directly, from which you then can deduce or derive the desired performance metric. Developing an appropriate indirect measurement strategy, and minimizing its overhead, relies almost completely on the cleverness and creativity of the performance analyst.

The unique characteristics of these measurement strategies make them more or less appropriate for different situations. Program tracing can provide the most detailed information about the system being monitored. An event-driven measurement tool, on the other hand, typically provides only a higher-level summary of the system behavior, such as overall counts or average durations. The information supplied both by an event-driven measurement tool and by a tracing tool is exact, though, such as the precise number of times a certain subroutine is executed. In contrast, the information provided by a sampling strategy is statistical in nature. Thus, repeating the same experiment with an event-driven or tracing tool will produce the same results each time whereas the results produced with a sampling tool will vary slightly each time the experiment is performed.

The system resources consumed by the measurement tool itself as it collects data will strongly affect how much perturbation the tool will cause in the system. As mentioned above, the overhead of an event-driven measurement tool is directly proportional to the number of occurrences of the event being measured. Events that occur frequently may cause this type of tool to produce substantial perturbation as a byproduct of the measurement process. The overhead of a sampling-based tool, however, is independent of the number of times any specific event occurs. The perturbation caused by this type of tool is instead a function of the sampling interval, which can be controlled by the experimenter or the tool builder. A trace-based tool consumes the largest amount of system resources, requiring both processor resources (i.e. time) to record each event and potentially enormous amounts of storage resources to save each event in the trace. As a result, tracing tends to produce the largest system perturbation.

Each indirect measurement tool must be uniquely adapted to the particular aspect of the system performance it attempts to measure. Therefore, it is impossible to make any general statements about a measurement tool that makes use of an indirect strategy. The key to implementing a tool to measure a specific performance metric is to match the characteristics of the desired metric with the appropriate measurement strategy. Several of the fundamental techniques that have been used for implementing the various measurement strategies are described in the following sections.

6.2   Interval timers

One of the most fundamental measuring tools in computer-system performance analysis is the *interval timer*. An interval timer is used to measure the execution time of an entire program or any section of code within a program. It can also provide the time basis for a sampling measurement tool. Although interval timers are relatively straightforward to use, understanding how an interval timer is constructed helps the performance analyst determine the limitations inherent in this type of measurement tool.

Interval timers are based on the idea of counting the number of clock pulses that occur between two predefined events. These events are typically identified by inserting calls to a routine that reads the current timer count value into a program at the appropriate points, such as shown previously in the example in Figure 2.1. There are two common implementations of interval timers, one using a hardware counter, and the other based on a software interrupt.

Hardware timers. The hardware-based interval timer shown in Figure 6.1 simply counts the number of pulses it receives at its clock input from a free-running clock source. The counter is typically reset to 0 when the system is first powered up so that the value read from the counter is the number of clock ticks that have occurred since that time. This value is used within a program by reading the memory location that has been mapped to this counter by the manufacturer of the system.

Assume that the value read at the start of the interval being measured is x_1 and the value read at the end of the interval is x_2. Then the total time that has elapsed between these two read operations is $T_e = (x_2 - x_1)T_c$, where T_c is the period of the clock input to the counter.

Software timers. The primary difference between a software-interrupt-based interval timer, shown in Figure 6.2, and a hardware-based timer is that the counter accessible to an application program in the software-based implementa-

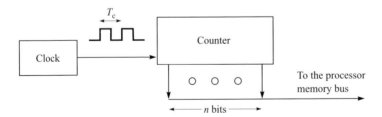

Figure 6.1 A hardware-based interval timer uses a free-running clock source to continuously increment an *n*-bit counter. This counter can be read directly by the operating system or by an application program. The period of the clock, T_c, determines the resolution of the timer.

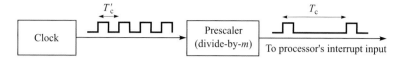

Figure 6.2 A software interrupt-based timer divides down a free-running clock to produce a processor interrupt with the period T_c. The interrupt service routine then maintains a counter variable in memory that it increments each time the interrupt occurs.

tion is not directly incremented by the free-running clock. Instead, the hardware clock is used to generate a processor interrupt at regular intervals. The interrupt-service routine then increments a counter variable it maintains, which is the value actually read by an application program. The value of this variable then is a count of the number of interrupts that have occurred since the count variable was last initialized. Some systems allow an application program to reset this counter. This feature allows the timer to always start from zero when timing the duration of an event.

The period of the interrupts in the software-based approach corresponds to the period of the timer. As before, we denote this period T_c so that the total time elapsed between two readings of the software counter value is again $T_e = (x_2 - x_1)T_c$. The processor interrupt is typically derived from a free-running clock source that is divided by m through a prescaling counter, as shown in Figure 6.2. This prescaler is necessary in order to reduce the frequency of the interrupt signal fed into the processor. Interrupts would occur much too often, and thus would generate a huge amount of processor overhead, if this prescaling were not done.

Timer rollover. One important consideration with these types of interval timers is the number of bits available for counting. This characteristic directly determines the longest interval that can be measured. (The complementary issue of the shortest interval that can be measured is discussed in Section 6.2.2.) A binary counter used in a hardware timer, or the equivalent count variable used in a software implementation, is said to 'roll over' to zero as its count undergoes a transition from its maximum value of $2^n - 1$ to the zero value, where n is the number of bits in the counter.

If the counter rolls over between the reading of the counter at the start of the interval being measured and the reading of the counter at the end, the difference of the count values, $x_2 - x_1$, will be a negative number. This negative value is obviously not a valid measurement of the time interval. Any program that uses an interval timer must take care to ensure that this type of roll over can never occur, or it must detect and, possibly, correct the error. Note that a negative value that occurs due to a single roll over of the counter can be converted to the appropriate value by adding the maximum count value, 2^n, to the negative value obtained when subtracting x_1 from x_2. Table 6.1 shows the maximum time between timer roll overs for various counter widths and input clock periods.

6.2.1   Timer overhead

The implementation of an interval timer on a specific system determines how the timer must be used. In general, though, we can think of using an interval timer to measure any portion of a program, much as we would use a stopwatch to time a runner on a track, for instance. In particular, we typically would use an interval time within a program as follows:

```
x_start = read_timer();
<event being timed>
x_end = read_timer();
elapsed_time = (x_end - x_start) * t_cycle;
```

When it is used in this way, we can see that the time we actually measure includes more than the time required by the event itself. Specifically, accessing the timer requires a minimum of one memory-read operation. In some implementations, reading the timer may require as much as a call to the operating-system kernel, which can be very time-consuming. Additionally, the value read from the timer must be stored somewhere before the event being timed begins. This requires at least one store operation, and, in some systems, it could require substantially more. These operations must be performed twice, once at the start of the event, and once again at the end. Taken altogether, these operations can add up to a significant amount of time relative to the duration of the event itself.

To obtain a better understanding of this timer overhead, consider the time line shown in Figure 6.3. Here, T_1 is the time required to read the value of the interval timer's counter. It may be as short as a single memory read, or as long as a call into the operating-system kernel. Next, T_2 is the time required to store the current time. This time includes any time in the kernel after the counter has been read, which would include, at a minimum, the execution of the return instruction. Time T_3 is the actual duration of the event we are trying to measure. Finally, the time from when the event ends until the program actually reads the counter value again is T_4. Note that reading the counter this second time involves the same set of operations as the first read of the counter so that $T_4 = T_1$.

Assigning these times to each of the components in the timing operation now allows us to compare the timer overhead with the time of the event itself, which is what we actually want to know. This event time, T_e is time T_3 in our time line, so that $T_e = T_3$. What we measure, however, is $T_m = T_2 + T_3 + T_4$. Thus, our

Table 6.1 The maximum time available before a binary interval timer with n bits and an input clock with a period of T_c rolls over is $T_c 2^n$

T_c	Counter width, n				
	16	24	32	48	64
10 ns	655 µs	168 ms	42.9 s	32.6 days	58.5 centuries
100 ns	6.55 ms	1.68 s	7.16 min	326 days	585 centuries
1 µs	65.5 ms	16.8 s	1.19 h	9.15 years	5,850 centuries
10 µs	655 ms	2.8 min	11.9 h	89.3 years	58,500 centuries
100 µs	6.55 s	28.0 min	4.97 days	893 years	585,000 centuries
1 ms	1.09 min	4.66 h	49.7 days	89.3 centuries	5,850,000 centuries

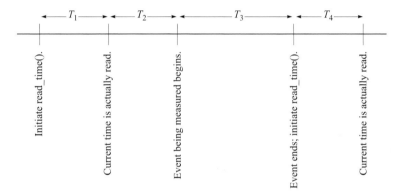

Figure 6.3 The overhead incurred when using an interval timer to measure the execution time of any portion of a program can be understood by breaking down the operations necessary to use the timer into the components shown here.

desired measurement is $T_e = T_m - (T_2 + T_4) = T_m - (T_1 + T_2)$, since $T_4 = T_1$. We call $T_1 + T_2$ the *timer overhead* and denote it T_{ovhd}.

If the interval being measured is substantially larger than the timer overhead, then the timer overhead can simply be ignored. If this condition is not satisfied, though, then the timer overhead should be carefully measured and subtracted from the measurement of the event under consideration. It is important to recognize, however, that variations in measurements of the timer overhead itself can often be quite large relative to variations in the times measured for the event. As a result, measurements of intervals whose duration is of the same order of magnitude as the timer overhead should be treated with great suspicion. A good rule of thumb is that the event duration, T_e, should be 100–1,000 times larger than the timer overhead, T_{ovhd}.

6.2.2   Quantization errors

The smallest change that can be be detected and displayed by an interval timer is its *resolution*. This resolution is a single clock tick, which, in terms of time, is the period of the timer's clock input, T_c. This finite resolution introduces a random *quantization error* into all measurements made using the timer.

For instance, consider an event whose duration is n ticks of the clock input, plus a little bit more. That is, $T_e = nT_c + \Delta$, where n is a positive integer and $0 < \Delta < T_c$. If, when one is measuring this event, the timer value is read shortly after the event has actually begun, as shown in Figure 6.4(a), the timer will count n clock ticks before the end of the event. The total execution time reported then will be nT_c. If, on the other hand, there is slightly less time between the actual start of the event and the point at which the timer value is read, as shown in Figure 6.4(b), the timer will count $n + 1$ clock ticks before the end of the event is detected. The total time reported in this case will then be $(n + 1)T_c$.

In general, the actual event time is within the range $nT_c < T_e < (n + 1)T_c$. Thus, the fact that events are typically not exactly whole number factors of the timer's clock period causes the time value reported to be rounded either up or down by one clock period. This rounding is completely unpredictable and is one readily identifiable (albeit possibly small) source of random errors in our measurements (see Section 4.2). Looking at this quantization effect another way, if we made ten measurements of the same event, we would expect that approximately five of them would be reported as nT_c with the remainder reported as $(n + 1)T_c$. If T_c is large relative to the event being measured, this quantization effect can make it impossible to directly measure the duration of the event. Consequently, we typically would like T_c to be as small as possible, within the constraints imposed by the number of bits available in the timer (see Table 6.1).

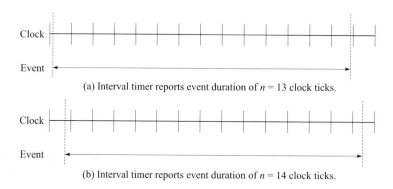

(a) Interval timer reports event duration of $n = 13$ clock ticks.

(b) Interval timer reports event duration of $n = 14$ clock ticks.

Figure 6.4 The finite resolution of an interval timer causes quantization of the reported duration of the events measured.

6.2.3   Statistical measures of short intervals

Owing to the above quantization effect, we cannot directly measure events whose durations are less than the resolution of the timer. Similarly, quantization makes it difficult to accurately measure events with durations that are only a few times larger than the timer's resolution. We can, however, make many measurements of a short duration event to obtain a statistical estimate of the event's duration.

Consider an event whose duration is smaller than the timer's resolution, that is, $T_e < T_c$. If we measure this interval once, there are two possible outcomes. If we happen to start our measurement such that the event straddles the active edge of the clock that drives the timer's internal counter, as shown in Figure 6.5(a), we will see the clock advance by one tick. On the other hand, since $T_e < T_c$, it is entirely possible that the event will begin and end within one clock period, as shown in Figure 6.5(b). In this case, the timer will not advance during this measurement. Thus, we have a Bernoulli experiment whose outcome is 1 with probability p, which corresponds to the timer advancing by one tick while are measuring the event. If the clock does not advance, though, the outcome is 0 with probability $1 - p$.

Repeating this measurement n times produces a distribution that approximates a binomial distribution. (It is only approximate since, for a true binomial dis-

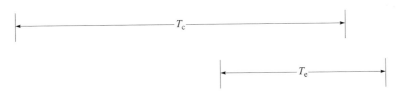

(a) Event T_e straddles the active edge of the interval timer.

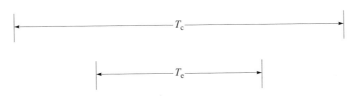

(b) Event T_e begins and ends within the resolution of the interval timer.

Figure 6.5 When one is measuring an event whose duration is less than the resolution of the interval timer, that is, $T_e < T_c$, there are two possible outcomes for each measurement. Either the event happens to straddle the active edge of the timer's clock, in which case the counter advances by one tick, or the event begins and completes between two clock edges. In the latter case, the interval timer will show the same count value both before and after the event. Measuring this event multiple times approximates a binomial distribution.

tribution, each of the n measurements must be independent. However, in a real system it is possible that obtaining an outcome of 0 in one measurement makes it more likely that one will obtain a 0 in the next measurement, for instance. Nevertheless, this approximation appears to work well in practice.) If the number of outcomes that produce 1 is m, then the ratio m/n should approximate the ratio of the duration of the event being measured to the clock period, T_e/T_c. Thus, we can estimate the average duration of this event to be

$$T_e = \frac{m}{n} T_c. \qquad (6.1)$$

We can then use the technique for calculating a confidence interval for a proportion (see Section 4.4.3) to obtain a confidence interval for this average event time.[1]

Example. We wish to measure an event whose duration we suspect is less than the 40 μs resolution of our interval timer. Out of $n = 10{,}482$ measurements of this event, we find that the clock actually advances by one tick during $m = 852$ of them. For a 95% confidence level, we construct the interval for the ratio $m/n = 852/10{,}482$ as follows:

$$(c_1, c_2) = \frac{852}{10{,}482} \mp (1.96) \sqrt{\frac{\frac{852}{10{,}482} \left(1 - \frac{852}{10{,}482}\right)}{10{,}482}} = (0.0786, 0.0840). \qquad (6.2)$$

Scaling this interval by the timer's clock period gives us the 95% confidence interval $(3.14, 3.36)$μs for the duration of this event.   ◇

6.3   Program profiling

A *profile* provides an overall view of the execution behavior of an application program. More specifically, it is a measurement of how much time, or the fraction of the total time, the system spends in certain states. A profile of a program can be useful for showing how much time the program spends executing each of its various subroutines, for instance. This type of information is often used by a programmer to identify those portions of the program that consume the largest fraction of the total execution time. Once the largest time consumers have been identified, they can, one assumes, be enhanced to thereby improve performance.

Similarly, when a profile of an entire system multitasking among several different applications is taken, it can be used by a system administrator to find system-level performance bottlenecks. This information can be used in turn to

---

[1] The basic idea behind this technique was first suggested by Peter H. Danzig and Steve Melvin in an unpublished technical report from the University of Southern California.

tune the performance of the overall system by adjusting such parameters as buffer sizes, time-sharing quanta, disk-access policies, and so forth.

There are two distinct techniques for creating a program profile – program-counter (PC) sampling and basic-block counting. Sampling can also be used to generate a profile of a complete system.

6.3.1　PC sampling

Sampling is a general statistical measurement technique in which a subset (i.e. a sample) of the members of a population being examined is selected at random. The information of interest is then gathered from this subset of the total population. It is assumed that, since the samples were chosen completely at random, the characteristics of the overall population will approximately follow the same proportions as do the characteristics of the subset actually measured. This assumption allows conclusions about the overall population to be drawn on the basis of the complete information obtained from a small subset of this population.

While this traditional population sampling selects all of the samples to be tested at (essentially) the same time, a slightly different approach is required when using sampling to generate a profile of an executing program. Instead of selecting all of the samples to be measured at once, samples of the executing program are taken at fixed points in time. Specifically, an external periodic signal is generated by the system that interrupts the program at fixed intervals. Whenever one of these interrupts is detected, appropriate state information is recorded by the interrupt-service routine.

For instance, when one is generating a profile for a single executing program, the interrupt-service routine examines the return-address stack to find the address of the instruction that was executing when the interrupt occurred. Using symbol-table information previously obtained from the compiler or assembler, this program-instruction address is mapped onto a specific subroutine identifier, i. The value i is used to index into a single-dimensional array, H, to then increment the element H_i by one. In this way, the interrupt-service routine generates a histogram of the number of times each subroutine in the program was being executed when the interrupt occurred.

The ratio H_i/n is the fraction of the program's total execution time that it spent executing in subroutine i, where n is the total number of interrupts that occurred during the program's execution. Multiplying the period of the interrupt by these ratios provides an estimate of the total time spent executing in each subroutine.

It is important to remember that sampling is a statistical process in which the characteristics of an entire population (in our present situation, the execution behavior of an entire program or system) are inferred from a randomly selected subset of the overall population. The calculated values of these inferences are, therefore, subject to random errors. Not surprisingly, we can calculate a confidence interval for these proportions to obtain a feel for the precision of our sampling experiment.

Example. Suppose that we use a sampling tool that interrupts an executing program every $T_c = 10$ ms. Including the time required to execute the interrupt-service routine, the program executes for a total of 8 s. If $H_X = 12$ of the $n = 800$ samples find the program counter somewhere in subroutine X when the interrupt occurred, what is the fraction of the total time the program spends executing this subroutine?

Since there are 800 samples in total, we conclude that the program spends 1.5% ($12/800 = 0.015$) of its time in subroutine X. Using the procedure from Section 4.4.3, we calculate a 99% confidence interval for this proportion to be

$$(c_1, c_2) = 0.015 \mp 2.576\sqrt{\frac{0.015(1 - 0.015)}{800}} = (0.0039, 0.0261). \quad (6.3)$$

So, with 99% confidence, we estimate that the program spends between 0.39% and 2.6% of its time executing subroutine X. Multiplying by the period of the interrupt, we estimate that, out of the 8 s the program was executing, there is a 99% chance that it spent between 31 (0.0039×8) and 210 (0.0261×8) ms executing subroutine X. ◇

The confidence interval calculated in the above example produces a rather large range of times that the program could be spending in subroutine X. Put in other terms, if we were to repeat this experiment several times, we would expect that, in 99% of the experiments, from three to 21 of the 800 samples would come from subroutine X. While this 7 : 1 range of possible execution times appears large, we estimate that subroutine X still accounts for less than 3% of the total execution time. Thus, we most likely would start our program-tuning efforts on a routine that consumes a much larger fraction of the total execution time.

This example does demonstrate the importance of having a sufficient number of samples in each state to produce reliable information, however. To reduce the size of the confidence interval in this example we need more samples of each event. Obtaining more samples per event requires either sampling for a longer period of time, or increasing the sampling rate. In some situations, we can simply let the program execute for a longer period of time. This will increase the total number of samples and, hence, the number of samples obtained for each subroutine.

Some programs have a fixed duration, however, and cannot be forced to execute for a longer period. In this situation, we can run the program multiple times and simply add the samples from each run. The alternative of increasing the sampling frequency will not always be possible, since the interrupt period is often fixed by the system or the profiling tool itself. Furthermore, increasing the sampling frequency increases the number of times the interrupt-service routine is executed, which increases the perturbation to the program. Of course, each run of the program must be performed under identical conditions. Otherwise, if the test conditions are not identical, we are testing two essentially different systems. Consequently, in this case, the two sets of samples cannot be simply added together to form one larger sample set.

It is also important to note that this sampling procedure implicitly assumes that the interrupt occurs completely asynchronously with respect to any events in the program being profiled. Although the interrupts occur at fixed, predefined intervals, if the program events and the interrupt are asynchronous, the interrupts will occur at random points in the execution of the program being sampled. Thus, the samples taken at these points are completely independent of each other. This sample independence is critical to obtaining accurate results with this technique since any synchronism between the events in the program and the interrupt will cause some areas of the program to be sampled more often than they should, given their actual frequency of occurrence.

6.3.2   Basic-block counting

The sampling technique described above provides a statistical profile of the behavior of a program. An alternative approach is to produce an exact execution profile by counting the number of times each *basic block* is executed. A basic block is a sequence of processor instructions that has no branches into or out of the sequence, as shown in Figure 6.6. Thus, once the first instruction in a block begins executing, it is assured that all of the remaining instructions in the block will be executed. The instructions in a basic block can be thought of as a computation that will always be executed as a single unit.

A program's basic-block structure can be exploited to generate a profile by inserting into each basic block additional instructions. These additional instructions simply count the number of times the block is executed. When the program terminates, these values form a histogram of the frequency of the basic-block executions. Just like the histogram produced with sampling, this basic-block histogram shows which portions of the program are executed most frequently. In this case, though, the resolution of the information is at the basic-block level instead of the subroutine level. Since a basic block executes as an indivisible unit, complete instruction-execution-frequency counts can also be obtained from these basic-block counts.

```
 1.  $37:    la      $25, __iob
 2.           lw      $15, 0($25)
 3.           addu    $9, $15, -1
 4.           sw      $9, 0($25)
 5.           la      $8, __iob
 6.           lw      $11, 0($8)
 7.           bge     $11, 0, $38
 8.           move    $4, $8
 9.           jal     __filbuf
10.           move    $17, $2
11.  $38:    la      $12, __iob
              . . .
```

Figure 6.6 A basic block is a sequence of instructions with no branches into or out of the block. In this example, one basic block begins at statement 1 and ends at statement 7. A second basic block begins at statement 8 and ends at statement 9. Statement 10 is a basic block consisting of only one instruction. Statement 11 begins another basic block since it is the target of an instruction that branches to label $38.

One of the key differences between this basic-block profile and a profile generated through sampling is that the basic-block profile shows the *exact* execution frequencies of all of the instructions executed by a program. The sampling profile, on the other hand, is only a statistical estimate of the frequencies. Hence, if a sampling experiment is run a second time, the precise execution frequences will most likely be at least slightly different. A basic-block profile, however, will produce exactly the same frequencies whenever the program is executed with the same inputs.

Although the repeatability and exact frequencies of basic-block counting would seem to make it the obvious profiling choice over a sampling-based profile, modifying a program to count its basic-block executions can add a substantial amount of run-time overhead. For instance, to instrument a program for basic-block counting would require the addition of at least one instruction to increment the appropriate counter when the block begins executing to each basic block. Since the counters that need to be incremented must be unique for each basic block, it is likely that additional instructions to calculate the appropriate offset for the current block into the array of counters will be necessary.

In most programs, the number of instructions in a basic block is typically between three and 20. Thus, the number of instructions executed by the instrumented program is likely to increase by at least a few percent and possibly as much as 100% compared with the uninstrumented program. These additional instructions can substantially increase the total running time of the program.

Furthermore, the additional memory required to store the counter array, plus the execution of the additional instructions, can cause other substantial perturbations. For instance, these changes to the program can significantly alter its memory behavior.

So, while basic-block counting provides exact profile information, it does so at the expense of substantial overhead. Sampling, on the other hand, distributes its perturbations randomly throughout a program's execution. Also, the total perturbation due to sampling can be controlled somewhat by varying the period of the sampling interrupt interval. Nevertheless, basic-block counting can be a useful tool for precisely characterizing a program's execution profile. Many compilers, in fact, have compile-time flags a user can set to automatically insert appropriate code into a program as it is compiled to generate the desired basic-block counts when it is subsequently executed.

6.4   Event tracing

The information captured through a profiling tool provides a summary picture of the overall execution of a program. An often-useful type of information that is ignored in this type of profile summary, however, is the time-ordering of events. A basic-block-counting profile can show the type and frequency of each of the instructions executed, for instance, but it does not provide any information about the order in which the instructions were executed. When this sequencing information is important to the analysis being performed, a program trace is the appropriate choice.

A *trace* of a program is a dynamic list of the events generated by the program as it executes. The events that comprise a trace can be any events that you can find a way to monitor, such as a time-ordered list of all of the instructions executed by a program, the sequence of memory addresses accessed by a program, the sequence of disk blocks referenced by the file system, the sizes and destinations of all messages sent over a network, and so forth. The level of detail provided in a trace is entirely determined by the performance analyst's ability to gather the information necessary for the problem at hand.

Traces themselves can be analyzed to characterize the overall behavior of a program, much as a profile characterizes a program's behavior. However, traces are probably more typically used as the input to drive a simulator. For instance, traces of the memory addresses referenced by a program are often used to drive cache simulators. Similarly, traces of the messages sent by an application program over a communication network are often used to drive simulators for evaluating changes to communication protocols.

6.4.1   Trace generation

The overall tracing process is shown schematically in Figure 6.7. A tracing system typically consists of two main components. The first is the application being traced, which is the component that actually *generates* the trace. The second main component is the trace *consumer*. This is the program, such as a simulator, that actually uses the information being generated. In between the trace generator and the consumer is often a large disk file on which to store the trace. Storing the trace allows the consumer to be run many times against an unchanging trace to allow comparison experiments without the expense of regenerating the trace. Since the trace can be quite large, however, it will not always be possible or desirable to store the trace on an intermediate disk. In this case, it is possible to consume the trace *online* as it is generated.

A wide range of techniques have been developed for generating traces. Several of these approaches are summarized below.

1. **Source-code modification.** Perhaps the most straightforward approach for generating a program trace is to modify the source code of the program to be traced. For instance, the programmer may add additional tracing statements to the source code, as shown in Figure 6.8. When the program is subsequently compiled and executed, these additional program statements will be executed, thereby generating the desired trace. One advantage of this approach is that the programmer can trace only the desired events. This can help reduce the volume of trace data generated. One major disadvantage is that inserting trace points is typically a manual process and is, therefore, very time-consuming and prone to error.

2. **Software exceptions.** Some processors have been constructed with a mode that forces a software exception just before the execution of each instruction. The

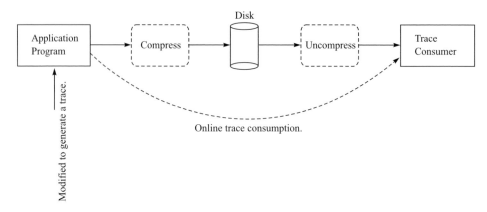

Figure 6.7 The overall process used to generate, store, and consume a program trace.

```
sum_x  =  0.0;
trace(1);
sum_xx  =  0.0;
trace(2);
for (i  =  1;  i  <=  n;  i++)
trace(3);
    {
        sum_x  +=  x[i];
        trace(4);
        sum_xx  +=  (x[i]*x[i]);
        trace(5);
    }
mean  =  sum_x  /  n;
trace(6);
var  =  ((n  *  sum_xx)  -  (sum_x  *  sum_x))  /  (n  *  (n-1));
trace(7);
std_dev  =  sqrt(var);
trace(8);
z_p  =  unit_normal(1  -  (0.5  *  alpha));
trace(9);
half_int  =  z_p  *  std_dev  /  sqrt(n);
trace(10);
c1  =  mean  -  half_int;
trace(11);
c2  =  mean  +  half_int;
        trace(12);
```

(a) The original source program with calls to the tracing routine inserted.

```
trace(i)
{ print(i,time);}
```

(b) The trace routine simply prints the statement number, i, and the current time.

Figure 6.8 Program tracing can be performed by inserting additional statements into the source code to call a tracing subroutine at appropriate points.

exception-processing routine can decode the instruction to determine its operands. The instruction type, address, and operand addresses and values can then be stored for later use. This approach was implemented using the T-bit in Digital Equipment Corporation's VAX processor series and in the Motorola 68000 processor family. Executing with the trace mode enabled on these processors slowed down a program's execution by a factor of about 1,000.

3. **Emulation.** An emulator is a program that makes the system on which it executes appear to the outside world as if it were something completely different. For example, the Java Virtual Machine is a program that executes application programs written in the Java programming language by emulating the operation of a processor that implements the Java byte-code instruction set. This emulation obviously slows down the execution of the application program compared with direct execution. Conceptually, however, it is a straightforward task to modify the emulator program to trace the execution of any application program it executes.

4. **Microcode modification.** In the days when processors executed microcode to execute their instruction sets through interpretation, it was possible to modify the microcode to generate a trace of each instruction executed. One important advantage of this approach was that it traced every instruction executed on the processor, including operating-system code. This feature was especially useful for tracing entire systems, including the interaction between the application programs and the operating system. The lack of microcode on current processors severely limits the applicability of this approach today.

5. **Compiler modification.** Another approach for generating traces is to modify the executable code produced by the compiler. Similar to what must be done for generating basic-block counts, extra instructions are added at the start of each basic block to record when the block is entered and which basic block is being executed then. Details about the contents of the basic blocks can be obtained from the compiler and correlated to the dynamic basic-block trace to produce a complete trace of all of the instructions executed by the application program. It is possible to add this type of tracing facility as a compilation option, or to write a post-compilation software tool that modifies the executable program generated by the compiler.

These trace-generation techniques are by no means the only ways in which traces can be produced. Rather, they are intended to give you a flavor of the types of approaches that have been used successfully in other trace-generation systems. Indeed, new techniques are limited only by the imagination and creativity of the performance analyst.

6.4.2   Trace compression

One obvious concern when generating a trace is the execution-time slowdown and other program perturbations caused by the execution of the additional tracing instructions. Another concern is the volume of data that can be produced in a very short time. For example, say we wish to trace every instruction executed by a processor that executes at an average rate of 10^8 instructions per second. If each item in the trace requires 16 bits to encode the necessary information, our tracing will produce more than 190 Mbytes of data per uninstrumented second of execution time, or more than 11 Gbytes per minute! In addition to obtaining the disks necessary to store this amount of data, the input/output operations required to move this large volume of data from the traced program to the disks create additional perturbations. Thus, it is desirable to reduce the amount of information that must be stored.

6.4.2.1 Online trace consumption

One approach for dealing with these large data volumes is to consume the trace *online*. That is, instead of storing the trace for later use, the program that will be driven by the trace is run simultaneously with the application program being traced. In this way, the trace is consumed as it is generated so that it never needs to be stored on disk at all.

A potential problem with online trace consumption in a multitasked (i.e. time-shared) system is the potential interdeterminate behavior of the program being traced. Since system events occur asynchronously with respect to the traced program, there is no assurance that the next time the program is traced the exact same sequence of events will occur in the same relative time order. This is a particular concern for programs that must respond to real-time events, such as system interrupts and user inputs.

This potential lack of repeatability in generating the trace is a concern when performing one-to-one comparison experiments. In this situation, the trace-consumption program is driven once with the trace and its output values are recorded. It is then modified in some way and then driven again with the same trace. If the identical input trace is used both times, it is reasonable to conclude that any change in performance observed is due to the change made to the trace-consumption program. However, if it cannot be guaranteed that the trace is identical from one run to the next, it is not possible to determine whether any change in performance observed is due to the change made, or whether it is due to a difference in the input trace itself.

6.4.2.2 Compression of data

A trace written to intermediate storage, such as a disk, can be viewed just like any other type of data file. Consequently, it is quite reasonable to apply a data-compression algorithm to the trace data as it is written to the disk. For example, any one of the large number of compression programs based on the popular Lempel–Ziv algorithm is often able to reduce the size of a trace file by 20–70%. Of course, the tradeoff for this data compression is the additional time required to execute the compression routine when the trace is generated and the time required to uncompress the trace when it is consumed.

6.4.2.3 Abstract execution

An interesting variation of the basic trace-compression idea takes advantage of the semantic information within a program to reduce the amount of information that must be stored for a trace. This approach, called *abstract execution*, separates the tracing process into two steps. The first step performs a compiler-style analysis of the program to be traced. This analysis identifies a small subset of the entire trace that is sufficient to later reproduce the full trace. Only this smaller subset is actually stored. Later, the trace-consumption program must execute some special trace-regeneration routines to convert this partial trace information into the full trace. These regeneration routines are automatically generated by the tracing tool when it performs the initial analysis of the program.

The data about the full trace that are actually stored when using the abstract-execution model consist of information describing only those transitions that may change during run-time. For example, consider the code fragment extracted from a program to be traced shown in Figure 6.9. The compiler-style analysis that would be performed on this code fragment would produce the control flow graph shown in Figure 6.10. From this control flow graph, the trace-generation tool can determine that statement 1 always precedes both statements 2 and 3. Furthermore, statement 4 always follows both statements 2 and 3. When this program is executed, the trace through this sequence of statements will be either 1–2–4, or 1–3–4. Thus, the only information that needs to be recorded during run-time is which of statements 2 and 3 actually occurred. The trace-regeneration routine is then able to later reconstruct the full trace using the previously recorded control flow graph.

Measurements of the effectiveness of this tracing technique have shown that it slows down the execution of the program being traced by a factor of typically 2–10. This slowdown factor is comparable to, or slightly better than, those of most other tracing techniques. More important, however, may be that, by recording information only about the changes that actually occur during run-time, this technique is able to reduce the size of the stored traces by a factor of ten to several hundred.

```
1.  if (i > 5)
2.      then a = a + i;
3.      else b = b + 1;
4.  i = i + 1;
```

Figure 6.9 A code fragment to be processed using the abstract execution tracing technique..

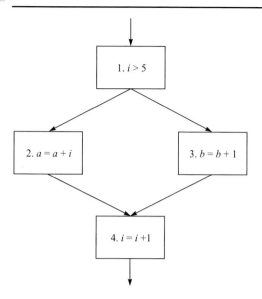

Figure 6.10 The control flow graph corresponding to the program fragment shown in Figure 6.9.

6.4.2.4 Trace sampling

Trace sampling is another approach that has been suggested for reducing the amount of information that must be collected and stored when tracing a program. The basic idea is to save only relatively small sequences of events from locations scattered throughout the trace. The expectation is that these small samples will be statistically representative of the entire program's trace when they are used. For instance, using these samples to drive a simulation should produce overall results that are similar to what would be produced if the simulation were to be driven with the entire trace.

Consider the sequence of events from a trace shown in Figure 6.11. Each sample from this trace consists of k consecutive events. The number of events between the starts of consecutive samples is the *sampling interval*, denoted by P. Since only the samples from the trace are actually recorded, the total amount of storage required for the trace can be reduced substantially compared with storing the entire raw trace.

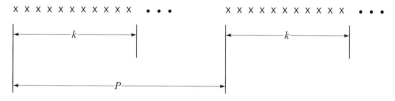

Figure 6.11 In trace sampling, k consecutive events comprise one sample of the trace. A new sample is taken every P events (P is called the sampling interval).

Unfortunately, there is no solid theoretical basis to help the experimenter determine how many events should be stored for each sample (k), or how large the sampling interval (P) should be. The best choices for k and P typically must be determined empirically (i.e. through experimentation). Furthermore, the choice of these parameters seems to be dependent on how the traces will be used. If the traces are used to drive a simulation of a cache to estimate cache-miss ratios, for instance, it has been suggested (see Laha *et al.* (1988)) that, in a trace of tens of millions of memory references, it is adequate to have several thousand events per sample. The corresponding sampling interval then should be chosen to provide enough samples such that 5–10% of the entire trace is recorded. These results, however, appear to be somewhat dependent on the size of the cache being simulated. The bottom line is that, while trace sampling appears to be a reasonable technique for reducing the size of the trace that must be stored, a solid theoretical basis still needs to be developed before it can be considered 'standard practice.'

6.5   Indirect and *ad hoc* measurements

Sometimes the performance metric we need is difficult, if not impossible, to measure directly. In this case, we have to rely on our ingenuity to develop an *ad hoc* technique to somehow derive the information indirectly. For instance, perhaps we are not able to directly measure the desired quantity, but we may be able to measure another related value directly. We may then be able to deduce the desired value from these other measured values.

For example, suppose that we wish to determine how much load a particular application program puts on a system when it is executed. We then may want to make changes to the program to see how they affect the system load. The first question we need to confront in this experiment is that of establishing a definition for the 'system load.'

There are many possible definitions of the system load, such as the number of jobs on the run queue waiting to be executed, to name but one. In our case, however, we are interested in how much of the processor's available time is spent executing our application program. Thus, we decide to define the average system load to be the fraction of time that the processor is busy executing users' application programs.

If we had access to the source code of the operating system, we could directly measure this time by modifying the process scheduler. However, it is unlikely that we will have access to this code. An alternative approach is to directly measure how much time the processor spends executing an 'idle' process that we create. We then use this direct measurement of idle time to deduce how much time the processor must have been busy executing real application programs during the given measurement interval.

Specifically, consider an 'idle' program that simply counts up from zero for a fixed period of time. If this program is the only application running on a single processor of a time-shared system, the final count value at the end of the measurement interval is the value that indirectly corresponds to an unloaded processor. If two applications are executed simultaneously and evenly share the processor, however, the processor will run our idle measurement program half as often as when it was the only application running. Consequently, if we allow both programs to run for the same time interval as when we ran the idle program by itself, its total count value at the end of the interval should be half of the value observed when only a single copy was executed.

Similarly, if three applications are executed simultaneously and equally share the processor for the same measurement interval, the final count value in our idle program should be one-third of the value observed when it was executed by itself. This line of thought can be further extended to n application programs simultaneously sharing the processor. After calibrating the counter process by running it by itself on an otherwise unloaded system, it can be used to indirectly measure the system load.

Example. In a time-shared system, the operating system will share a single processor evenly among all of the jobs executing in the system. Each available job is allowed to run for the *time slice* T_s. After this interval, the currently executing job is temporarily put to sleep, and the next ready job is switched in to run. Indirect load monitoring takes advantage of this behavior to estimate the system load. Initially, the load-monitor program is calibrated by allowing it to run by itself for a time T, as shown in Figure 6.12(a). At the end of this time, its counter value, n, is recorded. If the load monitor and another application are run simultaneously so that in total two jobs are sharing the processor, as shown in Figure 6.12(b), each job would be expected to be executing for half of the total time available. Thus, if the load monitor is again allowed to run for time T, we would expect its final count value to be $n/2$. Similarly, running the load monitor with two other applications for time T would result in a final count value of $n/3$, as shown in Figure 6.12(c). Consequently, knowing the value of the count after running the load monitor for time T allows us to deduce what the average load during the measurement interval must have been   ◇

One of the curious (and certainly most annoying!) aspects of developing tools to measure computer-systems performance is that instrumenting a system or pro-

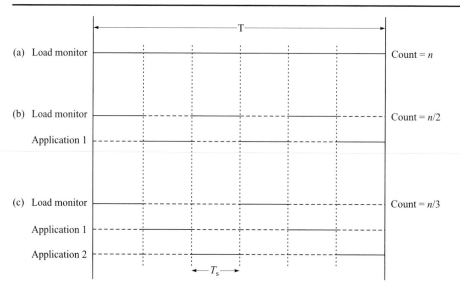

Figure 6.12 An example of using an indirect measurement technique to estimate the average system load in a time-shared system. The solid lines indicate when each application is running.

gram changes what we are trying to measure. Obtaining more information, or obtaining higher resolution measurements, for instance, requires more instrumentation points in a program. However, more instrumentation causes there to be more perturbations in the program than there are in its uninstrumented execution behavior. These additional perturbations due to the additional instrumentation then make the data we collect less reliable. As a result, we are almost always forced to use insufficient data to infer the behavior of the system in which we are interested.

To further confound the situation, performance perturbations due to instrumentation are nonlinear and nonadditive. They are nonlinear in the sense that doubling the amount of instrumentation in a program will not necessarily double its impact on performance, for instance. Similarly, instrumentation perturbation is nonadditive in the sense that adding more instrumentation can cancel out the perturbation effects of other instrumentation. Or, in some situations, additional instrumentation can multiplicatively increase the perturbations.

For example, adding code to an application program to generate an instruction trace can significantly change the spatial and temporal patterns of its memory accesses. The trace-generation code will cause a large number of extra store instructions to be executed, for instance, which can cause the cache to be effectively flushed at each trace point. These frequent cache flushes will then increase the number of caches missed, which will substantially impact the overall performance. If additional instrumentation is added, however, it may be possible that the additional memory locations necessary for the instrumentation could change the pattern of conflict misses in the cache in such a way as to actually improve the cache performance perceived by the application. The bottom line is that the effects of adding instrumentation to a system being tested are entirely unpredictable.

Besides these direct changes to a program's performance, instrumenting a program can cause more subtle indirect perturbations. For example, an instrumented program will take longer to execute than will the uninstrumented program. This increase in execution time will then cause it to experience more context switches than it would have experienced if it had not been instrumented. These additional context switches can substantially alter the program's paging behavior, for instance, making the instrumented program behave substantially differently than the uninstrumented program.

6.7   Summary

Event-driven measurement tools record information about the system being tested whenever some predefined event occurs, such as a page fault or a network operation, for instance. The information recorded may be a simple count of the number of times the event occurred, or it may be a portion of the system's state at the time the event occurred. A time-ordered list of this recorded state information is called a trace. While event-driven tools record all occurrences of the defined events, sampling tools query some aspect of the system's state at fixed time intervals. Since this sampling approach will not record every event, it provides a statistical view of the system. Indirect measurement tools are used to deduce some aspect of a system's performance that it is difficult or impossible to measure directly.

Some perturbation of a system's behavior due to instrumentation is unavoidable. Furthermore, and more difficult to compensate for, perhaps, is the unpredictable relationship between the instrumentation and its impact on performance. Through experience and creative use of measurement techniques, the performance analyst can try to minimize the impact of these perturbations, or can sometimes compensate for their effects.

It is important to bear in mind, though, that measuring a system alters it. While you would like to measure a completely uninstrumented program, what you actually end up measuring is the instrumented system. Consequently, you must always remain alert to how these perturbations may bias your measurements and, ultimately, the conclusions you are able to draw from your experiments.

6.8   For further reading

There is an extensive body of literature dealing with program tracing and a very large variety of tools has been developed. Although the following references only begin to scratch the surface of this field, they should provide you with some useful starting points.

- The Lempel–Ziv data-compression algorithm, on which many data compression programs have been based, is described in

  Terry A. Welch, 'A Technique for High Performance Data Compression,' *IEEE Computer*, Vol. 17, No. 6, June 1984, pp. 8–19.

- The abstract-execution idea, which was developed by James Larus, is described in the following papers, along with some related ideas. These papers also provide a good summary of the program-tracing process in general.

  James R. Larus, 'Efficient Program Tracing,' *IEEE Computer*, Vol. 26, No. 5, May 1993, pp. 52–61.

  James R. Larus, 'Abstract Execution: A Technique for Efficiently Tracing Programs,' *Software Practices and Experience,* Vol. 20, No. 12, December 1990, pp 1241–1258.

  Thomas Ball and James R. Larus, 'Optimally Profiling and Tracing Programs,' *ACM SIGPLAN-SIGACT Principles of Programming Languages (POPL)*, January 1992, pp. 59–70.

- This paper talks about some of the problems encountered when trying to trace applications running on multiprocessor systems, and describes the various types of perturbations that can occur due to tracing.

  Allen D. Malony and Daniel A. Reed, 'Performance Measurement Intrusion and Perturbation Analysis,' *IEEE Transactions on Parallel Distributed Systems*, Vol. 3, No. 4, July 1992, pp. 433–450.

- Paradyn is an interesting set of performance tools for parallel- and distributed-computing systems. The following paper provides a good overview of these tools:

  Barton P. Miller, Mark D. Callaghan, Jonathan M. Cargille, Jeffrey K. Hollingsworth, R. Bruce Irvin, Karen L. Karavanic, Krishna Kunchithapadam, and Tia Newhall. 'The Paradyn Parallel Performance Measurement Tools,' *IEEE Computer*, Vol. 28, No. 11, November 1995, pp. 37–46.

- The idea behind the indirect-load-measurement technique was presented in

  Edward D. Lazowska, John Zahorjan, David R. Cheriton, and Willy Zwaenepoel, 'File Access Performance of Diskless Workstations,' *IEEE Transactions on Software Engineering*, Vol. 4, No. 3, August 1986, pp. 238–268.

- The SimOS tool, described in the following paper, is an interesting example of how to trace an entire computer system, including both the application program and the operating system:

  Mendel Rosenblum, Stephen A. Herrod, Emmett Witchel, and Anoop Gupta, 'Complete Computer Simulation: The SimOS Approach,' *IEEE Parallel and Distributed Technology*, Fall 1995.

- The idea of sampling traces to reduce the amount of trace information that must be collected and stored is described in

  Subhasis Laha, Janak H. Patel, and Ravishankar K. Iyer, 'Accurate Low-Cost Methods for Performance Evaluation of Cache Memory Systems,' *IEEE Transactions on Computers*, Vol. 37, No. 11, November 1998, pp. 1325–1336.

6.9   Exercises

1. Determine the maximum time between rollovers for the interval timer available on your system.
2. What are the most important differences between tracing and basic-block counting?
3. Develop a technique for measuring the time a processor spends waiting for input/output requests.
4. Develop a technique for determining the associativity of a cache.
5. Measure the overhead of the interval timer on your system.
6. How would you measure the average number of jobs running on a time-shared system?
7. What interrupt period is needed to ensure that each of the 12 subroutines of a program that runs for 30 s has a 99% chance of having at least ten samples? Assume that each subroutine executes for at least 5% of the total time.
8. Use a program counter-sampling tool to compare the differences in performance between two versions of some appropriate benchmark program. Repeat your comparisons using a basic-block-counting tool. Compare and contrast the results you obtain when using these two different types of tools to profile the execution of this program. For instance, what are the fundamental differences between the techniques used by the basic-block-counting tool and those used by the sampling tool? How do the differences between these two tools affect your comparisons of the two versions of the benchmark program?
9. Compare the time penalties and the storage requirements of the various trace-compression techniques.

10. Are there any pathological situations in which these trace compression techniques can backfire and actually expand the input data set?

11. Devise an experiment to determine the following parameters of a computer system with a data cache:
    (a) the memory delay observed by the processor on a data-cache hit, and
    (b) the memory delay observed by the processor on a data-cache miss.
    Then
    (c) construct a simple model of the average memory delay observed by a program, given its hit-or-miss ratio. Use the parameters you measured above.

12. Write a test program that you can use to control the miss-ratio obtained in a system with a data cache. Use this program to validate the model of the average memory delay developed above. That is, measure the execution time of your test program and compare it with the time predicted by your model. What simplifications and approximations are you implicitly making? How could you improve your model or your test program? *Hint*: think about measuring the time required to scan through a large array with a fixed stride (the stride is the number of elements between successive references to the array – a stride of one accesses every element sequentially, a stride of two accesses every second element, a stride of three accesses every third element, and so on). By varying the stride, you should be able to determine the cache-block size. Then, knowing the block size, you can determine the miss ratio.

13. Section 6.5 discussed a technique for indirectly measuring the system load.
    (a) Write a program to perform this counting process.
    (b) Calibrate your counter by running two copies of it simultaneously. Show the results of your calibration with appropriate confidence intervals.
    (c) Use your counter process to determine how the load on a system varies over the course of day on a large time-shared system. For instance, you might try measuring the system load for 1 min every hour on each of several different days. Plot this system load as a function of time. Include appropriate error bars for each of the data points on your plot to give an indication of the variance in your measurements. (These error bars are simply the end-points of the confidence interval for each measured data point. Note that you must repeat the experiment several times to obtain enough independent measurements to generate a confidence interval.)

7 Benchmark programs

'It is not simply how busy you are, but why you are busy. The bee is praised; the mosquito is swatted.'

Marie O'Conner

To measure the maximum speed of an automobile, it must be in motion. Similarly, a computer must be executing some sort of program when you attempt to measure any aspect of its performance. Since you are ultimately interested in how the computer performs on your application programs, the best program to run is, obviously, one of your own applications. Unfortunately, this is not always possible since a substantial amount of time and effort may be required to port your existing application to a new computer system. It will perhaps not be cost-effective to port the application if the only goal is to measure the performance of the new system. Or, it may be that you are evaluating computer systems to determine which one is most appropriate for developing a completely new application. Since the application does not yet exist, it would be impossible to use it as your test program.

Owing to these practical and logistical difficulties in running your application program on the system or systems being evaluated, you instead are often forced to rely on making measurements while the computer system is executing some other program. This surrogate program is referred to as a *benchmark program* since it is used as a standard reference for comparing performance results.[1] The hope is that this standardized benchmark program is in some way characteristic of the applications that you plan to execute on the machine you are evaluating. If it is, you can use the measurements obtained when executing the benchmark program to predict how well the system will execute your application. The accuracy of these predictions determines the quality of a benchmark program, or a set of such programs, for your specific needs.

---

[1] The term "benchmark" was originally used by land surveyors to identify a mark made on some permanent object showing the elevation at that point. This mark is then used as the standard reference point in subsequent topological surveys.

7.1   Types of benchmark programs

Since different application domains have different execution characteristics, a wide range of benchmark programs has been developed in the attempt to characterize these different domains. Furthermore, different types of benchmarks satisfy the needs of many different types of users. Designers of new computer systems, for instance, often need benchmarks during the early stages of the design process that are focused on exercising specific components of the system. Since these early design stages typically rely on simulations to estimate performance, these benchmarks must be relatively small and easy to use. A large organization deciding which of several systems to purchase, on the other hand, may be committing a large sum of money on the basis of results of their performance tests. Consequently, they need much more complete benchmark programs that more accurately characterize their application environment.

It is important to note that a benchmark program should be easy to use and should be relatively simple to execute on a variety of different systems. If it is not easy to use, it is likely that the benchmark will not be used at all. Additionally, a benchmark that is difficult to use is more likely to be used incorrectly. Furthermore, if it is not easy to port the benchmark to various systems, it is probably a better use of the performance analyst's time to port the actual application of interest and measure its performance instead of spending time trying to run the benchmark program.

7.1.1   The single-instruction-execution time

Improving performance has been a primary goal of computer designers ever since the development of the first computer systems. Then, as now, however, the definition of performance was elusive. One of the earliest and most commonly accepted measures of performance was the time required to perform a single operation, such as an addition. Since almost all of a computer's instructions required the same amount of time to execute, knowing the time required to execute a single instruction was sufficient to completely characterize the performance of the system. Quite simply, the machine with the fastest addition operation would produce the best overall performance when executing any application program.

7.1.2   Instruction-execution mixes

To improve system performance, computer architects began to design processor-instruction sets in which each instruction would take only the minimum number of cycles required to complete its particular operation. For example, an instruction that accessed main memory might take longer than a simple arithmetic operation that accessed only the registers within the processor. Similarly, an addition instruction would be executed in less time than a multiplication or a division instruction. These performance-improvement techniques caused processors and systems to become increasingly more complex. As a result, the execution time of a single instruction was no longer adequate to summarize performance.

In response to this problem, in the late 1950s Jack C. Gibson proposed the *Gibson instruction mix* as a performance metric. The basic idea of this instruction mix is to categorize all of the instructions into different classes such that each instruction in the same class requires the same number of processor cycles to execute. The number of instructions of each class executed by a particular collection of programs is used to form a weighted average. This weighted average then is the performance metric used to compare systems. Gibson proposed some specific weights for a set of predefined instruction classes based on measurements of programs running on IBM 704 and 650 systems.

Given this type of weighted average of the mix of instructions executed, the total time required to execute a program can be expressed as

$$T_{program} = N \times CPI \times T_{clock}. \tag{7.1}$$

In this expression, N is the total number of instructions executed by the program, CPI is the weighted average of the number of processor clocks required to execute all of the instructions in the program, and T_{clock} is the period of one processor clock cycle. Note that CPI corresponds to Gibson's instruction-mix idea, except that the weights are determined for the specific program executed. Note that, when it is used as a metric to summarize a system's performance, a lower CPI value implies better overall performance.

Example. Table 7.1 shows the percentages of instructions executed in each of several classes by a particular processor executing a specific benchmark program. The average CPI for this situation is calculated as

$$CPI = 2(0.334) + 3(0.232) + 3(0.181) + 4(0.103) + 5(0.078) + 7(0.072)$$
$$= 3.213. \tag{7.2}$$

If the processor's clock cycle time is $T_{clock} = 8$ ns, the total execution time for this program would be estimated to be $T_{program} = 23,842,128 \times 3.213 \times 8 \times 10^{-9} = 0.61$ s.   ◇

From the above discussion, it is easy to see that one of the problems with using CPI to measure performance is that it depends on the mix of instructions actually executed. That is, the CPI value for a specific system depends completely on the particular application program executed. Furthermore, the number of instructions required to execute a program is not constant across all systems. Some

Table 7.1 The fractions of instructions executed in each class out of the 23,842,128 total instructions executed for a particular benchmark program

Instruction class	Fraction of instructions executed (%)	Clocks required
1	33.4	2
2	23.2	3
3	18.1	3
4	10.3	4
5	7.8	5
6	7.2	7

processors may require fewer instructions to execute the same program, although each individual instruction may require additional clocks. Other factors, such as the capability of the compiler to optimize the program's mix of instructions, can further distort this measure. Finally, simple instruction mixes ignore the important performance effects of input/output operations, complex memory hierarchies, and so forth.

7.1.3   Synthetic benchmark programs

In spite of the problems of using the instruction mix to compare performance, there is still something intuitively appealing about this type of weighted-average measure. One problem with the Gibson mix mentioned above is that, over time, it no longer reflected the mix of instructions executed by subsequent generations of systems and application programs. While the instruction mix reports performance based on the actual instructions executed by an application program, the basic idea behind the development of a *synthetic benchmark* program is to write a program that matches the expected or desired mix of instructions. In this sense, a synthetic benchmark program is essentially the complement of Gibson's instruction-mix idea.

Specifically, synthetic benchmark programs are artificial programs that do no real, useful work. Instead, the mixes of operations performed by these benchmarks are carefully chosen to match the relative mix of operations observed in some class of application programs. The hope is that, since the instruction mix is the same as that of the real application programs, the performance obtained when executing the synthetic program should provide an accurate indication of what would be obtained when executing an actual application.

Although this idea is intuitively appealing, these programs do not actually behave like real application programs. The primary problem is that these synthetic benchmarks do not accurately model the impact on performance caused by interactions among instructions that occur due to specific orderings of instructions. Different orderings of instructions can produce different patterns of dependences among the instructions, which can significantly change the number and type of pipeline stalls that occur, for instance. Similarly, the memory-referencing patterns of real applications are very hard to duplicate in a synthetic program. These patterns determine the memory locality, however, which profoundly affects the performance of a hierarchical memory subsystem. As a result, hardware and compilation optimizations can produce execution times on synthetic benchmarks that are substantially different than the execution times produced on actual application programs, even though the relative mix of instructions is the same in both cases.

The complexity of real application programs makes them difficult to use as benchmark programs. One of the strong attractions of synthetic benchmarks is that they abstract away many of the nitty-gritty details of real application programs. Unfortunately, experience has shown that it is exactly these details that are the major determinants of computer-system performance.

7.1.4 Microbenchmarks

Microbenchmarks are small, specially designed programs used to test some specific portion of a system. For example, a small program written to test only the processor–memory interface, the input/output subsystem, or the floating-point-execution unit, independent of the other components of the system, would be a microbenchmark. Microbenchmarks are typically used to characterize the maximum possible performance that could be achieved if the overall system performance were limited by that single component.

Carefully targeted microbenchmarks can be used to determine whether the performance capabilities of all of the components within a system are balanced, for instance. Or, as another example, they are often used to determine the performance characteristics of a system's components to provide values for important parameters for a simulation of the system. Writing this type of benchmark typically requires the programmer to have a deep understanding of the system component to be tested.

7.1.5 Program kernels

While microbenchmarks are used to examine the behavior of a specific component of a system, *kernel benchmarks*, on the other hand, are used to characterize the central or essential portion of a specific type of application program. A kernel benchmark program is a small program that has been extracted from a larger application program. It may consist of the inner portion of a loop that consumes a large fraction of the total execution time of a complete application program, for instance. It is hoped that, since this loop is executed frequently, it is somehow characteristic of the most important operations performed by the overall application program.

Since a program kernel is typically small, consisting of perhaps only a dozen lines of code, it should be easy to port to many different computer systems. Measuring the performance of this small kernel on several different systems, then, could provide some relative indication of how the different systems would perform when executing the complete application. Unfortunately, although these kernels can accurately predict how the different systems will perform for the type of operations in the kernel itself, these small benchmarks ignore major components of the system, such as the entire operating system, for instance. Furthermore, and perhaps more importantly, they typically do not stress the memory hierarchy in any realistic fashion. Unfortunately, it is exactly the system components that are not well exercised by kernel benchmarks that often become the performance bottlenecks. As a result, kernel benchmarks are of only limited usefulness in making overall comparisons or predictions regarding performance.

7.1.6　Application benchmark programs

To improve on the limited capabilities of kernel and synthetic benchmarks, standardized sets of real application programs have been collected into various *application-program benchmark suites*. These applications are complete, real programs that actually produce a useful result, in contrast to kernel and synthetic benchmark programs. Collections of programs are often selected to emphasize one particular class of applications, such as scientific and engineering applications, 'typical' engineering workstation applications, applications appropriate for parallel-computer systems, and so forth.

These real application programs can more accurately characterize how actual applications are likely to use a system than can the other types of benchmark programs. However, to reduce the time required to run the entire set of programs, they often use artificially small input data sets. This constraint may limit the applications' ability to accurately model the memory behavior and input/output requirements of a user's application programs. However, even with these limitations, these types of benchmark programs are the best to have been developed to date.

In selecting an appropriate set of application benchmark programs, one must be careful of avoiding 'toy' benchmarks. Although these programs are real applications that produce an actual result, they are too small to accurately characterize the application programs that are likely to be executed by the users of a system. Examples of these types of benchmarks include *quicksort, the prime-number sieve, the* N-*queens problem,* and *the Towers of Hanoi.* These toy benchmarks were popular with processor designers during the mid-1980s since they allowed an entire program to be executed on a simulated processor. With advances in system performance leading to faster simulators, however, these small benchmark programs have lost their usefulness.

7.2   Benchmark strategies

Most of the types of benchmark programs discussed in the previous section base the measure of performance on the time required to execute the benchmark. There are several other strategies that can be employed in a benchmark program, however. Specifically, the three different strategies for using a benchmark program to measure the performance of a computer system are the following.

1. Measure the time required to perform a *fixed amount of computation.*
2. Measure the amount of computation performed within a *fixed period of time.*
3. *Allow both the amount of computation performed and the time to vary.* Another measure of performance that is a function both of the time elapsed and of the amount of computation performed then must be defined.

7.2.1   Fixed-computation benchmarks

A common use of a benchmark program is to provide a vehicle for measuring a computer system's 'speed.' In the physical world, *speed* is defined to be the distance traveled per unit time. For example, the distance traveled by an object within a measured time provides a rigorous definition of the rate at which the object is traveling. For computer systems, however, we lack a mathematically rigorous definition of the 'distance traveled' by a computer system. Instead, we finesse the analogy of distance traveled by making our measurements relative to some basis system.

What we would like to do is define a computer system's *speed* or *execution rate*, denoted R_1, to be $R_1 = W_1/T_1$, where T_1 is the time required to execute the computation W_1. Unfortunately, for a given benchmark program, the value of W_1 is not precisely or commonly definable. To compensate for this problem, we define the execution rate of another system to be $R_2 = W_2/T_2$, where T_2 is the time required to execute the computation W_2 on this system. We then define the *speedup* value S such that $R_1 = SR_2$. This value allows us to say that the execution rate, or speed, of system 1 is S times faster than that of system 2.

Substituting for R_1 and R_2 into this equation gives the speedup of system 1 relative to system 2 as

$$S = \frac{R_1}{R_2} = \frac{W_1/T_1}{W_2/T_2}. \tag{7.3}$$

The problem with this definition of relative speedup, though, is that we still have no way to measure the actual amounts of computation performed by each machine, W_1 and W_2. The discussion of MIPS and MFLOPS in Sections 2.3.2 and 2.3.3 pointed out the difficulties of accurately defining W_1 and W_2. Instead, we define the amount of computation performed by a specific program to be constant regardless of how many instructions are actually required to execute the program on either system. Thus, we simply define the amount of computation completed by the system when executing the benchmark program to be W so that $W_1 \equiv W_2 \equiv W$. Then the speedup of machine 1 relative to machine 2 is

$$S = \frac{R_1}{R_2} = \frac{W/T_1}{W/T_2} = \frac{T_2}{T_1}. \tag{7.4}$$

By defining the amount of computation performed when executing a specific benchmark program to be constant, we can use the time required to perform this computation as a relative measure of performance. Thus, we fix the amount of computation to be performed in the benchmark program and use as a performance metric the time required to actually perform this computation.

7.2.1.1 Amdahl's law

The concept of fixing the amount of computation to be executed in a program leads to an upper bound on how much the overall performance of any computer system can be improved due to changes in only a single component of the system. This idea was first proposed in 1967 in a short paper by Gene Amdahl in which he pointed out the inherent limitations in trying to improve computer-system performance by using multiple processors. Although this original paper contained no formal analysis, the concept has come to be known as *Amdahl's law*.

Amdahl's argument is essentially that the overall performance improvement observed in an application program is limited by that portion of the application that is *unaffected* by whatever change was made to the system. In particular, consider the execution time lines shown in Figure 7.1. The top line shows the time required to execute some given program on the system before any changes are made. Call this time T_{old}. Now assume that some change that reduces the execution time for some operations in the program by a factor of q is made to the

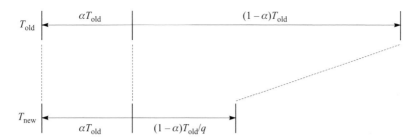

Figure 7.1 The execution time of a program can be divided into a fraction α that is unaffected by a system enhancement, and the fraction $1 - \alpha$ that is improved by a factor of q. Then, according to Amdahl's law, the limit on the overall speedup obtained through this enhancement is $S < 1/\alpha$.

system . The program now runs in time T_{new}, where $T_{\text{new}} < T_{\text{old}}$, as shown in the bottom line.

Since the change to the system improves the performance of only some operations in the program, there are many other operations in the program that are unaffected by this change. Let α be the fraction of all operations that are unaffected by the enhancement. Then, as shown in the bottom line of Figure 7.1, the new execution time, T_{new}, can be divided into two components. The first component, αT_{old}, is the execution time of that fraction of the program that is unaffected by the change. The second component of T_{new}, which is the remaining fraction $1 - \alpha$ of the original execution time, has its performance improved by the factor q. Thus, the time required for this component is $(1 - \alpha)T_{\text{old}}/q$. The overall speedup caused by this improvement is then found to be

$$S = \frac{T_{\text{old}}}{T_{\text{new}}} = \frac{T_{\text{old}}}{\alpha T_{\text{old}} + (1 - \alpha)T_{\text{old}}/q} = \frac{1}{1/q + \alpha(1 - 1/q)}. \tag{7.5}$$

This equation is interesting by itself since it can be used to calculate the overall speedup obtained due to some improvement in the system, assuming that q and α can be determined. However, it is interesting to ask what happens as the impact on performance of the improvement becomes large, that is, as $q \to \infty$.

It is easy to show that, in the limit as $q \to \infty$, $(1 - \alpha)T_{\text{old}}/q \to 0$. Thus, the overall speedup, S, is bounded by $1/\alpha$. That is,

$$\lim_{q \to \infty} S = \lim_{q \to \infty} \frac{1}{1/q + \alpha(1 - 1/q)} = \frac{1}{\alpha}. \tag{7.6}$$

This result says that, no matter how much one type of operation in a system is improved, the overall performance is inherently limited by the operations that still must be performed but are unaffected by the improvement. For example, the best (ideal) speedup that could be obtained in a parallel computing system with p

processors is p. However, if 10% of a program cannot be executed in parallel, the overall speedup when using the parallel machine is at most $1/\alpha = 1/0.1 = 10$, even if an infinite number of processors were available. The constraint that 10% of the total program must be executed sequentially limits the overall performance improvement that could be obtained.

An obvious corollary to Amdahl's law is that any system designer or programmer should concentrate on making the common case fast. That is, operations that occur most often will have the largest value of α. Thus, improving these operations will have the biggest impact on overall performance. Interestingly, the common cases also tend to be the simplest cases. As a result, optimizing these cases first tends to be easier than optimizing the more complex, but rarely used, cases.

7.2.2   Fixed-time benchmarks

Benchmark programs that measure the amount of time required to perform a fixed amount of computation tend to be the most popular. It is likely that this popularity occurs because these types of benchmarks tend to fit our intuition of what improvements in computer performance should mean. For example, if you purchase a faster system, you generally expect that it should require less time to execute your applications.

An alternative view argues that users with large problems to solve are willing to wait a fixed amount of time to obtain a solution. The allowable time may be determined simply by the users' patience, or by some external factor. For instance, a system that is used to compute a weather forecast is useless if it takes more than 24 h to produce the next day's forecast.

When a user with this type of application purchases a faster system, they often want to solve a larger problem within the same amount of time as they were willing to wait for a solution when using the previous (slower) system. Thus, instead of holding the amount of computation performed by the benchmark constant, the amount of time that the benchmark program is allowed to run is held constant. Then the amount of computation performed by the system when executing this benchmark program is allowed to vary. At the end of the allotted execution time, the total amount of computation completed, which must be carefully defined, is used as the measure of the relative speeds of the different systems.

The SLALOM benchmark was the first to implement this fixed-time, variable-computation strategy. It was based on a scientific application for calculating radiosity. The measure of performance in this case was the accuracy of the answer that could be computed in 1 min. This benchmark did not specify a particular algorithm for computing the result, but rather defined the accuracy of the answer produced as the number of 'patches,' or areas, into which a given geometric shape was subdivided in the 1-min interval. The more patches produced, the more accurate the final answer.

One of the nice features of this type of benchmark is that it automatically scales the problem being solved to the capabilities of the system being tested. More powerful systems end up solving larger problems than do less powerful machines. As result, these fixed-time benchmarks are useful for comparing systems with wide ranges of processing capabilities.

Some of the weaknesses of this benchmarking strategy, and SLALOM in particular, are due to the loosely defined statement of the problem. Because the benchmark defines only the problem to be solved without specifying the steps to solve it, clever programmers are free to develop better algorithms for solving the problem. The original complexity of SLALOM, for instance, was $O(n^3)$. Improvements in the algorithm, however, reduced the complexity first to $O(n^2)$, and, eventually, to $O(n \log n)$. These algorithmic improvements resulted in the self-contradictory situation of observing a substantial jump in performance on one system, as measured by this benchmark, simply by executing the better algorithm. The nonlinear complexity of the algorithm also makes the resultant performance metric nonlinear. (See Section 2.2 for a discussion of what makes a good performance metric.) Thus, it is impossible to say that a system that can compute $2N$ patches in the given time is twice as powerful as a system that computes only N.

Finally, SLALOM's use of memory was not proportional to its computational requirements. As a result, it was not unusual for a system to run out of memory and have to abort the program before the entirety of the allotted time had elapsed. Despite these problems, the SLALOM benchmark has provided important insights for the development of subsequent benchmark programs.

7.2.2.1 Scaling Amdahl's law

One of the major criticisms concerning Amdahl's law has been that it emphasizes the wrong aspect of the performance potential of parallel-computing systems. The argument is that purchasers of parallel systems are most likely to fall into the category of users who want to solve larger problems within the available time. Following this line of argument leads to the following 'scaled' or 'fixed-time' version of Amdahl's law.

It is common to judge the performance of an application executing on a parallel system by comparing the parallel execution time with p processors, T_p, with the time required to execute the equivalent sequential version of the application program, T_1, using the speedup $S_p = T_1/T_p$. With the fixed-time interpretation, however, the assumption is that there is no single-processor system that is capable of executing an equivalent sequential version of the parallel application. The single-processor may not have a large enough memory, for example, or the time required to execute the sequential version would be unreasonably long.

In this case, then, the parallel-execution time is divided into the parallel component, $1 - \alpha$, and the inherently sequential component, α, giving $T_p = T_1 = \alpha T_1 + (1 - \alpha)T_1$, as shown in Figure 7.2. Note that T_1 is the time required to produce the answer originally. That is, T_1 is the time that the user is willing to allow the application to run. Since no single-processor system exists that is capable of executing an equivalent problem of this size, it is assumed that the parallel portion of the execution time would increase by a factor of p if it were executed on a hypothetical single-processor system. This gives a hypothetical sequential execution time of $T'_1 = \alpha T_1 + (1 - \alpha)pT_1$.

The parallel speedup is found to be

$$S_p = \frac{T'_1}{T_p} = \frac{\alpha T_1 + (1 - \alpha)pT_1}{T_1} = p + \alpha(1 - p). \tag{7.7}$$

Thus, with this fixed-time, variable-problem-size interpretation of Amdahl's law, the performance of a parallel machine is not limited by the portion that is inherently sequential. Rather, as the system is made larger, the size of the problems that can be solved increases proportionally.[2]

7.2.3   Variable-computation and variable-time benchmarks

Fixed-computation benchmarks generally fit our intuition about what improvements in computer performance should do to the execution time of an applica-

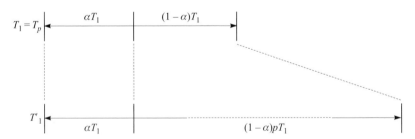

Figure 7.2 In the fixed-time interpretation of Amdahl's law, an application is always allowed time T_1 to execute. When the application is executed on a parallel system, the time is divided into the inherently sequential component, α, and the parallel component, $1 - \alpha$. It is assumed that the parallel portion of the execution time would increase by a factor of p if it were executed on a hypothetical single-processor system. This gives a corresponding speedup for the parallel system of $S_p = p + \alpha(1 - p)$.

---

[2] Kumar *et al.* (1994) have proposed the *isoefficiency function* as a way of more precisely capturing the idea of scaled speedup.

tion program. Fixed-time benchmarks, on the other hand, allow the problem size to scale up to match the capabilities of the system under test. The third and most general benchmark-program strategy fixes neither the available time nor the amount of computation to be done. These types of benchmarks instead try to measure some other aspect of performance that is a function of the computation and the execution time. This derived metric is then used as the measure of performance when executing the benchmark.

The HINT benchmark is a good example of this variable-computation, variable-time benchmark-program strategy. It rigorously defines the 'quality' of a solution for a given mathematical problem that is to be solved by the benchmark program. The solution's quality, based on the problem's definition, can be continually improved by doing additional computation. The ratio of this quality metric to the time required to achieve that level of quality is then used as the measure of performance. The HINT benchmark expresses this final performance metric as QUIPS, or *quality improvements per second*.

The specific problem to be solved in the HINT benchmark is to find rational bounds from above and below for

$$\int_0^1 \frac{(1-x)}{(1+x)} \, dx. \tag{7.8}$$

The problem statement for the benchmark specifies that a technique called *interval subdivision* must be used to find these bounds. This technique divides the x and y ranges into a number of intervals that are an integer power of two. It then simply counts the number of squares that are in the area completely below the curve, and those that completely contain the area, including the curve itself. These two counts give the lower and upper bounds, respectively, on the area under the curve.

The actual *quality* of the solution is defined to be $1/(u-l)$, where u is the estimate of the upper bound and l is the estimate of the lower bound. That is, u is the number of squares that completely contain the area, while l is the number of squares completely below the curve. The quality is then improved by splitting the intervals into smaller subintervals and performing repeated interval subdivision on these subintervals. An example of this process is shown in Figure 7.3.

By fixing neither the available time nor the total amount of computation to be completed, this type of benchmark automatically scales to find the performance limits of a wide range of systems. With the HINT benchmark, for instance, the quality of the solution theoretically can be improved forever. Practical limits in a computer system's available memory, arithmetic precision, and instruction-execution rate, however, limit the ultimate quality value that a particular system can obtain. Consequently, this type of benchmark is useful for comparing the limits of various computer systems in addition to the more typical performance

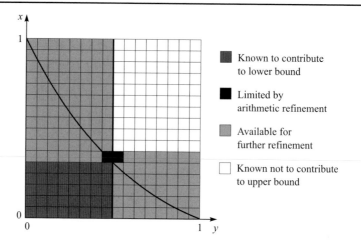

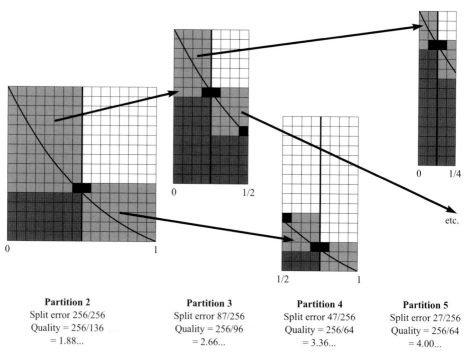

Partition 2	**Partition 3**	**Partition 4**	**Partition 5**
Split error 256/256	Split error 87/256	Split error 47/256	Split error 27/256
Quality = 256/136	Quality = 256/96	Quality = 256/64	Quality = 256/64
= 1.88...	= 2.66...	= 3.36...	= 4.00...

Figure 7.3 An example of the sequence of interval subdivisions used to bound the area of the function $f(x) = (1 - x)/(1 + x)$ in the HINT benchmark program. Reprinted from J. L. Gustafson and Q. O. Snell, 'HINT: A New Way to Measure Computer Performance,' in *Proceedings of the Twenty-Eighth Hawaii International Conference on System Sciences, Wailea, Hawaii*, January 3–6, 1995, Volume II, pp. 392–401.

comparison of which machine produces the best (i.e. highest-quality) result in the least amount of time.

7.3   Example benchmark programs

A variety of different benchmark programs has been developed over the years to measure the performance of many different types of computer systems in different application domains. This section summarizes some of the key features of several of these benchmarks. Although this list is by no means complete, it should provide some idea of how the various benchmarks are similar and where they differ. It also provides some historical context for the development of benchmark programs.

7.3.1   Scientific and engineering

The scientific and engineering research community has long driven the need for high-performance computing. The computational needs of the USA's national laboratories, for instance, helped encourage the development of vector supercomputers, such as the Control Data CDC-6600, the CDC-7600, and the several generations of systems developed by Seymour Cray and his associates at Cray Research, Inc. As some of the primary users of these systems, the national laboratories had a vested interest in developing benchmark programs for testing their actual delivered performance.

7.3.1.1 Livermore loops

The *Livermore Fortran kernels*, also known more casually as the *Livermore loops*, were developed at the Lawrence Livermore National Laboratory. These loops, which eventually grew to consist of 24 kernels, were chosen to represent the most critical sections of Fortran programs used in a broad range of numerical application programs. Each loop is a common type of programming construct used by computational scientists at the laboratory and spans the range of good to poor programming practice.

Using program kernels instead of entire applications to measure performance derived from the observation that most of the execution time in an application was spent in one or two critical loops, or was distributed across numerous similar loops. It was assumed that the performance that could be achieved for an entire application executed on a specific system could be extrapolated by measuring the execution time for the appropriate representative kernel. The performance metric reported for the benchmark was the MFLOPS rate for each individual loop. Additionally, the aggregate arithmetic, harmonic, and geometric means were calculated for all of the loops taken together. Since running these small kernels was much easier than running an entire application program, they became a popular set of programs for comparing supercomputer systems.

7.3.1.2 NAS kernels

Another set of numerical benchmark programs developed primarily to test the performance of vector supercomputers is the *numerical aerodynamic simulation (NAS) kernel benchmark*. This benchmark developed at the NASA Ames Research Center consists of seven kernels representative of the types of Fortran programs developed for computational fluid-dynamics calculations. These kernels perform such operations as a two-dimensional fast Fourier transform (FFT) with complex numbers, Cholesky decomposition, matrix multiplication, and Gaussian elimination. Although several of the kernels do perform nontrivial numbers of integer and logical operations, the performance metric is again MFLOPS. This benchmark kernel was designed to focus on a computer system's vector performance and so specifically excluded input/output and operating system times from the measured execution time.

7.3.1.3 LINPACK

The *LINPACK* benchmark program is probably one of the most successful benchmark programs developed in terms of both its longevity and the total number and range of unique types of computer systems for which corresponding performance results have been reported. This widespread use and recognition is due primarily to the vigorous efforts of one of its developers, Dr Jack Dongarra. It was originally developed in Fortran, but it has subsequently been ported to a wide variety of different languages and is still in active use today.

This benchmark program uses LU factorization and back substitution to solve a dense $N \times N$ system of linear equations. The actual computations used in the solution of this system are contained within the *basic linear-algebra subroutines* (BLAS). These subroutines have seen widespread usage themselves in actual application programs beyond their use in this benchmark program. The final performance metrics reported are the total execution time and the MFLOPS rate.

An important feature of this benchmark is the addition of a 'wrapper' program that generates the matrices to be used in the solution process. This wrapper also computes the norms of the residual vectors to ensure that the solution process produces a final answer that is within a prespecified tolerance. This approach ensures that consistent execution of the benchmark is achieved. It also ensures that any optimizations that may be made in order to improve its performance (by a compiler, for instance) do not adversely affect the final answer.

7.3.1.4 PERFECT club

The *PERFECT club* benchmark suite is a set of 13 complete Fortran application programs drawn from the fields of computational fluid dynamics, chemical and physical modeling, engineering design, and signal processing. The programs were selected to represent the range of computations that might be performed on a high-performance computing system.

PERFECT is actually an acronym for *performance evaluation of cost-effective transformations*. This name reflects one of the primary goals of assembling these benchmarks, which was to evaluate the effectiveness of compiler transformations for automatically converting a sequential program into a form suitable for execution on a parallel-computing system. The programs included instrumentation to report the total elapsed execution time as well as the CPU time. Each program in the benchmark set also included an internal test that compared critical values produced by the program with known correct values to thereby validate the final output.

7.3.1.5 SPEC CPU

The *System Performance Evaluation Cooperative (SPEC)* was founded in 1988 by a group of workstation manufacturers (Apollo/Hewlett-Packard, Digital Equipment Corporation, MIPS, and Sun Microsystems) to provide a standardized set of application benchmark programs and, perhaps more importantly, a standardized methodology for running the programs and reporting the results. The original benchmark set, SPEC89, consisted of four programs written in C and six Fortran programs.

One of SPEC's strengths has been its recognition that benchmarks 'age' as computer-system performance increases. As a result, SPEC has frequently issued new sets of benchmark programs that attempt to provide more realistic tests of the capabilities of changing systems. Furthermore, SPEC has recognized that different application domains require different types of benchmarks. To accommodate these needs, SPEC has expanded to include the Open Systems Group (OSG), the High-Performance Group (HPG), and the Graphics Performance Characterization Group (GPC).

The SPEC OSG is the successor to the original SPEC committee. The primary focus of this group is on benchmark programs for characterizing component and system-level performance of workstations and servers that run open operating systems, such as the various flavors of UNIX. The benchmarks of the CPU committee, which focus on the processor, memory hierarchy, and compiler components of a computer system, are the follow-on to the original SPEC89 benchmark suite. This benchmark set actually consists of two sets of programs, the ten floating-point intensive programs in CFP95, which are summarized in Table 7.2,

Table 7.2. The programs that comprise the SPEC CFP95 benchmark suite (reprinted from the SPEC web site `www.spec.org`, used with permission.)

Benchmark	Reference Time (sec)	Application areas	Description
101.tomcatv	3,700	Fluid dynamics; geometric translation	Generation of a two-dimensional boundary-fitted coordinate system around general geometric domains
102.swim	8,600	Weather prediction	Solves shallow-water equations using finite-difference approximations (the only single-precision benchmark in CFP95)
103.su2cor	1,400	Quantum physics	Masses of elementary particles are computed in the quark–gluon theory
104.hydro2d	2,400	Astrophysics	Hydrodynamical Navier–Stokes equations are used to compute galactic jets
107.mgrid	2,500	Electromagnetism	Calculation of a three-dimensional potential field
110.applu	2,200	Fluid dynamics; maths	Solves matrix system with pivoting
125.turb3d	4,100	Simulation	Simulates turbulence in a cubic area
141.apsi	2,100	Weather prediction	Calculates statistics on temperature and pollutants in a grid
145.fpppp	9,600	Chemistry	Calculates multi-electron derivatives
146.wave	3,000	Electromagnetism	Solves Maxwell's equations on a Cartesian mesh.

and the eight integer benchmarks in SPEC CINT95, which are summarized in Table 7.3.

The SPEC documentation specifies a rigorous methodology for running the benchmark programs. Each program in the set produces a value called the *SPECratio*, which is the ratio of the *SPEC reference time* given for the benchmark divided by the total execution time of the benchmark measured on the system under test. This reference time is supplied by SPEC (see Tables 7.2 and 7.3) and was obtained by running the programs on a Sun SPARCstation 10/40 with 128 MB of memory using the Sun SC3.0.1 compilers. The final composite metric is then the geometric mean of the SPECratios for all of the programs in either the CFP95 or the CINT95 subset. (However, see the discussion of the geometric mean in Section 3.3.4.) Note that, by definition, the SPECint95 and SPECfp95 values for the Sun SPARCstation 10/40 must be 1.

The next generation of the SPEC CPU benchmarks is currently under development. In addition, SPEC's HPG has developed the SPEChpc96 benchmark set to measure complete application-level performance for large high-performance

Table 7.3. The programs that comprise the SPEC CINT95 benchmark suite (reproduced from the SPEC web site: `www.spec.org`, used with permission)

Benchmark	Reference Time (sec)	Application area	Description
099.go	4600	Game playing; AI	Plays the game Go against itself
124.m88ksim	1900	Simulation	Simulates the Motorola 88100 processor running Dhrystone and a memory-testing program
126.gcc	1700	Programming; compilation	Compiles pre-processed source into optimized SPARC assembly code
129.compress	1800	Compression	Compresses large text files (about 16 MB) using adaptive Limpel–Ziv coding
130.li	1900	Language interpreter	Lisp interpreter
132.ijpeg	2400	Imaging	Performs jpeg image compression with various parameters
134.perl	1900	Shell interpreter	Performs text and numeric manipulations (anagrams/prime-number factoring)
147.vortex	2700	Database	Builds and manipulates three interrelated databases

computing systems. Currently, this benchmark set includes two large programs that have been used heavily in industry. The *seismic* program performs calculations of the type used by the oil industry to locate gas and oil deposits. The GAMESS (general atomic and molecular electronic structure system) program contains the types of routines for drug design and bonding analysis used by the pharmaceutical and chemical industries.

7.3.1.6 Whetstone and Dhrystone

Good examples of synthetic benchmark programs include the *Whetstone* and the *Dhrystone*. Even though these two programs are no longer used for serious performance testing, they are interesting for their historical perspective. The operations in the Whetstone benchmark were determined by studying the behavior of 1970s-era scientific application programs written in ALGOL. Its primary goal was to measure floating-point performance. One of its important components, for instance, consists of several floating-point additions and multiplications, and several trigonometric operations. The primary focus of the Dhrystone benchmark, on the other hand, was to measure integer performance using primarily a variety of character-string-copy and string-compare operations.

7.3.2 Transaction processing

The *Transaction Processing Council* (*TPC*) was established to develop benchmark programs for systems that perform online transaction processing (OLTP). These types of systems consist of numerous users making requests to read and potentially update the records in a large shared database. OLTP systems include such applications as airline reservation systems, networks of automatic teller machines (ATMs), and inventory-control systems.

One of the most important performance characteristics of OLTP applications is the rate at which transactions can be processed within a given response-time limit. For instance, a typical performance specification would be that 95% of all transactions must complete in less than 1 s. Other critical requirements for these systems include the need to always maintain consistent data, and the need to be operational essentially all of the time.

The first benchmark from TPC, known as *TPC-A*, was based on an early *DebitCredit* benchmark that was meant to simulate the types of transactions that would be likely to occur in an ATM-type of environment. A key feature of this benchmark was that it did not specify the actual program to be executed. Rather, it specified a high-level functional requirement. Furthermore, the number of simulated requests, and the size of the database serving the requests, increased in proportion to the capability of the system being tested. Thus, this benchmark fixed neither the amount of computation to be performed nor the time for which the test was allowed to run. Rather, the performance requirement was that 90% of the transactions must complete in less than 2 s. The final performance metric reported by this benchmark was the number of transactions completed per minute while satisfying this requirement.

The second benchmark from TPC, called *TPC-B*, was a batch-mode version of TPC-A. That is, it eliminated the simulated terminals and the network over which the terminals communicated. The commands were instead applied directly to the database from a script in an off-line batch-mode configuration. (Given the highly competitive nature of the OLTP business, it was a very controversial decision to release the TPC-B benchmark.) The stated intent of this benchmark was to model a database-server application environment.

The successor to the TPC-A benchmark for OLTP systems is *TPC-C*. This benchmark is essentially a more complex version of TPC-A that simulates the transactions against a database required in an order-entry environment. These transactions include entering orders into the database, updating payment information, inventory control, and so forth. Performance is again measured in transactions per second. *TPC-D*, which focuses on decision-support systems, continues the series of TPC benchmarks. Finally, the *TPC-W* benchmark has been developed to simulate Web-based electronic-commerce applications.

7.3.3   Servers and networks

Client–server computer systems are loosely defined as those in which several independent computer systems (the clients) communicate over some network with another computer system (the server) that responds to the clients' requests, such as to have access to shared files. Benchmarks for characterizing the performance of client–server systems typically execute synthetic programs on the clients that send a stream of file-access commands, or other types of requests, to the server. The mix of requests is usually determined by measuring the types of requests that are generated in some given type of application environment. The performance metric in this type of test is typically the number of requests that can be served per unit time, or the average time required to respond to these requests.

7.3.3.1 SFS/LADDIS

The SPEC System File Server (SFS) 1.1 benchmark was designed to measure the throughput of UNIX servers running the Network File System (NFS) protocol. The program has also been known by the name LADDIS which was an acronym for the companies that collaborated to develop the program, specifically Legato, Auspex, Digital, Data General, Interphase, and Sun.

The benchmark program itself runs on a client system to generate a variety of NFS commands, such as *lookup*, *read*, *write*, *create*, and *remove*, that are sent to a system running an NFS server. The specific mix of requests was chosen to match the characteristics observed in several actual NFS installations. The server sends a response to the client after the request has been satisfied. The client continues to send additional requests at a faster rate until either the server's throughput begins to deteriorate, or its response time exceeds a predefined threshold. The final performance metric is then the maximum number of NFS operations that can be served per second.

SFS 2.0, which is a substantially improved version of SFS 1.1, was released in late 1997 to replace SFS 1.1. This new version includes many enhancements, such as a larger and updated workload that reflects the mix of operations observed in more than 1,000 NFS application environments. It also includes support for both TPC and UDP network transmission protocols. Because of these and other differences, results obtained using SFS 2.0 cannot be compared directly with those obtained with SFS 1.1.

7.3.3.2 SPECweb

With the explosive growth of the Internet and the World Wide Web has come a need for benchmarks similar to SFS to measure the throughput rates of Web servers. The SPECweb benchmark built on the framework of the SFS/LADDIS

Table 7.4. Some of the additional benchmarks developed for various application domains

Benchmark	Source	Application domain
AIM benchmarks	AIM Technology	UNIX workstation and server tests
Business Benchmark	Neal Nelson and Assoc.	UNIX server throughput
GPC	SPEC	UNIX graphics subsystems
MacBench	Ziff-Davis	General Apple Macintosh performance
MediaStones	Providenza and Boekelheide	Windows PC multimedia performance
NetBench	Ziff-Davis	PC file server
PCBench	Ziff-Davis	MS-DOS PC benchmark
ServerBench	Ziff-Davis	PC subsystems (disk, processor, network)
SYSmarks	BAPCo[3]	Retail PC software packages
WinBench	Ziff-Davis	Windows PC graphics and disks
WinStone	Ziff-Davis	Windows PC performance

benchmark discussed above, consists of client programs that continuously send HTTP requests to a Web-server system. The rate at which these requests are sent is gradually increased until the server can no longer respond within the predefined response-time threshold. The maximum rate at which requests can be served before the server's response time begins to decrease is then the performance metric reported.

7.3.4 Miscellaneous benchmarks

In addition to the benchmarks summarized above, many other benchmark programs have been developed for several other specific application domains, including graphics performance, personal computers (PCs), and tests of multimedia performance. Some of these benchmarks are summarized in Table 7.4.

7.4 Summary

Now that you have read this chapter, you should have some appreciation for the fact that there is little to no agreement within the computer-performance-analysis community on what constitutes a good benchmark program. Table 7.5 summarizes the strategies that can be used in a benchmark program to exercise the

Table 7.5. Benchmark programs can employ these strategies to measure performance

Benchmark strategy		Performance metric
Time	Computation	
Variable	Fixed	Total execution time
Fixed	Variable	Total amount of computation completed within the given time
Variable	Variable	Third dimension derived from the statement of the problem, such as *quality*

system under test. Probably the most common benchmark strategy is the fixed-computation approach in which the total time required to execute all of the computation specified in the benchmark program is used as the performance metric. This strategy seems to most closely match our intuition of what we mean when we say that the performance of a computer system has improved, as measured by some given benchmark program. The complementary approach is to fix the amount of time the system is allowed to execute the benchmark program. The total amount of computation it completes in this fixed time period then is used as the metric of performance. An advantage of this approach is that it automatically scales the amount of computation in the problem to the performance capabilities of the system being measured.

In the most flexible benchmark strategy, neither the amount of computation that needs to be performed by the system, nor the amount of time it is allowed to compute, is fixed. Instead, a third dimension is derived from some combination of the execution time and the amount of computation completed within this time. This derived quantity is then the metric of performance. In the HINT benchmark, for instance, the metric of performance is *quality improvements per second* (abbreviated QUIPS), where the definition of 'quality' is rigorously defined as a function of the problem being solved by the benchmark program. This variable-time, variable-computation benchmark strategy seems to effectively capture all of the best aspects of the other two strategies.

As summarized in Table 7.6, benchmark programs themselves can be classified into several different types. In general, benchmarks based on instruction times or instruction-execution profiles are inadequate for any real performance comparisons since they ignore critical aspects of a system's overall performance. Microbenchmarks are appropriate for analyzing one component of a system, or one aspect of its performance, in isolation from the rest of the system. Program kernels and toy benchmarks are often appealing since their small sizes and limited execution times generally make them easy to run on a wide

Table 7.6. A wide variety of benchmark programs has been developed to satisfy a range of specific needs and goals

Benchmark type	Description
Instruction time	Time required to execute one instruction
Instruction-execution profile	Weighted average execution time
Microbenchmark	Small program that exercises one specific component of a system
Program kernels	Central or essential loop extracted from a larger program
Toy benchmark	Complete program that executes a small, often trivial, operation
Synthetic benchmark	Program that matches the execution profile of a set of real application programs
Application benchmark	Reduced or scaled-down version of an actual application that produces a useful result
Your application program	The best benchmark program

variety of systems. However, it is precisely their small sizes and limited execution times that make them inappropriate for analyzing the entire capabilities of a system.

Synthetic benchmarks also have a certain intellectual appeal in that they attempt to capture the essential behavior of a variety of programs within a class of applications in a single benchmark program. Although synthetic benchmarks typically provide numerous parameters that can be used to adjust their run-time characteristics, it is difficult to duplicate the actual low-level details of a real application program in a synthetic benchmark. Unfortunately for the developers of synthetic benchmark programs, it is precisely these low-level details of real applications that seem to have the biggest impact on system performance. Thus, any results based on a synthetic benchmark should be treated with a great deal of caution.

Although the best benchmark program will continue to be your particular mix of applications, standardized application benchmark programs are often a reasonable substitute. They provide the advantage of standardization in that they can easily be used by many different performance analysts. As a result, they can provide a common basis for comparing the performances of different systems when they are measured by different individuals. Even though users of computer systems want to run their real application programs, not some standard benchmark program, all of these various types of benchmark programs are nevertheless likely to remain an important component of the overall computer-systems-performance-analysis picture.

7.5 For further reading

- The basic idea behind Amdahl's law was first presented in

  Gene M. Amdahl, 'Validity of the Single Processor Approach to Achieving Large Scale Computing Capabilities,' *AFIPS Conference Proceedings, Spring Joint Computer Conference,* April 1967, Atlantic City, NJ, pp. 483–485,

  with additional details described in:

  Gene M. Amdahl, 'Limits of Expectation,' *International Journal of Supercomputer Applications,* Vol. 2, No. 1, Spring 1988, pp. 88–97.

- The following papers discuss the many variations of Amdahl's law:

  J. L. Gustafson, 'Reevaluating Amdahl's Law,' *Communications of the ACM,* May 1988, Vol. 31, No. 5, pp. 532–533,

  Xiaofeng Zhou, 'Bridging the Gap Between Amdahl's Law and Sandia Laboratory's Results,' *Communications of the ACM,* August 1989, Volume 32, No. 8, pp. 1014–1015,

  Dilip Sarkar 'Cost and Time-Cost Effectiveness of Multiprocessing,' *IEEE Transactions on Parallel and Distributed Systems,* Vol. 4, No. 6, June 1993, pp. 704–712.

- This book discusses benchmarking and scalability of high-performance parallel-computing systems:

  David J. Kuck, *High Performance Computing: Challenges for Future Systems,* Oxford University Press, New York, 1996.

- The following books provide good summaries of several common benchmark programs:

  Rich Grace, *The Benchmark Book,* Prentice Hall, Upper Saddle River, NJ, 1996,

  J. Dongarra and W. Gentzsch (eds.), *Computer Benchmarks,* North-Holland Publishers, 1993.

- The details of the SLALOM benchmark are given in

  John Gustafson, Diane Rover, Stephen Elbert, and Michael Carter, 'The Design of a Scalable, Fixed-Time Computer Benchmark,' *Journal of Parallel and Distributed Computing,* Vol. 11, No. 8, August 1991, pp. 388–401.

- The following three papers discuss the HINT benchmark. The first paper by Sylvester describes in glowing terms how the HINT benchmark can be used to compare the performances of client–server computing systems. The response by Mashey then points out some of the flaws in this benchmark. The Gustafson and Snell paper is the detailed description of the benchmark program by its authors.

T. Sylvester, 'HINT Benchmark Ideal for Fair C/S Testing,' *Client–Server Today,* September 1994, pp. 83–84.

J. Mashey, 'Counterpoint: Here's a Good Hint on Performance,' *Client–Server Today,* October 1994, pp. 53–55.

J. L. Gustafson and Q. O. Snell, 'HINT: A New Way to Measure Computer Performance,' *Hawaii International Conference on System Sciences,* 1995, pp. II:392–401.

- This paper summarizes several different benchmark suites that have been developed to characterize scientific application programs and shows the results of executing these programs on a Cray Research parallel-vector super-computer:

  M. Berry, G. Cybenko, and J. Larson, 'Scientific Benchmark Characterizations,' *Parallel Computing,* Vol. 17, 1991, pp. 1173–1194.

- These papers discuss some of the pros and cons of the popular SPEC benchmark suite:

  Ran Giladi and Niv Ahituv, 'SPEC as a Performance Evaluation Measure,' *IEEE Computer,* Vol. 28, No. 8, August 1995, pp. 33–42,

  Nikki Mirghafori, Margret Jacoby, and David Patterson, 'Truth in SPEC Benchmarks,' *ACM Computer Architecture News,* Vol. 23, No. 5, December 1995, pp. 34–42.

- A detailed example of how microbenchmark programs can be used to characterize a particular aspect of a system's performance is described in

  Rafael H. Saavedra, R. Stockton Gaines, and Michael J. Carlton, 'Characterizing the Performance Space of Shared-Memory Computers Using Micro-Benchmarks,' University of Southern California Department of Computer Science Technical Report no. USC-CS-93-547, `http://www.usc.edu/dept/cs/tech.html`.

- The Gibson mix is described in

  J. C. Gibson, *The Gibson Mix,* IBM Systems Development Division, Poughkeepsie, NY, technical report no. 00.2043.

- The Whetstone and Dhrystone benchmarks are described in the following papers:

  H. J. Curnow and B. A. Wichmann, 'A Synthetic Benchmark,' *The Computer Journal,* Vol. 19, No. 1, 1976, p. 80,

  R. P. Weicker, 'Dhrystone: A Synthetic Systems Programming Benchmark,' *Communications of the ACM,* Vol. 27, No. 10, October 1984, pp. 1013–1030.

- Chapter 2, 'The Role of Performance,' in the following computer architecture text provides some useful insights into how benchmark programs have been used in evaluating processor designs.

David A. Patterson and John L. Hennessy, *Computer Organization and Design: The Hardware/Software Interface,* (Second Edition), Morgan Kaufmann Publishers, San Francisco, CA, 1998.

- The *isoefficiency* function is described in
  V. Kumar, A. Grama, A. Gupta, and G. Karypis, *Introduction to Parallel Computing: Design and Analysis of Algorithms,* Benjamin/Cummings Publishing, Redwood City, CA, 1994.
- Finally, a great deal of information about the various benchmark sets is available on the Web. These sites often allow access to the source code of the benchmark programs themselves. A few examples are listed below.

Basic Linear Algebra Subroutines (BLAS),

    http://www.cfm.brown.edu/people/ce107/blas.html.

HINT Benchmark,

    http://www.scl.ameslab.gov/scl/HINT/HINT.html.

NAS Parallel Benchmarks,

    http://science.nas.nasa.gov/Software/NPB/.

Parkbench Parallel Benchmarks,

    http://www.netlib.org/parkbench/.

Perfect Club benchmarks,

    http://www.csrd.uiuc.edu/benchmark/benchmark.html.

SPEC Benchmarks,

    http://www.spec.org/.

Transaction Processing Performance Council (TPC) benchmarks,

    http://www.tpc.org/.

7.6   Exercises

1. What are some possible measures of 'computation' in a computer system? What are the strengths and limitations of each of these measures?
2. How could these measures of computation be used to develop a benchmark program?
3. How do MFLOPS, MIPS, and QUIPS relate to benchmark programs?

4. Compare the advantages and disadvantages of each of the different types of benchmark programs.

5. Explain the key differences between the two variations of Amdahl's law discussed in this chapter.

6. In designing a new computer system, we make an enhancement that improves some mode of execution by a factor of ten. This enhanced mode is used 50% of the time, measured as a percentage of the execution time when the enhanced mode is in use. (Recall that Amdahl's law uses the fraction of the original, unenhanced execution time that could make use of the enhanced mode. Thus, we cannot directly use this 50% measurement to compute the net speedup using Amdahl's law.)

   (a) What is the speedup that we have obtained by using this fast mode?

   (b) What percentage of the original execution time has been converted to fast mode?

7. Three different enhancements are being proposed for a new computer system. Enhancement 1 produces a speedup of 30, enhancement 2 produces a speedup of 20, and enhancement 3 produces a speedup of 10. Only one enhancement can be in use at any time.

   (a) If enhancements 1 and 2 are each usable for 30% of the (unenhanced) execution time, what fraction of this time must enhancement 3 be used to achieve an overall speedup of 10?

   (b) Assume that the distribution of enhancement usage is 30%, 30%, and 20% of the unenhanced execution time for enhancements 1, 2, and 3, respectively. If all three enhancements are in use, during what fraction of the reduced (i.e. enhanced) execution time is no enhancement in use?

8. What are the advantages of fixing the execution time of a benchmark program while allowing the amount of computation it completes to vary? What are the disadvantages?

9. Develop a new microbenchmark program to characterize the input/output performance of a computer system. You will have to define what 'input/output performances' means, and how to measure it. After you have completed your benchmark program, use it to compare the input/output performances of three different computer systems. Use some appropriate analysis technique for your comparison, such as the ANOVA test.

8 Linear regression models

'I see your point ... and raise you a line.'

Elliot Smorodinsky

Measuring the performance of a computer system for all possible input values would allow us to answer any question someone might have about how the system will perform under any set of conditions. Unfortunately, it would be prohibitively expensive, if not impossible, to make all of these measurements. Instead, we can measure the system's performance for a limited number of inputs and use these measured values to produce a mathematical model that describes the behavior of the system over a range of input values. We can then use this model, which is called a *regression model*, to predict how the system will perform when given an input value that we did not actually measure.

A linear-regression model begins with a system that has one continuous (or nearly so) input factor whose value we can control. If we plot the measured response values as a function of the input values, we may find that there appears to be a linear relationship between the input and the output, as shown in Figure 8.1. We can then use the method of *least-squares minimization* to produce a *linear-regression equation* to model the system. This model will allow us to *predict* how the system will respond to input values that we did not actually measure.

8.1 Least squares minimization

A simple linear regression model is of the form

$$y = a + bx \tag{8.1}$$

where x is the input variable, y is the predicted output response, and a and b are the regression parameters that we wish to estimate from our set of measurements. If y_i is the value we actually measure when we set the input value to x_i, then each of these (x_i, y_i) pairs can be written as

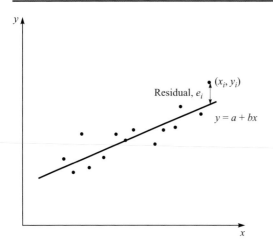

Figure 8.1 A scatter plot of the measured data points with the calculated regression line. The experimenter controls the input value, x_i, and measures the corresponding output value, y_i. The residual, e_i, is the difference between the regression line and the measured data point, (x_i, y_i).

$$y_i = a + bx_i + e_i \tag{8.2}$$

where e_i is the difference between the measured value for y_i and the value that would have been predicted for y_i from the regression model (see Figure 8.1). This difference is called the *residual* for this measurement.

To find the regression parameters a and b that will form a line that most closely fits the n measured data points, we can minimize the sum of squares of these residuals, denoted SSE. That is, we wish to find a and b to minimize

$$SSE = \sum_{i=1}^{n} e_i^2 = \sum_{i=1}^{n} (y_i - a - bx_i)^2. \tag{8.3}$$

We begin by differentiating SSE first with respect to a and then with respect to b. We then set both of these partial derivatives to zero to produce the following system of equations

$$na + b \sum_{i=1}^{n} x_i = \sum_{i=1}^{n} y_i \tag{8.4}$$

$$a \sum_{i=1}^{n} x_i + b \sum_{i=1}^{n} x_i^2 = \sum_{i=1}^{n} x_i y_i. \tag{8.5}$$

Solving this system for b produces

$$b = \frac{n \sum_{i=1}^{n} x_i y_i - \left(\sum_{i=1}^{n} x_i\right)\left(\sum_{i=1}^{n} y_i\right)}{n \sum_{i=1}^{n} x_i^2 - \left(\sum_{i=1}^{n} x_i\right)^2}. \tag{8.6}$$

Table 8.1. Measured times required to read various input file sizes

File size (bytes) (x_i)	Time (μs) (y_i)
10	3.8
50	8.1
100	11.9
500	55.6
1,000	99.6
5,000	500.2
10,000	1,006.1

We then can use Equation (8.4) to find that

$$a = \bar{y} - b\bar{x}. \tag{8.7}$$

Example. We wish to develop a regression model to relate the time required to perform a file-read operation to the number of bytes read.

We perform an experiment in which we vary the number of bytes read from 10 to 10,000 and measure the corresponding reading time. Our resulting measurements are shown in Table 8.1.

From these data, we calculate

$$\sum_{i=1}^{7} x_i = 16,660.0 \tag{8.8}$$

$$\sum_{i=1}^{7} y_i = 1,685.3 \tag{8.9}$$

$$\sum_{i=1}^{7} x_i y_i = 12,691,033.0 \tag{8.10}$$

$$\sum_{i=1}^{7} x_i^2 = 126,262,600.0 \tag{8.11}$$

$$\bar{x} = 2,380 \tag{8.12}$$

$$\bar{y} = 240.76. \tag{8.13}$$

Plugging these values into the above equations for a and b produces

$$b = \frac{(7)(12{,}691{,}033.0) - (16{,}660.0)(1685.3)}{(7)(126{,}262{,}600.0) - (16{,}660.0)^2} = 0.1002 \tag{8.14}$$

$$a = 240.76 - (0.1002)(2{,}380) = 2.24. \tag{8.15}$$

Thus, using these estimates for the parameters for a linear regression model for this system produces

$$y = 2.24 + 0.1002x. \tag{8.16}$$

From this equation we can say that the time required to read a file from the disk is approximately 2.24 µs plus an additional 0.1002 µs per byte read. We can then predict that the time required to read a file of 3,000 bytes would be about 2.24 + 0.1002(3,000) = 303 µs, for instance. ◇

8.2   Confidence intervals for regression parameters

It is important to bear in mind that the regression model parameters a and b calculated using this technique are estimates based on experimentally measured values. Thus, they are subject to all of the types of experimental errors described in Chapter 4. Additionally, the output values we predict when using the regression model also are affected by the experimental errors since they are simple linear combinations of the measured values. Confidence intervals are again useful in quantifying the precision of our estimates of the regression parameters and the predicted output values.

To derive a confidence interval for the regression parameters, we first need some estimate of their variance. It can be shown that the best estimate of this variance is obtained by dividing the sum of squares of the residuals, SSE, by the number of degrees of freedom available for this term. Since we used n measurements to derive the two regression parameters, there are $n - 2$ degrees of freedom for SSE. Thus,

$$s^2 = \frac{SSE}{n - 2}. \tag{8.17}$$

To simplify the calculation of this sample variance, it useful to expand SSE as follows:

$$SSE = \sum_{i=1}^{n} e_i^2 = \sum_{i=1}^{n} (y_i - a - bx_i)^2 = \sum_{i=1}^{n} [(y_i - \bar{y}) - b(x_i - \bar{x})]^2 \tag{8.18}$$

$$= S_{yy} - 2bS_{xy} + b^2 S_{xx} = S_{yy} - bS_{xy}$$

where

$$S_{xx} = \sum_{i=1}^{n}(x_i - \bar{x})^2 = \sum_{i=1}^{n}x_i^2 - \frac{\left(\sum_{i=1}^{n}x_i\right)^2}{n} \tag{8.19}$$

$$S_{yy} = \sum_{i=1}^{n}(y_i - \bar{y})^2 = \sum_{i=1}^{n}y_i^2 - \frac{\left(\sum_{i=1}^{n}y_i\right)^2}{n} \tag{8.20}$$

$$S_{xy} = \sum_{i=1}^{n}(x_i - \bar{x})(y_i - \bar{y}) = \sum_{i=1}^{n}x_iy_i - \frac{\left(\sum_{i=1}^{n}x_i\right)\left(\sum_{i=1}^{n}y_i\right)}{n}. \tag{8.21}$$

Using these intermediate terms gives the following estimate of the variance of the regression parameters

$$s^2 = \frac{SSE}{n-2} = \frac{S_{yy} - bS_{xy}}{n-2}. \tag{8.22}$$

Using this sample variance, it is easily shown that the confidence interval for the slope of the regression equation, b, is

$$(b_1, b_2) = b \mp \frac{t_{[1-\alpha/2;n-2]}s}{\sqrt{S_{xx}}} \tag{8.23}$$

where $t_{[1-\alpha/2;n-2]}$ is from a t distribution with $n-2$ degrees of freedom. As before, when n is sufficiently large, we can approximate the t distribution using a standard normal distribution. Similarly, the confidence interval for the intercept in the regression equation, a, is

$$(a_1, a_2) = a \mp \frac{t_{[1-\alpha/2;n-2]}s\sqrt{\sum_{i=1}^{n}x_i^2}}{\sqrt{nS_{xx}}}. \tag{8.24}$$

Finally, we are often interested in using a regression model to predict a future observed response. That is, we would like to estimate the system's response for a particular input level that we did not (or could not) actually measure. Our prediction of the system's response, y_p, when the input value is x_p is found simply by inserting these values into the regression equation. Thus, $y_p = a + bx_p$. A corresponding confidence interval for this prediction is

$$(y_{p1}, y_{p2}) = y_p \mp t_{[1-\alpha/2;n-2]}s\sqrt{1 + \frac{1}{n} + \frac{(x_p - \bar{x})^2}{S_{xx}}}. \tag{8.25}$$

Example. Using the data in Table 8.1, we found the corresponding regression model to be $y = 2.24 + 0.1002x$. Calculate appropriate confidence intervals for these regression parameters.

We first calculate S_{xx}, S_{yy}, and S_{xy} to be

$$S_{xx} = 126{,}262{,}600 - \frac{(16{,}660)^2}{7} = 86{,}611{,}800 \tag{8.26}$$

$$S_{yy} = 1{,}275{,}670.43 - \frac{(1{,}685.3)^2}{7} = 869{,}922.42 \tag{8.27}$$

$$S_{xy} = 12{,}691{,}033 - \frac{(16{,}660)(1{,}685.3)}{7} = 8{,}680{,}019. \tag{8.28}$$

The variance of the regression parameters is then calculated to be

$$s^2 = \frac{869{,}922.42 - 0.1002(8{,}680{,}019)}{7 - 2} = 36.9027. \tag{8.29}$$

The corresponding standard deviation is

$$s = \sqrt{36.9027} = 6.0748. \tag{8.30}$$

The 90% confidence intervals for the regression parameters a and b are then found to be

$$(b_1, b_2) = 0.1002 \mp \frac{2.015(6.0748)}{\sqrt{86{,}611{,}800}} = 0.1002 \mp 0.0013 = (0.099, 0.102) \tag{8.31}$$

$$(a_1, a_2) = 2.24 \mp \frac{2.015(6.0748)\sqrt{126{,}262{,}600}}{\sqrt{7(8{,}680{,}019)}} = 2.24 \mp 5.59 = (-3.35, 7.83). \tag{8.32}$$

Since the confidence interval for a includes zero, at the 90% confidence level, we cannot conclude that this y-intercept is significantly different than zero.

We also used this model to predict that the time required to read a file of 3,000 bytes would be $y_{3000} = 303$ μs. We can then calculate the 90% confidence interval for this prediction to be

$$(y_{3000;1}, y_{3000;2}) = 303 \mp 2.015(6.0748)\sqrt{1 + \frac{1}{7} + \frac{(3{,}000 - 2{,}380)^2}{86{,}611{,}800}} \tag{8.33}$$

$$= 303 \mp 13.11 = (290, 316).$$

Thus, we are 90% confident that it will take between 290 and 316 μs to read a file of 3,000 bytes. ◇

These confidence intervals allow us to determine how much measurement noise there is in our estimates of the regression parameters. Confidence intervals that are large relative to the size of the parameters would suggest that there is a large amount of error in our regression model. This error could be due to systematic or random errors in the measurements, or it could be due to the fact that the underlying process we are measuring does not, in fact, exhibit a linear relationship. As a result, we should be careful when drawing conclusions from a regression model with large variances (and, therefore, large confidence intervals) in the parameters.

Furthermore, when a linear-regression model is used to predict system-response values for inputs that are outside of the range of measurements that were used to develop the model, we would expect to have less confidence in the values predicted. In fact, it may be that the system is linear only within the range that we happened to measure. Thus, great care should also be taken when trying to predict values outside of the range of measurements. This situation is investigated further in the exercises at the end of the chapter.

8.3   Correlation

After developing a linear-regression model, it is useful to know how well the equation actually models the measured data. That is, we are interested in knowing how strong the linear *correlation* between the input and output is. The *coefficient of determination*, and its square root, called the *correlation coefficient*, are quantitative measures of this observed linearity.

8.3.1   The coefficient of determination

We start by using the method of *allocation of variation* to determine how much of the total variation is explained by the linear model. In Equation (8.18), we saw that

$$SSE = S_{yy} - bS_{xy}.\tag{8.34}$$

If we let $SST = S_{yy}$ and $SSR = bS_{xy}$, then we have

$$SST = SSR + SSE.\tag{8.35}$$

In this form of the expression, we readily see that the total variation in the measured system outputs, i.e. SST, is partitioned into two components. The first component, SSR, is the portion of the total variation explained by the regression model. The remaining component, SSE, is due to measurement error. In a scatter plot of the measurements, we see this error as the variation of the measurements around the regression line.

The fraction of the total variation explained by the regression model is called the *coefficient of determination*. It is denoted r^2 and, similar to what we have seen before, it is found as

$$r^2 = \frac{SSR}{SST} = \frac{SST - SSE}{SST}.\tag{8.36}$$

Since $SST = SSR + SSE$, it should be apparent that $0 \le r^2 \le 1$. If there is a perfect linear relationship between the input and the output, then all of the variation in the measured outputs will be explained by the regression model. In this case, all of the measured data points would fall directly on the regression line so that all of the residuals, e_i, are zero, giving $SSE = 0$. In this case, then, $r^2 = 1$. If, on the other hand, none of the variation in the outputs is explained by the regression model, then $SSE = SST$ and $r^2 = 0$.

Thus, the coefficient of determination provides an indication of how well the regression model fits the data. Values of r^2 near 1 indicate a close linear relationship between the input and output values. Conversely, values of r^2 near 0 indicate that there is little to no linear relationship. The latter situation would occur if the output were a horizontal line, for instance, so that knowing any of the input values would be of no help in predicting the output values. Similarly, even if there were a functional relationship between the inputs and outputs, but it was not linear (it could be quadratic, perhaps), then r^2 would be near zero.

8.3.2 The correlation coefficient

The square root of the coefficient of determination is called the *correlation coefficient*, denoted r. It can be shown that

$$r = \frac{S_{xy}}{\sqrt{S_{xx} S_{yy}}}. \tag{8.37}$$

Note that, equivalently,

$$r = b \sqrt{\frac{S_{xx}}{S_{yy}}} = \sqrt{\frac{SSR}{SST}} \tag{8.38}$$

where $b = S_{xy}/S_{xx}$ is the slope from the linear regression model.

The value of r ranges between -1 and $+1$. A value of $r = +1$ indicates a perfect positive linear correlation between the input and output variables. In this case, any increase in the magnitude of the input will produce an appropriately scaled increase in the output. A value of $r = -1$, on the other hand, means that any change in the input will produce a corresponding change in the output in the opposite direction. That is, an increase in the input will produce an appropriate decrease in the output. Values of r between -1 and $+1$ indicate different degrees of linear correlation.

It is important to understand the differences between the coefficient of determination and the correlation coefficient. Suppose that we have two different systems for which we have developed linear regression models. For one of them we calculate a correlation coefficient of $r_1 = 0.6$ while for the other we find $r_2 = -0.9$. From these correlation coefficients we cannot conclude that the linear relationship for the second system is 50% 'better' than that for the first. All we can conclude is that the linear relationship in the second system appears stronger.

Looking at the coefficient of determination, though, we find $r_1^2 = 0.36$ and $r_2^2 = 0.81$. Now we see that, for the first system, only 36% of the variation in the output is explained by the linear-regression model. For the second system, however, 81% of the change in the output values is explained by the regression model. We can thus conclude that the linear relationship between the inputs and the output for the second system is much stronger than that for the first.

Example. Again using the data from Table 8.1, we can calculate the correlation coefficient for the regression model relating the time required to read a file of a given number of bytes as follows:

$$r = 0.1002 \sqrt{\frac{86,611,800}{869,922.4171}} = 0.9998. \tag{8.39}$$

The coefficient of determination is $r^2 = (0.9998)^2 = 0.9996$. Thus, we conclude that 99.96% of the variation in the time required to read a file is explained by this linear-regression model.   ◇

8.3.3   Correlation and causation

Finally, it is important to appreciate the difference between *correlation* and *causation*. Causation implies that an observed change in the output is the direct result of a change in the input. That is, there is some process within the system that somehow links the input and the output. If the process is linear, we would expect to find a large correlation coefficient. For example, reading a large file takes longer than reading a small file because more data must be transferred from the disk to the memory. Thus, we are not surprised to find a high correlation between the file-reading time and the number of bytes read in the example above.

However, the converse is not always true. That is, the output could be highly correlated to the input without the input *causing* the output. For example, we may find that there is a high correlation between the time required to send a message on some shared network and the time of day. Thus, knowing the time of day allows us to predict with some accuracy how long it will take to send a message. However, the time of day does not *cause* there to be a certain transmission time. Rather, the number of people using the system changes throughout the day according to work schedules. It is the actions of these users that change the load on the network, which then causes the changes observed in the message-transmission times. Thus, although there is a strong correlation between the time required to send a message and the time of day, the analyst must be careful not to conclude that one causes the other. This admonition is commonly summarized in the aphorism 'correlation does not imply causation.'

8.4　Multiple linear regression

A multiple-linear-regression model is a straightforward extension of the simple one-input regression model. It allows the model to include the effects of several input variables that are all linearly related to a single output variable. For example, it may be that the total execution time of a program is a linear function of the number of memory and file input/output operations it performs. The multiple-regression model would then allow the prediction of execution times on the basis of these two input factors.

For simplicity of explanation, we first consider the case of a multiple linear model with two independent input variables, x_1 and x_2. In this case, we are trying to fit a plane to the collection of measurements instead of a simple line. The basic form of this two-dimensional regression model is

$$y = b_0 + b_1 x_1 + b_2 x_2 \tag{8.40}$$

where b_0, b_1, and b_2 are the regression parameters we wish to estimate. By making n measurements of the output y for various combinations of the inputs x_1 and x_2, we obtain n data points (x_{1i}, x_{2i}, y_i), where y_i is the output value observed when input x_1 is set to the specific value x_{1i} and input x_2 is set to x_{2i}. Each of these data points can be expressed as

$$y = b_0 + b_1 x_{1i} + b_2 x_{2i} + e_i \tag{8.41}$$

where e_i is again the residual for the data point (x_{1i}, x_{2i}, y_i).

Just like in the simple regression case, we wish to minimize the sum of the squares of the residuals:

$$SSE = \sum_{i=1}^{n} e_i^2 = \sum_{i=1}^{n} (y_i - b_0 - b_1 x_{1i} - b_2 x_{2i})^2. \tag{8.42}$$

As before, this expression takes on its minimum value when the partial derivatives of SSE with respect to b_0, b_1, and b_2 are all set to zero. This procedure then leads to the following system of equations:

$$n b_0 + b_1 \sum_{i=1}^{n} x_{1i} + b_2 \sum_{i=1}^{n} x_{2i} = \sum_{i=1}^{n} y_i \tag{8.43}$$

$$b_0 \sum_{i=1}^{n} x_{1i} + b_1 \sum_{i=1}^{n} x_{1i}^2 + b_2 \sum_{i=1}^{n} x_{1i}x_{2i} = \sum_{i=1}^{n} x_{1i}y_i \tag{8.44}$$

$$b_0 \sum_{i=1}^{n} x_{2i} + b_1 \sum_{i=1}^{n} x_{1i}x_{2i} + b_2 \sum_{i=1}^{n} x_{2i}^2 = \sum_{i=1}^{n} x_{2i}y_i. \tag{8.45}$$

We now have three equations that we can solve to find the three unknowns b_0, b_1, and b_2. The wide availability of software for solving these types of systems of equations should make this a relatively simple task, although the solution could also be found by using any of the standard methods for solving systems of equations.

This same procedure can be generalized to find a multiple linear regression model of the form

$$y = b_0 + b_1 x_1 + \cdots + b_k x_k \tag{8.46}$$

for k independent inputs. Again, we wish to minimize

$$SSE = \sum_{i=1}^{n} e_i^2 = \sum_{i=1}^{n} (y_i - b_0 - b_1 x_{1i} - b_2 x_{2i} - \cdots - b_k x_{ki})^2 \tag{8.47}$$

where y_i is the output value measured when the k inputs are set to $(x_{1i}, x_{2i}, \cdots, x_{ki})$ and there are in total n measurements available. After setting the partial derivatives of SSE with respect to the b_i values to zero, we obtain a system of equations that can be solved to find the b_i regression parameters.

To solve this system, it is convenient to organize the input values used when making all of the measurements of the system into a matrix $\mathbf{X}$ defined as

$$\mathbf{X} = \begin{bmatrix} 1 & x_{11} & x_{21} & \cdots & x_{k1} \\ 1 & x_{12} & x_{22} & \cdots & x_{k2} \\ \vdots & \vdots & \vdots & \vdots & \vdots \\ 1 & x_{1i} & x_{2i} & \cdots & x_{ki} \\ \vdots & \vdots & \vdots & \vdots & \vdots \\ 1 & x_{1n} & x_{2n} & \cdots & x_{kn} \end{bmatrix}. \tag{8.48}$$

Next define the matrix

$$\mathbf{A} = \mathbf{X}^{\mathsf{T}}\mathbf{X} \tag{8.49}$$

and the two column vectors

$$b = \begin{bmatrix} b_0 \\ b_1 \\ \vdots \\ b_i \\ \vdots \\ b_k \end{bmatrix} \qquad (8.50)$$

$$d = \begin{bmatrix} \sum_{i=1}^{n} y_i \\ \sum_{i=1}^{n} x_{1i} y_i \\ \vdots \\ \sum_{i=1}^{n} x_{ki} y_i \end{bmatrix}. \qquad (8.51)$$

Then, if A is invertible, the regression coefficients are found by solving

$$b = A^{-1} d. \qquad (8.52)$$

Owing to the effort required to solve linear systems of equations with a large number of variables, it is recommended that you use one of the several commonly available software packages designed for this purpose. Many versions of these packages intended for use by statisticians also can calculate confidence intervals for the regression parameters, predicted outputs, and so forth. This approach is generally much more convenient, and much less error-prone, than is trying to solve these systems manually.

8.5   Verifying linearity

An important consideration in developing linear regression models is that the relationship you are trying to model might not in fact be linear. Even if the relationship is not linear, you can still mechanically apply the formulas to calculate values for the regression-model parameters that will minimize the sum of the squares of the residuals. However, the resulting model will be wrong in the sense that it will give poor predictions for output values.

Furthermore, applying a linear model to a nonlinear system will give a misleading impression about the system's overall behavior. Consequently, it is very important to verify that the inputs and outputs appear to be linearly related. A simple plot of the output values as a function of the inputs is often sufficient to verify this assumption of linearity. Constructing this type of plot before beginning any regression calculation should be considered mandatory.

8.6   Nonlinear models

For systems with nonlinear input–output relationships, it is sometimes possible to transform the nonlinear data into a linear form. The linear-regression formulas can then be applied to these transformed data.

For example, say that we know (or suspect) that the input–output relationship of a system is exponential such that

$$y = ab^x. \tag{8.53}$$

In this case, if we take the logarithm of both sides we obtain

$$\ln y = \ln a + (\ln b)x. \tag{8.54}$$

By letting $y' = \ln y$, $a' = \ln a$, and $b' = \ln b$, we can rewrite this equation in our standard form

$$y' = a' + b'x. \tag{8.55}$$

The regression formulas can then be used to find a' and b', from which a and b in the nonlinear model can be obtained.

The conversion of a nonlinear function into a linear function to which the above linear-regression techniques can be applied is called *curvilinear regression*. There is also a variety of other general *transformations* that can be used to convert measured data from one form to another. There is a large body of literature dealing with this topic of *curve fitting*, to which the interested reader should refer. Many of these curve-fitting techniques have been implemented in readily available software packages.

Example. You are given the task of estimating the growth over time in the number of transistors on a certain type of integrated-circuit chip that your company produces. In particular, you are asked to estimate how many transistors are likely to be integrated on the chip 4 years from now, assuming that the growth in transistor density continues at the same rate as it has over the past several years.

You begin by collecting the data in Table 8.2, which shows the estimated number of transistors integrated on this type of chip for the past 6 years. After plotting this data, as shown in Figure 8.2, it is apparent that the growth in transistor density is nonlinear. In fact, the growth appears to be exponential. Consequently, you expect that you can model this growth using a regression equation of the form

$$y = ab^x. \tag{8.56}$$

To apply the linear regression techniques, however, you must first *linearize* the model by letting $y' = \ln y$, $a' = \ln a$, and $b' = \ln b$, to give

Table 8.2. Estimates of the number of transistors on a certain type of integrated-circuit chip during several consecutive years

Year (x_i)	Number of transistors (y_i)	Transformed data $(y_i' = \ln y_i)$
1	9,500	9.1590
2	16,000	9.6803
3	23,000	10.0432
4	38,000	10.5453
5	62,000	11.0349
6	105,000	11.5617

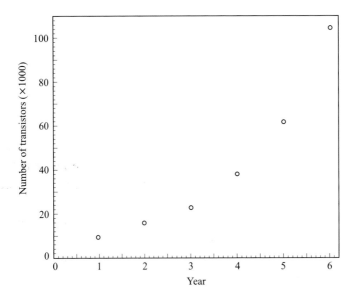

Figure 8.2 A scatter plot of the measured data points from Table 8.2.

$$y' = a' + b'x. \tag{8.57}$$

The corresponding values you calculate for y_i' are shown in Table 8.2, and a scatter plot of these linearized values is shown in Figure 8.3.

Using the linear regression equations, you calculate the following intermediate values:

$$\sum_{i=1}^{6} x_i = 21 \tag{8.58}$$

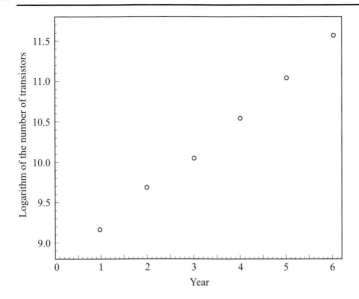

Figure 8.3 A scatter plot of the transformed (linearized) data points from Table 8.2.

$$\sum_{i=1}^{6} x_i^2 = 91 \tag{8.59}$$

$$\sum_{i=1}^{6} y_i' = 62.0246 \tag{8.60}$$

$$\sum_{i=1}^{6} (y_i')^2 = 645.1103 \tag{8.61}$$

$$\sum_{i=1}^{6} x_i y_i' = 225.3756 \tag{8.62}$$

$$S_{xx} = 17.5 \tag{8.63}$$

$$S_{yy} = 3.9354 \tag{8.64}$$

$$S_{xy} = 8.2895. \tag{8.65}$$

You then find the regression parameters to be $a' = 8.68$ and $b' = 0.474$, from which you can calculate $a = e^{a'} = 5{,}881$ and $b = e^{b'} = 1.61$. This produces the regression model for growth in transistor density

$$y = (5{,}881)1.61^x. \tag{8.66}$$

It is a good idea to find confidence intervals for these regression parameters to provide some indication of how well they model the data. We first calculate the standard deviation as follows:

$$s = \sqrt{\frac{S_{yy} - b'S_{xy}}{n-2}} = \sqrt{\frac{3.9354 - (0.474)(8.2895)}{4}} = 0.0465. \tag{8.67}$$

Note that we must use b' in this expression instead of b since the standard deviation is applicable only to the linearized version of the regression model. For a 90% confidence interval for b', we find from the t table $t_{1-0.95;4} = 2.132$. Then the interval itself is found to be

$$(b'_{lo}, b'_{hi}) = 0.4737 \mp \frac{2.132(0.0465)}{\sqrt{17.5}} = (0.4500, 0.4974). \tag{8.68}$$

The corresponding interval for b is

$$(b_{lo}, b_{hi}) = (e^{0.4500}, e^{0.4974}) = (1.57, 1.64). \tag{8.69}$$

Similarly, the confidence interval for a' is

$$(a'_{lo}, a'_{hi}) = 8.68 \mp \frac{2.132(0.0465)\sqrt{91}}{\sqrt{6(17.5)}} = (8.59, 8.77). \tag{8.70}$$

The corresponding confidence interval for a is then found to be

$$(a_{lo}, a_{hi}) = (e^{8.59}, e^{8.77}) = (5,360, 6,450). \tag{8.71}$$

Finally, we predict what the transistor density will be 4 years in the future by setting $x = 10$ in the above regression equation (since $x = 6$ corresponds to the present) to give

$$y_{10} = (5,881)1.61^{10} = 670,000. \tag{8.72}$$

To calculate an appropriate confidence interval for this prediction, we must again work with the linearized parameters. Thus, $y'_{10} = 8.68 + (0.474)(10) = 13.42$. The 90% confidence interval for this prediction is

$$(y'_{10;lo}, y'_{10;hi}) = 13.42 \mp (2.132)(0.0465)\sqrt{1 + \frac{1}{6} + \frac{(10-3.5)^2}{17.5}} \tag{8.73}$$
$$= (13.23, 13.60).$$

The corresponding confidence interval for y'_{10} is $(556,000, 809,000)$. Thus, we conclude that, if the growth in transistor densities maintains the same rate as it has over the past 6 years, there is a 90% chance that we will see between 556,000 and 809,000 transistors per chip 4 years from now.

◇

Note that this conclusion relies on the assumption that the variation in transistor densities that we estimated follows a normal (Gaussian) distribution. This variation in this case corresponds to the 'noise' in the data in Table 8.2. Since these are not actually measurements in the sense in which we typically think of measurements in computer-performance-analysis experiments, however, this assumption is not in fact necessarily reasonable. As a result, our conclusions must be treated with an appropriate measure of caution. In particular, the confidence-interval width perhaps does not accurately reflect what would be actually observed. Nevertheless, without some additional information about the error in these 'measurements,' this approach to modeling the growth in transistor densities is probably as reasonable as is any other alternative.

8.7   Summary

Linear regression uses the least-squares-minimization technique to develop a mathematical model of a system from a set of measured data values. This model relates a single output response of a system to the values presented at its inputs. Since this model is derived from measured data, which are subject to measurement noise, confidence intervals are again used to quantify the precision of the regression parameters. Confidence intervals can also be calculated for output values predicted from the model. Before blindly applying the linear-regression formulas, it is important to verify that the output indeed appears to be linearly related to the inputs. The coefficient of determination and the correlation coefficient provide quantitative measures of the linearity between the output and the inputs. Inputs and outputs that are not linearly related can often be 'linearized' by using an appropriate transformation. The linear regression models then can be applied to the linearized data.

8.8   For further reading

- Chapter 15 of this text describes the mathematics behind linear regression, and discusses the general problem of fitting measured data to a parameterized model. William H. Press, Saul A. Teukolsky, William T. Vetterling, and Brian P. Flannery, *Numerical Recipes in C* (Second Edition), Cambridge University Press, New York, NY, 1992.

8.9   Exercises

1. What error distribution is assumed to exist in the measurements used to develop a linear-regression model? What are the consequences of this assumption being wrong for your data?

2. What is an outlier? How should outliers be handled in regression modeling?

3. What can you say about a regression model whose coefficient of determination is 0.87? 0.54? 0.29?

4. What other criteria besides the least-squares error criterion could be used to find a line that fits the measured data?

5. Using the data values shown in Table 8.1, calculate confidence intervals for input file-size values ranging from 100 bytes to 10,500 bytes in steps of 100 bytes. Plot these confidence intervals and the corresponding linear-regression model on the same graph. What happens to the confidence intervals towards the ends of the measured values?

6. Show that the coefficient of determination is the square of the correlation coefficient.

7. Develop a linear-regression model to predict the time required to perform a recursive subroutine call as a function of the depth of the recursion. We are interested only in the overhead of the call and return, not the user work that would be performed within the subroutine.

   (a) Measure and plot the time required to perform a recursive call n levels deep using appropriate values of n in the range [100, 100,000]. Superimpose on this plot your linear-regression model. Also, determine 90% confidence intervals for the regression parameters and include appropriate information about the correlation between the inputs and outputs of your model.

   (b) Use this model to predict the time required to perform this recursive call m levels deep (with an appropriate confidence interval), where m is near the middle of the range of values you measured, but not a value you actually measured.

   (c) Now measure the time required to perform this recursive call m levels deep and calculate a 90% confidence interval. Compare your prediction from part (b) with these measurements, and explain your results.

   (d) Repeat parts (b) and (c) for two additional values of m, one that is larger than the largest value you measured in part (a), and one that is smaller than the smallest value you measured.

8. Repeat the above problem for the time required to read a file of b bytes.

9. Using the data in Table 8.2, estimate the number of transistors that will be on a chip in year 20 and year 25. Calculate a 90% confidence interval for your predictions.

9 The design of experiments

'The fundamental principle of science, the definition almost, is this: the sole test of the validity of any idea is experiment.'

Richard P. Feynman

The primary goal of the *design of experiments* is to determine the maximum amount of information about a system with the minimum amount of effort. A well-designed experiment guides the experimenter in choosing what experiments actually need to be performed. From the resulting measurements, the experimenter can determine the effects on performance of each individual input factor, and the effects of their interactions. The form of the experimental design also allows a quantitative evaluation of the error inherent in the experimental measurements relative to the overall system response.

A key assumption behind the design of experiments is that there is a nonzero cost associated with performing an experiment. This cost includes the time and effort required to gather the necessary data, plus the time and effort needed to analyze these data to draw some appropriate conclusions. Consequently, it is important to minimize the number of experiments that must be performed while maximizing the information obtained.

Good experiment design allows the experimenter to

- isolate the effects of each individual input variable,
- determine the effects due to interactions of the input variables,
- determine the magnitude of the change in the system's output due to the experimental error, and
- obtain the maximum amount of information with the minimum amount of effort by limiting and controlling the number of experiments that must be performed.

9.1   Types of experiments

The simplest design for an experiment *varies one input* (factor) while holding all of the other inputs constant. Unfortunately, this approach ignores possible inter-actions between two input variables, which could lead one to draw erroneous conclusions. The opposite extreme is a *full factorial design with replication* in which the system's response is measured for all possible input combinations. With this type of data, it is possible to determine the effects of all input variables and all of their interactions, along with an indication of the magnitude of the measurement error. However, a full factorial design can require a very large number of experiments. For example, a system with five factors (input variables), each of which has four possible levels, requires $4^5 = 1,024$ separate experiments. Repeating all of the measurements twice to obtain some estimate of the measure-ment error increases the total number of experiments to $1,024 \times 3 = 3,072$.

To reduce the total number of experiments that must be performed, the experi-menter can reduce either the number of levels used for each input variable, or the total number of inputs. Both of these choices restrict the conclusions that can be drawn from the resulting measurements, of course. The $n2^m$ factorial design limits the number of levels for each input variable to two, either high or low. Although not as much information is provided by this reduced experiment design as with the complete design, it does provide a way to more quickly determine which input variables are the most important. A complete design restricted to only these important variables can then be performed.

9.2   Terminology

The terminology used in the design of experiments can sometimes be confusing. Here we define some of the most important terms.

- **The response variable.** The response variable is the output value that is mea-sured as the input values are changed. A common response variable is the total execution time, for instance.
- **Factors.** The input variables of an experiment that can be controlled or chan-ged by the experimenter are called the factors. For example, the factors of an experiment might include the cache size, the size of a disk file, the processor type or clock rate, the number of bytes to be sent on a communications net-work, and so forth.
- **Levels.** The levels of a factor are the specific values to which it may be set. These values may be continuous (or nearly so), such as the number of bytes

moved in an input/output operation, or they may be categorical, such as the type of system being used.

- **Replication.** Replicating an experiment means completely rerunning it with all of the same input levels. Since the measurements of the response variable are subject to random variations, replications of an experiment are used to determine the impact of measurement error on the response variable.
- **Interaction.** An interaction between factors occurs when the effect of one factor depends on the level of another factor.

9.3   Two-factor experiments

Previously, in Section 5.2.1, we examined a *one-factor* experiment for comparing alternatives. The only factor, or input variable, in this experiment was the type of system we were comparing. The number of levels in this experiment corresponded to the number of different alternatives being compared. Recall that we used the analysis of variance (ANOVA) technique to separate the total variation observed in all of the measurements into (i) the variation due to measurement error within each alternative separately, and (ii) the variation across alternatives. Further recall that this variation across alternatives could be due both to actual differences in the alternatives and to measurement error. Thus, we used the *F*-test to determine whether this cross-alternative variation was statistically significant compared with the variation known to be due to measurement error alone. If it was, we could conclude that there was indeed a statistically significant difference between the alternatives.

9.3.1   Interaction of factors

We now extend this basic idea to experiments with two factors, calling them factor *A* and factor *B*. As you might guess, we want to separate the total variation we observe among our measurements into the *effect* due to *A*, the effect due to *B*, and the variation due to measurement errors. However, there is one additional effect we need to consider here – specifically, the effect due to the *interaction* of factors *A* and *B*.

For example, consider an experiment in which we want to observe the effect on the system's response time of varying the size of the main memory available in the system and the degree of multiprogramming allowed. (The degree of multiprogramming is the number of applications that are allowed to time-share the processor.) If we have three different memory sizes available, say 32, 64, and 128 Mbytes, and we allow from one to four applications to share the system, we have in total 12 combinations of the two factors that we must consider. Table 9.1

Table 9.1. The user-response times in seconds measured with various combinations of system memory size and degree of multiprogramming

	B (MBytes)		
A	32	64	128
1	0.25	0.21	0.15
2	0.52	0.45	0.36
3	0.81	0.66	0.50
4	1.50	1.45	0.70

shows the user-response times of the system measured for each of these combinations, where factor A is the degree of multiprogramming and factor B is the memory size.

A common (and inappropriate) shortcut that is often made in these types of experiments is to vary only one factor at a time. For instance, say the experimenter fixes the memory size at 64 Mbytes while varying the degree of multiprogramming. Then, the degree of multiprogramming is fixed, say at 3, while the memory size is varied. The experimenter may then feel that they now have a complete view of the system's performance as a function of these two factors since, after all, they allowed both of them to vary. The problem with this reasoning is that it corresponds to measuring only along the '64' column in Table 9.1, followed by measuring along the '3' row. However, all of the other possible combinations of the two factors have been ignored. Thus, the experimenter would be unable to determine whether there is any interaction between the memory size and the degree of multiprogramming. In this example, in fact, it appears that there could be some interaction. Specifically, when the degree of multiprogramming is 4, the response time decreases nonlinearly with the memory size. With smaller degrees of multiprogramming, however, the response time appears to be more directly correlated to the available memory size.

9.3.2 ANOVA for two-factor experiments

The development of the ANOVA technique for a two-factor experiment closely parallels the one-factor development of ANOVA in Section 5.2.1. Begin by letting y_{ijk} be the kth measurement made with factor A set to its ith level and factor B set to its jth level. Assume that A has a possible levels, B can take on b possible levels, and n measurements in total have been made for each combination of the two factors. It is convenient to summarize all of these abn total measurements as shown in Table 9.2.

Table 9.2. Entry y_{ijk} in this table is the kth measurement made with factor A set to its ith level and factor B set to its jth level when using the ANOVA technique in a two-factor experiment

				B				
A	1	2	$\cdots$	j	$\cdots$	b	Sum	Mean
1	y_{111}	y_{121}	$\cdots$	y_{1j1}	$\cdots$	y_{1b1}	$S_{1..}$	$\bar{y}_{1..}$
	y_{112}	y_{122}	$\cdots$	y_{1j2}	$\cdots$	y_{1b2}		
	$\vdots$	$\vdots$		$\vdots$		$\vdots$		
	y_{11n}	y_{12n}	$\cdots$	y_{1jn}	$\cdots$	y_{1bn}		
2	y_{211}	y_{221}	$\cdots$	y_{2j1}	$\cdots$	y_{2b1}	$S_{2..}$	$\bar{y}_{2..}$
	y_{212}	y_{222}	$\cdots$	y_{2j2}	$\cdots$	y_{2b2}		
	$\vdots$	$\vdots$		$\vdots$		$\vdots$		
	y_{21n}	y_{22n}	$\cdots$	y_{2jn}	$\cdots$	y_{2bn}		
$\vdots$	$\vdots$	$\vdots$		$\vdots$		$\vdots$		
i	y_{i11}	y_{i21}	$\cdots$	y_{ij1}	$\cdots$	y_{ib1}	$S_{i..}$	$\bar{y}_{i..}$
	y_{i12}	y_{i22}	$\cdots$	y_{ij2}	$\cdots$	y_{ib2}		
	$\vdots$	$\vdots$		$\vdots$		$\vdots$		
	y_{i1n}	y_{i2n}	$\cdots$	y_{ijn}	$\cdots$	y_{ibn}		
$\vdots$	$\vdots$	$\vdots$		$\vdots$		$\vdots$		
a	y_{a11}	y_{a21}	$\cdots$	y_{aj1}	$\cdots$	y_{ab1}	$S_{a..}$	$\bar{y}_{a..}$
	y_{a12}	y_{a22}	$\cdots$	y_{aj2}	$\cdots$	y_{ab2}		
	$\vdots$	$\vdots$		$\vdots$		$\vdots$		
	y_{a1n}	y_{a2n}	$\cdots$	y_{ajn}	$\cdots$	y_{abn}		
Sum	$S_{.1.}$	$S_{.2.}$	$\cdots$	$S_{.j.}$	$\cdots$	$S_{.b.}$	$S_{...}$	
Mean	$\bar{y}_{.1.}$	$\bar{y}_{.2.}$	$\cdots$	$\bar{y}_{.j.}$	$\cdots$	$\bar{y}_{.b.}$		$\bar{y}_{...}$

Next, we find the mean of the n measurements made for each combination of levels, that is, when factor A is at level i and factor B is at level j. This gives

$$\bar{y}_{ij.} = \frac{\sum_{k=1}^{n} y_{ijk}}{n} = \frac{S_{ij.}}{n} \tag{9.1}$$

where $S_{ij.} = \sum_{k=1}^{n} y_{ijk}$. The value $\bar{y}_{ij.}$ then is the local mean value of the measurements within each cell of the table.

We can then write each individual measurement as the sum of its local mean value and a residual term, e_{ijk}. This produces

$$y_{ijk} = \bar{y}_{ij.} + e_{ijk} \tag{9.2}$$

which shows the deviation of each measurement from its local mean value. Thus, the e_{ijk} terms are an indication of the variation in the measurements around the mean for that set of levels (input values).

Extending what we did previously for the one-factor experiment, we can express the individual row and column means from Table 9.2 as the sum of the overall grand mean of all of the measurements, $\bar{y}_{...}$, and the deviations due to the *effects* of the factors. Note that, in this case, however, we have an inter-action effect from the combination of the two factors in addition to the main effects of each factor. This produces the following expression:

$$\bar{y}_{ij.} = \bar{y}_{...} + \alpha_i + \beta_j + \gamma_{ij} \tag{9.3}$$

where α_i is the main effect of the ith level of factor A, β_j is the main effect of the jth level of factor B, and γ_{ij} is the effect due to the interaction of factor A at level i and factor B at level j. Substituting Equation (9.3) into Equation (9.2) then gives

$$y_{ijk} = \bar{y}_{...} + \alpha_i + \beta_j + \gamma_{ij} + e_{ijk}. \tag{9.4}$$

The effects are constrained so that

$$\sum_{i=1}^{a} \alpha_i = 0 \tag{9.5}$$

$$\sum_{j=1}^{b} \beta_j = 0 \tag{9.6}$$

$$\sum_{i=1}^{a} \gamma_{ij} = 0 \tag{9.7}$$

$$\sum_{j=1}^{b} \gamma_{ij} = 0. \tag{9.8}$$

Expressing each individual measurement in this form now allows us to sepa-rate the total variation in the measurements into the components due to factor A, factor B, their interaction, AB, and the measurement error. This separation is called the *sum-of-squares identity* and is written as

$$SST = SSA + SSB + SSAB + SSE \tag{9.9}$$

where

$$SST = \sum_{i=1}^{a} \sum_{j=1}^{b} \sum_{k=1}^{n} (y_{ijk} - \bar{y}_{...})^2 \tag{9.10}$$

$$SSA = bn \sum_{i=1}^{a} (\bar{y}_{i..} - \bar{y}_{...})^2 \tag{9.11}$$

$$SSB = an \sum_{j=1}^{b} (\bar{y}_{.j.} - \bar{y}_{...})^2 \tag{9.12}$$

$$SSAB = n \sum_{i=1}^{a} \sum_{j=1}^{b} (\bar{y}_{ij.} - \bar{y}_{i..} - \bar{y}_{.j.} - \bar{y}_{...})^2 \tag{9.13}$$

$$SSE = \sum_{i=1}^{a} \sum_{j=1}^{b} \sum_{k=1}^{n} (y_{ijk} - \bar{y}_{ij.})^2. \tag{9.14}$$

The proof of this identity is done by algebraically expanding SST and noticing that all of the cross-product terms are zero due to the above constraints on α_i, β_j, and γ_{ij}.

To compute these sum of squares values it is useful to expand them as follows:

$$SST = \sum_{i=1}^{a} \sum_{j=1}^{b} \sum_{k=1}^{n} y_{ijk}^2 - \frac{S_{...}^2}{abn} \tag{9.15}$$

$$SSA = \frac{\sum_{i=1}^{a} S_{i..}^2}{bn} - \frac{S_{...}^2}{abn} \tag{9.16}$$

$$SSB = \frac{\sum_{j=1}^{b} S_{.j.}^2}{an} - \frac{S_{...}^2}{abn} \tag{9.17}$$

$$SSAB = \frac{\sum_{i=1}^{a} \sum_{j=1}^{b} S_{ij.}^2}{n} - \frac{\sum_{i=1}^{a} S_{i..}^2}{bn} - \frac{\sum_{j=1}^{b} S_{.j.}^2}{an} + \frac{S_{...}^2}{abn} \tag{9.18}$$

$$SSE = SST - SSA - SSB - SSAB. \tag{9.19}$$

In these expressions, $S_{ij.} = \sum_{k=1}^{n} y_{ijk}$ for each cell (i, j) in Table 9.2. The remaining S_x values are the row and column sums shown in Table 9.2.

We are interested in the sum-of-squares identity in Equation (9.9) since it partitions the total variation in our measurements into its constituent components. We need only divide each of these sum-of-squares terms by their respective degrees of freedom to find the variance for each term. We can then use the F-test to compare the variance of each component with the variance of the error term, to thereby determine which components are statistically significant and which are likely to be due to random error alone.

The number of degrees of freedom for each factor is simply one less than the total number of levels the factor can assume. Thus, SSA has $a - 1$ degrees of freedom and SSB has $b - 1$ degrees of freedom. The number of degrees of freedom for the interaction, $SSAB$, is then the product of these two terms, $(a - 1)(b - 1)$. Since there are n measurements for each combination of levels of the factors, the sum for each cell in Table 9.2 has $n - 1$ degrees of freedom. Additionally, since all ab cells contribute to the total error, the total number of degrees of freedom for SSE is $ab(n-1)$. Finally, since SST is calculated using all of the measurements, its number of degrees of freedom is $abn-1$. Note that the number of degrees of freedom partitions according to the sum-of-squares terms:

$$df(SST) = df(SSA) + df(SSB) + df(SSAB) + df(SSE) \tag{9.20}$$

$$abn - 1 = (a-1) + (b-1) + (a-1)(b-1) + ab(n-1). \tag{9.21}$$

Dividing the sum-of-squares terms by their corresponding numbers of degrees of freedom produces the following estimates of their variances (recall that these variances are also called the *mean-square* values):

$$s_a^2 = \frac{SSA}{a-1} \tag{9.22}$$

$$s_b^2 = \frac{SSB}{b-1} \tag{9.23}$$

$$s_{ab}^2 = \frac{SSAB}{(a-1)(b-1)} \tag{9.24}$$

$$s_e^2 = \frac{SSE}{ab(n-1)}. \tag{9.25}$$

Now recall that we use the F-test to compare two variances. First, we calculate the corresponding F statistic for each factor. This statistic is the ratio of the variance of the factor in which we are interested to the variance of the error term:

$$F_a = \frac{s_a^2}{s_e^2} \tag{9.26}$$

$$F_b = \frac{s_b^2}{s_e^2} \tag{9.27}$$

$$F_{ab} = \frac{s_{ab}^2}{s_e^2}. \tag{9.28}$$

If the resulting F statistic is 'sufficiently large,' meaning that the variance of the numerator is 'sufficiently larger' than the variance in the denominator, we conclude that the corresponding factor, or interaction of factors, is statistically significant. The calculated statistic is determined to be 'sufficiently large' and, therefore, statistically significant, if it is greater than the *critical F* value obtained from the F distribution. Thus, if

$$F_a > F_{[\alpha; a-1, ab(n-1)]} \tag{9.29}$$

Table 9.3. A summary of using an analysis-of-variance (ANOVA) test for a two-factor experiment: if the computed F statistic is larger than the critical F value obtained from the table, the effect of the corresponding factor or interaction can be considered statistically significant at the α level of significance.

	Source of variation			
	A	B	AB	Error
Sum of squares	SSA	SSB	$SSAB$	SSE
Degrees of freedom	$a - 1$	$b - 1$	$(a-1)(b-1)$	$ab(n-1)$
Mean square	$s_a^2 = \dfrac{SSA}{a-1}$	$s_b^2 = \dfrac{SSB}{b-1}$	$s_{ab}^2 = \dfrac{SSAB}{(a-1)(b-1)}$	$s_e^2 = \dfrac{SSE}{ab(n-1)}$
Computed F statistic	$F_a = \dfrac{s_a^2}{s_e^2}$	$F_b = \dfrac{s_b^2}{s_e^2}$	$F_{ab} = \dfrac{s_{ab}^2}{s_e^2}$	
F value from table	$F_{[\alpha;a-1,ab(n-1)]}$	$F_{[\alpha;b-1,ab(n-1)]}$	$F_{[\alpha;(a-1)(b-1),ab(n-1)]}$	

we conclude that the variation in measurements due to the effect of factor A is statistically significant at the α level of significance. In this expression, $F_{[\alpha;a-1,ab(n-1)]}$ is the critical value obtained from the F distribution with $a-1$ degrees of freedom in the numerator and $ab(n-1)$ degrees of freedom in the denominator.

Similarly, we conclude that the effect of factor B is statistically significant if

$$F_b > F_{[\alpha;b-1,ab(n-1)]} \tag{9.30}$$

and that the interaction of A and B is statistically significant if

$$F_{ab} > F_{[\alpha;(a-1)(b-1),ab(n-1)]}. \tag{9.31}$$

Conversely, if the calculated F statistics are not greater than the critical values, we conclude that the effect of the corresponding factor or interaction is not significant. The ANOVA test for this two-factor experiment can be summarized as shown in Table 9.3.

9.3.3 The need for replications

It is enlightening to observe what happens when we have only one measurement for each combination of levels, that is, when $n = 1$. In this case, the sum of all of the measurements within a single cell becomes

$$S_{ij.} = \sum_{k=1}^{1} y_{ijk} = y_{ijk}. \tag{9.32}$$

On substituting this value into Equation (9.18), we see that $SSAB = SST - SSA - SSB$. From Equation (9.19) we then see that this condition implies that $SSE = 0$. As a result, we are left without any information about the magnitude of the measurement errors. Another way of looking at this situation is that, when $n = 1$, we cannot separate the effect due to the interaction of the two factors from the measurement noise. To separate out information about both the interaction effect and the magnitude of the measurement errors, we must make more than one measurement at each of the combinations of the different levels. That is, we need $n > 1$. Note that these measurements should be true *replications* of the experiment, not simply another measurement of the identical configuration.

Example. We wish to use a two-factor-experiment design to examine the effects of the main memory size and the degree of multiprogramming on the response time of a given computer system beginning with the data collected in Table 9.1.

The first thing to notice is that, to separate both the interaction effect and the experimental error in this experiment, we need at least one additional measurement for each set of input combinations. More than two replications for each combination would be desirable, but two should be sufficient to obtain some indication both of the magnitude of the errors and of the interaction. Table 9.4 repeats the data from Table 9.1 along with an additional set of measurements and the sums necessary for calculating the sum-of-squares terms. Note that $a = 4$ and $b = 3$ in this experiment since there are four levels of factor A, the degree of multiprogramming, and three levels of factor B, the main memory size. Also, $n = 2$ since we have two measurements at each combination of levels.

Using the data in this table, we can now calculate the the sum of squares values as follows:

$$SST = (0.25^2 + 0.28^2 + \cdots + 0.68^2) - \frac{14.98^2}{4(3)(2)} = 13.6976 - 9.35 = 4.3476 \tag{9.33}$$

$$SSA = \frac{1.19^2 + \cdots + 7.26^2}{3(2)} - \frac{14.98^2}{4(3)(2)} = \frac{76.3286}{3(2)} - 9.35 = 3.3714 \tag{9.34}$$

$$SSB = \frac{6.21^2 + 5.36^2 + 3.41^2}{4(2)} - \frac{14.98^2}{4(3)(2)} = \frac{78.9218}{4(2)} - 9.35 = 0.5152 \tag{9.35}$$

Table 9.4. The user-response times in seconds measured with various combinations of system-memory size and degree of multiprogramming

	B (MBytes)			
A	32	64	128	Sum
1	0.25	0.21	0.15	
	0.28	0.19	0.11	
S_{1j}	0.53	0.40	0.26	1.19
2	0.52	0.45	0.36	
	0.48	0.49	0.30	
S_{2j}	1.00	0.94	0.66	2.60
3	0.81	0.66	0.50	
	0.76	0.59	0.61	
S_{3j}	1.57	1.25	1.11	3.93
4	1.50	1.45	0.70	
	1.61	1.32	0.68	
S_{4j}	3.11	2.77	1.38	7.26
Sum	6.21	5.36	3.41	14.98

$$SSAB = \frac{0.53^2 + 0.40^2 + \cdots + 1.38^2}{2} - \frac{76.3286}{3(2)} - \frac{78.9218}{4(2)} + \frac{14.98^2}{4(3)(2)} \qquad (9.36)$$
$$= 0.4317$$

$$SSE = 4.3476 - 3.3714 - 0.5152 - 0.4317 = 0.0293. \qquad (9.37)$$

The mean-square values computed from these sum-of-squares values are shown in Table 9.5 along with the corresponding computed and critical F values.

So, after all of this calculation, what can we say about the impact on the response time of varying the degree of multiprogramming and the main memory size? First, we can conclude that 77.6% (SSA/SST) of all of the variation in our measurements is due to factor A, the degree of multiprogramming. Also, only 11.8% (SSB/SST) is due to factor B, the size of the main memory, and only 9.9% ($SSAB/SST$) is due to the interaction of the two factors. Only 0.7% of the total variation is due to random errors, suggesting that the measurements are quite precise compared with the variation due to the factors.

Finally, since the computed F values both for the factors and for their interaction are larger than the corresponding critical F values obtained from the table, we can conclude with 95% confidence that the effects of both factors are indeed statistically significant. Furthermore, with the same level of confidence, we can conclude that the interaction of the memory size and the degree of multiprogramming is also statistically significant. Thus, our final conclusion is

Table 9.5. The computed mean-square values with the corresponding F values for the data in Table 9.4 with an $\alpha = 0.05$ level of significance

| | \multicolumn{5}{c}{Source of variation} |
	A	B	AB	Error	Total
Sum of squares	3.3714	0.5152	0.4317	0.0293	4.3476
Degrees of freedom	3	2	6	12	23
Mean square	$s_a^2 = 1.1238$	$s_b^2 = 0.2576$	$s_{ab}^2 = 0.0720$	$s_e^2 = 0.0024$	
Computed F statistic	$F_a = 460.2$	$F_b = 105.5$	$F_{ab} = 29.5$		
F value from table	\multicolumn{5}{l}{$F_{[0.05;3,12]} = 3.49 \quad F_{[0.05;2,12]} = 3.89 \quad F_{[0.05;6,12]} = 3.00$}

that the degree of multiprogramming has the largest impact on the response time, but we cannot dismiss either the impact of the size of the main memory, or the impact of the interaction of the memory size and the degree of multiprogramming. In fact, we find that the relative impacts of both the memory size (11.8%) and the interaction of the memory size and the degree of multiprogramming (9.9%) are about the same.   ◇

9.4 Generalized m-factor experiments

Generalizing the use of the analysis-of-variance (ANOVA) technique for experiments with $m > 2$ independent factors closely follows the development of the two-factor experiments in the previous section. However, owing to the additional factors and, more significantly, the increasing number of interactions, the calculations for multiple-factor experiments become progressively more tedious. For example, consider an experiment with $m = 3$ factors, A, B, and C. We have to consider not only the main effects of each factor individually, but also the additional interactions AB, AC, BC, and ABC.

In general, in an experiment with m factors there are m main effects, $\binom{m}{2}$ two-factor interactions, $\binom{m}{3}$ three-factor interactions, and so on up to $\binom{m}{m-1}$ interactions with $(m-1)$ factors, and $\binom{m}{m} = 1$ interaction with m factors. In total, there are $2^m - 1$ effects.

After determining the total number of effects that must be considered in an experiment, the ANOVA procedure for an m-factor experiment becomes essen-

tially the same as that for the two-factor case. In particular, the steps to follow
are these.

1. Calculate the $2^m - 1$ sum of squares terms, SSx, for each factor individually
   and for each of the interactions. Then find the sum of the squares of the
   errors, SSE, by subtraction.
2. Determine the number of degrees of freedom, $df(SSx)$, for each of the sum-of-
   squares terms.
3. Calculate $s_x^2 = SSx/df(SSx)$ to find the mean square (variance) for each
   effect.
4. Calculate the F statistic for each term by finding the ratio of the mean square
   of the term to the mean square error. That is, $F_x = s_x^2/s_e^2$.
5. Find the corresponding critical F value from the table using the appropriate
   number of degrees of freedom corresponding to the numerator and denominator used when calculating the F statistic in the previous step. The value
   from the table is $F_{[\alpha; df(numerator), df(denominator)]}$, where α is the desired significance
   level and $df(\cdot)$ is the number of degrees of freedom of the corresponding term.
6. Compare the calculated F statistic, F_x, with the value read from the table. If
   F_x is greater than the table value, you can conclude with $1 - \alpha$ confidence that
   the effect of term x is statistically significant.
7. You can also calculate SSx/SST to determine the fraction of the total variation that is attributable to effect x. This gives an indication of the relative
   importance of each effect while the previous step determines whether it is
   statistically significant. Note that an effect may be relatively unimportant
   even though it is *statistically* significant.

The only real potential difficulty with this procedure is calculating the sum of
squares terms, and determining the number of degrees of freedom. The necessary
computational formulas for $m = 3$ factors are shown below. It is then assumed
that the reader can generalize to the case when $m > 3$.

Assume that factor A can take on a different levels, factor B can take on b
different levels, and factor C can take on c different levels. Also, assume that n
complete replications of each experimental configuration have been made. That
is, there are n measurements for each combination of levels. We begin by defining
the following intermediate sums.

$$S_{....} = \sum_{i=1}^{a}\sum_{j=1}^{b}\sum_{k=1}^{c}\sum_{l=1}^{n} y_{ijkl} \tag{9.38}$$

$$S_{i...} = \sum_{j=1}^{b}\sum_{k=1}^{c}\sum_{l=1}^{n} y_{ijkl} \tag{9.39}$$

$$S_{.j..} = \sum_{i=1}^{a} \sum_{k=1}^{c} \sum_{l=1}^{n} y_{ijkl} \qquad (9.40)$$

$$S_{..k.} = \sum_{i=1}^{a} \sum_{j=1}^{b} \sum_{l=1}^{n} y_{ijkl} \qquad (9.41)$$

$$S_{ij..} = \sum_{k=1}^{c} \sum_{l=1}^{n} y_{ijkl} \qquad (9.42)$$

$$S_{i.k.} = \sum_{j=1}^{b} \sum_{l=1}^{n} y_{ijkl} \qquad (9.43)$$

$$S_{.jk.} = \sum_{i=1}^{a} \sum_{l=1}^{n} y_{ijkl} \qquad (9.44)$$

$$S_{ijk.} = \sum_{l=1}^{n} y_{ijkl} \qquad (9.45)$$

The sum-of-squares terms then are calculated as follows:

$$SST = \sum_{i=1}^{a} \sum_{j=1}^{b} \sum_{k=1}^{c} \sum_{l=1}^{n} y_{ijkl}^2 - S \qquad (9.46)$$

$$SSA = \frac{\sum_{i=1}^{a} S_{i...}^2}{bcn} - S \qquad (9.47)$$

$$SSB = \frac{\sum_{j=1}^{b} S_{.j..}^2}{acn} - S \qquad (9.48)$$

$$SSC = \frac{\sum_{k=1}^{c} S_{..k.}^2}{abn} - S \qquad (9.49)$$

$$SSAB = \frac{\sum_{i=1}^{a} \sum_{j=1}^{b} S_{ij..}^2}{cn} - \frac{\sum_{i=1}^{a} S_{i...}^2}{bcn} - \frac{\sum_{j=1}^{b} S_{.j..}^2}{acn} + S \qquad (9.50)$$

$$SSAC = \frac{\sum_{i=1}^{a} \sum_{k=1}^{c} S_{i.k.}^2}{bn} - \frac{\sum_{i=1}^{a} S_{i...}^2}{bcn} - \frac{\sum_{k=1}^{c} S_{..k.}^2}{abn} + S \qquad (9.51)$$

$$SSBC = \frac{\sum_{j=1}^{b} \sum_{k=1}^{c} S_{.jk.}^2}{an} - \frac{\sum_{j=1}^{b} S_{.j..}^2}{acn} - \frac{\sum_{k=1}^{c} S_{..k.}^2}{abn} + S \qquad (9.52)$$

Table 9.6. The number of degrees of freedom corresponding to each sum-of-squares term for an experiment with $m = 3$ factors

Sum of squares	Degrees of freedom
SSA	$a - 1$
SSB	$b - 1$
SSC	$c - 1$
SSAB	$(a - 1)(b - 1)$
SSAC	$(a - 1)(c - 1)$
SSBC	$(b - 1)(c - 1)$
SSABC	$(a - 1)(b - 1)(c - 1)$
SSE	$abc(n - 1)$
SST	$abcn - 1$

$$
SSABC = \frac{\sum_{i=1}^{a} \sum_{j=1}^{b} \sum_{k=1}^{c} S_{ijk.}^2}{n} - \frac{\sum_{i=1}^{a} \sum_{j=1}^{b} S_{ij..}^2}{cn} - \frac{\sum_{i=1}^{a} \sum_{k=1}^{c} S_{i.k.}^2}{bn}
$$
$$
- \frac{\sum_{j=1}^{b} \sum_{k=1}^{c} S_{.jk.}^2}{an} + \frac{\sum_{i=1}^{a} S_{i...}^2}{bcn} + \frac{\sum_{j=1}^{b} S_{.j..}^2}{acn}
$$
$$
+ \frac{\sum_{k=1}^{c} S_{..k.}^2}{abn} - S \tag{9.53}
$$

where

$$
S = \frac{S_{....}^2}{abcn}. \tag{9.54}
$$

The corresponding number of degrees of freedom for each of these sum-of-squares terms is shown in Table 9.6.

As you can see, the basic idea behind the ANOVA technique for experiments with many factors does not change. Rather, the computational complexity increases due to the large number of terms that now comprise the sum-of-squares identity. There are numerous statistical software packages that can be used to perform the calculations necessary for an ANOVA test. To intelligently interpret the results, though, it is important to understand how the various terms are calculated.

In addition to increasing the computational complexity of an ANOVA test, additional input factors and levels increase the number of measurements that must be made. We now look at some techniques for reducing this complexity by limiting the number of interactions that we take into account, or by limiting the number of levels that we consider. The penalty for this simplification, of course, is a loss of information. However, we often find that the high-order interactions turn out to be relatively small, and that, in some instances, examining many levels of the various factors does not provide any particularly useful new insights. As a result, they often can be safely ignored.

9.5 $n2^m$ experiments

The $n2^m$-experiment designs can be thought of as special cases of a generalized m-factor experiment in which each factor is allowed to take on only two possible levels (or values). These values could be categorical values, such as a compiler optimization being turned on or off, for instance, or they could be two different levels of a continuous value, such as two different memory sizes. We can take advantage of this restriction on the number of levels for each factor to simplify the analysis of the measured data. This allows us to design an experiment with more factors than we could comfortably handle in the generalized m-factor design to determine which factors have the largest impact on the system's response. We can then perform a more complete analysis, focusing on only the most important factors, with a larger number of input levels.

Just like with the previous experiment designs, we wish to apply the ANOVA technique to partition the variation in the measurements into the components due to each factor, due to their interactions, and due to the measurement error. To apply this analysis technique, we first need to find the sum-of-squares terms for each component.

9.5.1   Two factors

Let's begin by considering an experiment with only two factors, A and B, that can be set to two possible values. For convenience, we will refer to these two factors as being at either a 'high' level or a 'low' level. Recognize, however, that high and low are arbitrary for a categorical variable. For instance, high may refer to a compiler optimization being turned off, while low means the optimization was turned on. Similarly, high could refer to processor type X, while low refers to processor type Y. This situation gives us four possible configurations to measure: both A and B set to their high values, both set to their low values, A set to high and B set to low, and vice versa.

Assuming that we make measurements of n replications of each configuration, let

- y_{AB} = the sum of the n measured responses when both A and B are set to their high values,

- y_{ab} = the sum of the n measured responses when both A and B are set to their low values,
- y_{Ab} = the sum of the n measured responses when A is set to its high value and B is set to its low value, and
- y_{aB} = the sum of the n measured responses when A is set to its low value and B is set to its high value.

We then define the following contrasts:

$$w_A = y_{AB} + y_{Ab} - y_{aB} - y_{ab} \tag{9.55}$$

$$w_B = y_{AB} - y_{Ab} + y_{aB} - y_{ab} \tag{9.56}$$

$$w_{AB} = y_{AB} - y_{Ab} - y_{aB} + y_{ab}. \tag{9.57}$$

Intuitively, the contrast w_A is the difference between the system's responses when A is set to its high and low values. Similarly, w_B is the difference in response when B is set to its two extreme values, and w_{AB} is the response when A and B are set to opposing extremes. That is, w_{AB} is an indication of the interaction of the two factors.

While it is perhaps not a very interesting derivation, it can be shown that the sum-of-squares terms can be found simply by dividing the square of the above contrasts by the total number of observations made for all factors at all levels. Thus,

$$SSA = \frac{w_A^2}{n2^m} \tag{9.58}$$

$$SSB = \frac{w_B^2}{n2^m} \tag{9.59}$$

$$SSAB = \frac{w_{AB}^2}{n2^m}. \tag{9.60}$$

Since each factor has only two possible levels, each of these sum-of-squares terms has a single degree of freedom. As before, SSE can be found using the sum-of-squares identity:

$$SSE = SST - SSA - SSB - SSAB. \tag{9.61}$$

Since the number of degrees of freedom for SST is $n2^m - 1$, the number of degrees of freedom for SSE is $(n2^m - 1) - 1 - 1 - 1 = (n - 1)2^m$. The variances (or mean square values) for each sum-of-squares term are again found as the ratio of the sum-of-squares value and its corresponding number of degrees of freedom. Finally, the F-test is used to determine whether each component of the

Table 9.7. The use of the analysis-of-variance (ANOVA) test for an $n2^m$ factorial experiment in which there are n replications with each of the m factors taking on two possible values: if the computed F statistic is larger than the critical F value obtained from the table, the effect of the corresponding factor or interaction can be considered statistically significant at the α level of significance

			Source of variation		
	A	B	AB	Error	Sum
Sum of squares	SSA	SSB	$SSAB$	SSE	SST
Degrees of freedom	1	1	1	$2^m(n-1)$	$n2^m - 1$
Mean square	$s_a^2 = \dfrac{SSA}{1}$	$s_b^2 = \dfrac{SSB}{1}$	$s_{ab}^2 = \dfrac{SSAB}{1}$	$s_e^2 = \dfrac{SSE}{2^m(n-1)}$	
Computed F statistic	$F_a = \dfrac{s_a^2}{s_e^2}$	$F_b = \dfrac{s_b^2}{s_e^2}$	$F_{ab} = \dfrac{s_{ab}^2}{s_e^2}$		
F value from table	$F_{[\alpha;1,2^m(n-1)]}$	$F_{[\alpha;1,2^m(n-1)]}$	$F_{[\alpha;1,2^m(n-1)]}$		

variation is statistically significant. The ANOVA test for this experiment with two factors is summarized in Table 9.7.

Example. A certain compiler has two optimization options that can be turned on or off individually. Table 9.8 shows the execution times measured when running a test program compiled with all four combinations of the two optimizations being turned on and off. We measured $n = 3$ replications for each combination.

From these measured values, we find the corresponding contrasts to be $w_A = -20.5$, $w_B = 271.3$, and $w_{AB} = -22.1$. The contrasts are used to calculate the corresponding values for the ANOVA test shown in Table 9.9. From the table of critical F values in Appendix C.2, we see that $F_{[0.95;1,8]} \approx 5.4$. Since all of the computed F values are larger than this critical value, we conclude that both optimizations produce statistically significant variations in the execution time of this test program, as does the interaction of the two optimizations. However, we see that the fraction of the total variation due to optimization B being turned on is $(6{,}133.64/6{,}212.57) \times 100\% = 98.7\%$. Thus, even though both optimizations produce effects that are not simply due to random errors (that is, the effects are statistically significant), almost all of the change is due to this single compiler optimization.

Table 9.8. Execution-time measurements of a test program compiled with two different optimizations turned on and off

Optimization combination	Replication			Total
	1	2	3	
Both off (y_{AB})	45.7	46.4	44.1	136.2
A off, B on (y_{Ab})	3.8	4.1	3.7	11.6
A on, B off (y_{aB})	52.5	52.1	52.9	157.5
Both on (y_{ab})	3.6	3.7	3.5	10.8

9.5.2   More than two factors

The contrasts shown in the previous section are used to separate out the influences of the input factors and their various interactions on the system's response measured with the various combinations of input levels. The main effect of the input A, for instance, is found by comparing the system's response when A is set to its high value with that when it is set to its low value. Thus, we can assign a positive sign to A when it is at its high value and a negative sign when it is at its low value. The same holds true for finding the main effects of input B. The signs applied to the interaction effects are found by algebraically multiplying the corresponding signs for A and B. The signs for each combination of input factors for this two-factor case are summarized in Table 9.10.

For example, with the input combination ab, both inputs are at their low values, so the sign for the measured response term y_{ab} in the contrasts w_A and w_B is negative. Since $(-1) \times (-1) = +1$, the sign for the interaction contrast w_{AB} is positive. Given this type of sign table, the terms comprising each contrast can be found simply by reading down the table. For instance, the contrast for the main effect of A is found by reading down the first column to be $w_A = -y_{ab} + y_{Ab} - y_{aB} + y_{AB}$.

Extending this procedure to larger values of m is quite straightforward. Consider the case with $m = 3$ input factors. There are in total $2^3 = 8$ input combinations that must be measured. The resulting sign table for this experiment is shown in Table 9.11. With this type of sign-table representation, we can see that any pair of contrasts is orthogonal. This orthogonality allows each contrast to be used in calculating a corresponding sum-of-squares term for the ANOVA test.

For example, from Table 9.11, we find that the contrast for the interaction between factors B and C is

$$w_{AC} = y_{abc} - y_{Abc} + y_{aBc} - y_{abC} - y_{ABc} + y_{AbC} - y_{aBC} + y_{ABC}. \tag{9.62}$$

Table 9.9. The computed mean square values with the corresponding F values for the data in Table 9.8 with an $\alpha = 0.05$ level of significance

	A	B	AB	Error	Total
			Source of variation		
Sum of squares	35.02	6,133.64	40.70	3.21	6,212.57
Degrees of freedom	1	1	1	8	11
Mean square	$s_A^2 = 35.02$	$s_B^2 = 6,133.64$	$s_{AB}^2 = 40.70$	$s_e^2 = 0.4013$	
Computed F statistic	$F_A = 87.3$	$F_B = 15,286$	$F_{AB} = 101.4$		

Table 9.10. Determining the signs for the contrasts for an $n2^m$-factor experiment with $m = 2$

Measured response	Contrast		
	w_A	w_b	w_{AB}
y_{ab}	–	–	+
y_{Ab}	+	–	–
y_{aB}	–	+	–
y_{AB}	+	+	+

Table 9.11. Determining the signs for the contrasts for an $n2^m$-factor experiment with $m = 3$

Measured response	Contrast						
	w_A	w_B	w_C	w_{AB}	w_{AC}	w_{BC}	w_{ABC}
y_{abc}	–	–	–	+	+	+	–
y_{Abc}	+	–	–	–	–	+	+
y_{aBc}	–	+	–	–	+	–	+
y_{abC}	–	–	+	+	–	–	+
y_{ABc}	+	+	–	+	–	–	–
y_{AbC}	+	–	+	–	+	–	–
y_{aBC}	–	+	+	–	–	+	–
y_{ABC}	+	+	+	+	+	+	+

The corresponding sum-of-squares term is then

$$SSAC = \frac{w_{AC}^2}{2^3 n}.$$
(9.63)

As before, each of these effects has one degree of freedom. The sum of squares for the error term is again found as $SSE = SST - SSA - SSB - SSC - SSAB - SSAC - SSBC - SSABC$, with $(n-1)2^m$ degrees of freedom. Once these sum-of-squares terms have been computed, the ANOVA test is performed in the normal way.

9.6   Summary

The design-of-experiments technique presented in this chapter extends the one-factor ANOVA technique presented in Section 5.2.1 to m factors. This extension allows us to isolate the effects on the system's output of each individual input variable, the effects due to their interactions, and the magnitude of the measurement errors. We can compare the relative importances of these effects, and determine whether the effects are statistically significant. Although the number of experiments that must be performed grows very quickly with the number of factors and the number of levels of each factor, the $n2^m$ design provides a simplified analysis for quickly isolating the most important factors and interactions. A complete analysis on these factors alone can then be performed.

9.7   For further reading

- The ANOVA technique and the design of experiments concept have long been important tools in the statisticians' toolbox. See

  Ronald E. Walpole and Raymond H. Myers, *Probability and Statistics for Engineers and Scientists* (Second Edition), Macmillan Publishing, New York, 1978,

  for example. The concepts are also commonly used by physical scientists who must deal with noisy data, and by researchers of all types who must rely on sampling from large populations. With the notable exception of

  Raj Jain, *The Art of Computer Systems Performance Analysis,* John Wiley and Sons, Inc., 1991,

  however, the design-of-experiments concepts have not been a common tool for the computer-research community. This lack of statistical rigor has been a weakness in the field of computer-systems performance analysis. I hope that this chapter will encourage you to be more careful in the experiments and analyses you perform. This text by Jain also provides a good discussion of *fractional factorial* designs. These experiment designs provide a way of reducing the total number of input combinations that must be tested at the expense of grouping together the contributions to the total variation of some of the input factors and their interactions. This type of grouping is called *confounding* since the effects of some of the factors and their interactions cannot be separated.

9.8 Exercises

1. What is the difference between the 'variation' explained by a factor and the 'variance?'
2. The allocation of variation is used to determine the relative importance of each factor. What is used to determine whether it is statistically significant?
3. The use of confidence intervals for effects makes an implicit assumption about the distribution of measurement errors. What is this assumption?
4. What are the key differences between an $n2^m$-factor experiment and a one-factor experiment?
5. What type of experiment design should be used to determine the effect of the size of a processor's cache on performance? What are the factors that should be considered? What is the response variable?
6. What type of experiment should be used to determine which of three new disk drives should be purchased?
7. What is the difference between a 'contrast' and the 'effect' of a factor?
8. How many experiments are necessary to determine the effects of eight different input variables if three of them have five levels, and the remainder have two levels? Assume that n replications are necessary.
9. Find two different optimizations that can be used together or independently to improve the execution time of a program. For instance, loop unrolling and memory padding are two optimization techniques that can be used to reduce the execution time of simple loops. Loop unrolling attempts to reduce the relative overhead of a loop by executing several iterations of the original loop for each execution of the loop's control structure. Memory padding, on the other hand, inserts some unused memory locations between large arrays accessed in a loop to ensure that they do not cause cache and memory conflicts. These techniques are orthogonal and can also be used together. An example of these techniques is shown in the following programs:

```
c  original program

       program main

       parameter (n=1024*1024)
       common /com/ a(n), b1(n), b2(n), b3(n), b4(n)

       do 10 irep=1,10
         do 10 i=1,n
             a(i) = .25*(b1(i)+b2(i)+b3(i)+b4(i))
     10 continue

       end

c after padding

       program main

       parameter (n=1024*1024)
       common /com/ a(n), x1(32), b1(n), x2(32), b2(n), x3(32),
     * b3(n), x4(32), b4(n)

       do 10 irep=1,10
         do 10 i=1,n
             a(i) = .25*(b1(i)+b2(i)+b3(i)+b4(i))
     10 continue

       end


c after unrolling

       program main

       parameter (n=1024*1024)
       common /com/ a(n), b1(n), b2(n), b3(n), b4(n)

       do 10 irep=1,10
         do 10 i=1,n-2,3
           a(i) = .25*(b1(i)+b2(i)+b3(i)+b4(i))
           a(i+1) = .25*(b1(i+1)+b2(i+1)+b3(i+1)+b4(i+1))
```

```
      a(i+2) = .25*(b1(i+2)+b2(i+2)+b3(i+2)+b4(i+2))
10 continue

   end



c after unrolling and padding

   program main

   parameter (n=1024*1024)
   common /com/ a(n), x1(32), b1(n), x2(32), b2(n), x3(32),
   * b3(n), x4(32), b4(n)

   do 10 irep=1,10
     do 10 i=1,n-2,3
     a(i) = .25*(b1(i)+b2(i)+b3(i)+b4(i))
     a(i+1) = .25*(b1(i+1)+b2(i+1)+b3(i+1)+b4(i+1))
     a(i+2) = .25*(b1(i+2)+b2(i+2)+b3(i+2)+b4(i+2))
10 continue

   end
```

Design an appropriate experiment to determine the impacts on performance of loop unrolling, memory padding, and the combination used together for the above example loop. Note that you can view this experiment as having two factors – loop unrolling and padding – and each of these factors has two possible values – either on or off. Do a minimum of three replications and determine the percentages of the variation that are due to the factors, their combination, and the experimental error.

10. Design an appropriate experiment to compare the times required to perform some basic operation, such as a subroutine call and return, on three different types of systems; call them A, B, and C. Use appropriate contrasts to compare A–B, A–C, and B–C. Determine whether there is a statistically significant difference among the three machines in terms of the times required to perform this operation both at the 90% and at the 95% confidence levels.

10 Simulation and random-number generation

'Do not plan a bridge's capacity by counting the number of people who swim across the river today.'

Unknown

Oftentimes we wish to predict some aspect of the performance of a computer system before it is actually built. Since the real machine does not yet exist, we obviously cannot measure its performance directly. Instead, the best we can do is to *simulate* the important aspects of the system. We then try to extrapolate from these simulations information about how the system will behave once it is actually built. Simulation may also be appropriate when we want to investigate some aspect of a system's performance that we cannot easily measure directly or indirectly.

When the system does not yet exist, there are many assumptions that must be made about the, perhaps not completely defined, system before it can be simulated. Simplifying assumptions are also necessary when simulating an existing system since it would most likely be impossible to simulate every small detail. If these assumptions are not realistic, the simulation results will not accurately predict how the system will ultimately perform.

Simulation has the advantage of being much less expensive than actually building a machine. Additionally, it is much more flexible than measuring the performance of a real machine. In a simulated system, we can quickly change important parameters that would be difficult or impossible to change in a real system, such as the size or associativity of the cache, for instance, to determine how the system's performance will be affected. This ability to rapidly change the system configuration allows us to explore more of the design space than would be possible if we had only a real machine with which to experiment. As a result, we can more easily determine the system parameters that produce the best overall performance.

10.1   Simulation-efficiency considerations

An important limitation of simulation is, of course, precisely the fact that it is not a real system. Every simulator has built into it simplifying assumptions that limit its ability to exactly duplicate the behavior of a real system. There is, in general, a trade-off between the *accuracy* of a simulation and the *time* required to write the simulator and execute the necessary simulations. An extremely detailed simulator can take a very long time to write. Furthermore, since it simulates the system at a very fine level of granularity, it can take a very long time to execute to produce a single result. Consequently, a less detailed simulator may actually be preferable. Although the results it produces will probably not be as accurate as those pro-duced by a more detailed simulator, the simpler simulator might allow suffi-ciently detailed results to be produced more quickly.

Determining the level of detail necessary when writing a new simulator is more art than science. The 'correct' choice depends on the level of detail necessary in order to make the desired decision, and the consequences of being wrong. For example, the consequences of being wrong when using a simulator to determine the best cache size for a new system are relatively small. Either the cache specified will be too large, resulting in a slightly higher cost than necessary, or the cache will be too small, which will produce a degradation in performance. The incor-rect operation of a microprocessor used to control a heart pacemaker, though, can have much more serious consequences. Thus, in this case, a very detailed simulation may be warranted.

When developing a new simulator, it is important to explicitly consider the consequences and trade-offs of the simplifying assumptions that must be made. The following (incomplete) list highlights some of the simulation *efficiency* trade-offs that confront the simulation-model developer.

- **The complexity of the simulation model.** There is a nonlinear relationship between simulation-model complexity and the accuracy of the results obtained. In general, the results of a simulation will be more accurate as the model is made more detailed. However, since the simulation is only a model of the real system, increasing the level of detail beyond a certain point quickly leads to diminishing returns. That is, the programming effort and simulation time required for a very detailed model do not continue to produce corre-sponding improvements in the simulation results after a certain level of detail has been incorporated. Furthermore, simpler models are easier to validate than are very complex, detailed models.

- **The time factor for decisions.** The goal of developing a simulation model is to make a decision based on the results produced by executing the simulation. As a result, the simulation model developer must always bear in mind the time by which a decision will be required. For example, we may be given the job of developing a simulator that will be used to predict how certain system parameters should be set for the next time period in a time-shared system on the basis of the recent pattern of resource usage. Even though we may be able to produce highly accurate predictions with a very detailed simulator, the results will be useless if the results of the simulation are not available before they are needed by the scheduler for the next time period.

- **Allocation of human and machine resources.** There is typically a trade-off in the human time required to implement a complex piece of software such as a simulator and the time required to execute the resulting program. If the simulation is going to be executed only a few times, it may not be worth the programmer's time to implement a highly efficient, elegant algorithm. Instead, it may be a better use of resources to quickly implement a more inefficient algorithm, and then pay the resulting execution-time penalty. This trade-off may then allow the simulation developer to spend more time analyzing the results and less time actually writing the simulator program.

10.2   Types of simulations

There are several different types of simulations that are commonly used by the computer systems performance analyst. These include

1. emulation,
2. static (or *Monte Carlo*) simulation, and
3. discrete-event simulation.

10.2.1 Emulation

An *emulator program* is a simulation program that runs on some existing system to make that system appear to be something else. Since the goal of emulation is to make one type of system appear to be another type, an emulation program typically sacrifices performance for flexibility. For example, a terminal-emulator program is often executed on a personal computer to make that computer appear to be a specific type of terminal to a remote system. The *Java Virtual Machine* (JVM) is an example of a processor emulator.

The JVM is a program that executes on a wide variety of different computer systems. It simulates the execution of a *virtual* processor whose instruction set is that defined in the JVM specification. This emulation allows programs written in the Java programming language to be executed on any processor for which a JVM has been written. Thus, by *interpreting* the JVM instruction set, this program can make any computer system appear to be a processor that directly executes Java programs.

10.2.2 Static (Monte Carlo) simulation

A *static simulation* is one in which there typically is no time parameter. Instead, the simulation is run until some equilibrium state is reached, or until further refinement of the state of the simulated system is no longer useful or possible. Static simulations are often used to evaluate probabilistic systems, to model some physical phenomenon, or to numerically estimate the solution of some mathematical expression, such as a complex integral. Since static simulations are driven with sequences of random numbers, they are also commonly referred to as *Monte Carlo* simulations, after the casinos of Monte Carlo.

As an example of how a Monte Carlo simulation works, consider the problem of numerically determining the value of π. We begin with a geometric description that we can directly relate to the value of π, as shown in Figure 10.1. Since the area of a circle with a radius of 1 is $\pi(1)^2 = \pi$, the area of the quarter-circle within the first quadrant in Figure 10.1 is $\pi/4$. The area contained within the unit square in this quadrant is simply 1. Thus, the ratio of the area of the quarter-circle to the area of the square, which we denote R, is $R = \pi/4$. The numerical value of π then can be found from $\pi = 4R$.

We have now transformed the problem of computing the numerical value of π into the equivalent geometric problem of determining the ratio of the two areas, R. A Monte Carlo simulation can be used to find R by modeling an equivalent physical system. In particular, imagine throwing darts randomly at Figure 10.1

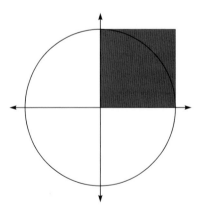

Figure 10.1 The area shown within the shaded quarter-circle is $\pi/4$ while the area contained within the unit square is 1. An estimate of the ratio of these two areas can be obtained with a simple Monte Carlo simulation, which then allows us to estimate the numerical value of π.

such that every dart hits within the unit square. After throwing a large number of darts, we count the number of times a dart hit within the quarter-circle, n_{circ}, and the total number of darts thrown, n_{total}. Then the desired ratio of the two areas is $R = n_{circ}/n_{total}$.

We can simulate this dart-throwing experiment by generating two random numbers, u_1 and u_2, for each dart thrown, such that u_1 and u_2 are both uniformly distributed between 0 and 1. If the distance from the origin of the point defined by $(x, y) = (u_1, u_2)$ is smaller than the radius of the circle, that is, $\sqrt{u_1^2 + u_2^2} < 1$, then the simulated dart has hit within the quarter-circle. By repeating this process a large number of times, we can theoretically compute the value of π to any level of precision desired. The key to this type of Monte Carlo simulation is identifying an appropriate physical model for the system being studied.

10.2.3   Discrete-event simulation

A *discrete-event simulator* is used to model a system whose global state changes as a function of time. The state may also be affected by events that are generated externally to the simulator as well as those that are spawned within the simulator by the processing of other events. The basic idea is that the global state is appropriately updated every time some event occurs. While the specific details of every simulator will be unique, discrete-event simulators all share a similar overall structure. Each discrete-event simulator will require at least some of the following components:

- an event scheduler,
- a global time variable and a method for updating this time,
- event-processing routines,
- event-generation mechanisms, and
- data-recording and -summarization routines.

10.2.3.1 The event scheduler

The event scheduler is the heart of a discrete-event simulator. It maintains a list of all pending events in their global time order. It is the responsibility of the scheduler to process the next event on the list by removing it from the list and dispatching the event to the appropriate event-processing routine. The scheduler also inserts new events into the appropriate point in the list on the basis of the time at which the event is supposed to be executed. Updates to the global time variable also are coordinated by the scheduler.

10.2.3.2 The global time variable

The global time variable records the current simulation time. It can be updated by the scheduler using one of two approaches. In the *fixed-increment* approach, the scheduler increments the global time variable by some fixed amount. It then checks the pending events on the event list. If the scheduled execution time for any of the pending events matches the current time, all of these events are dispatched for execution. After all of the events scheduled for the current time have been processed, the scheduler again increments the global time variable.

The alternative *event-driven* approach allows the global time to jump to the value of the next event at the head of the pending-event list. With this approach, the value of the global time variable will change nonuniformly, sometimes jumping by a large amount, sometimes not changing from one event to another. The choice of which approach to use depends on the specific details of the system being simulated. The event-driven approach is probably the most common in simulations of computer systems, however.

10.2.3.3 Event processing

Each event in the system will typically have its own event-processing routine to simulate what happens when that event occurs in a real system. These routines may update the global state and they may generate additional events that must be inserted into the pending-event list by the scheduler. The processing of each event depends entirely on the system being simulated, though.

For example, a memory-access event in a simulation of a processor may result in two possible outcomes. If the address being accessed is found in the simulated cache memory, the event may simply return the stored value.

If the address is not in the cache, however, the memory-access event-processing routine may generate a new event that returns the corresponding data value t_{miss} time units in the future, where t_{miss} is the time required to service a cache miss. This event must be inserted, in the correct time order, into the list of pending events. Then when the event is eventually serviced, it will appear to the rest of the simulated system as if the earlier memory access actually did produce a cache miss with a delay of t_{miss}. This ability to generate new events and insert them into the pending event list provides a powerful mechanism for simulating events that consist of multiple subevents separated in time.

10.2.3.4 Event generation

Discrete-event simulators are often classified according to the technique used to generate events. Commonly used classifications are *execution driven*, *trace driven*, and *distribution driven*.

Execution driven. An execution-driven simulation is somewhat similar to an emulation in that the simulator actually executes a benchmark program. Thus, the simulator actually produces the same output from the benchmark program as that which would be produced if the benchmark were executed on an actual machine. The primary difference between an execution driven simulation and an emulation is that, in addition to executing the program, the simulator models the necessary details of the system being tested. An emulation, on the other hand, simply executes the program without regard to how the execution is performed. The emulation is concerned only with producing the appropriate output from the benchmark program whereas the execution-driven simulator is concerned also with *how* the output is produced.

Execution-driven simulations are often considered the most accurate type of simulation since they must model all of the details necessary to actually execute a program. This advantage is also their primary disadvantage, however. Modeling a system at this level of detail can be quite expensive both in terms of simulation time, and in terms of the time required to develop and verify the simulator. To simulate a program that does floating-point-arithmetic operations or any input/output operations, for instance, the simulator must provide mechanisms for actually performing the necessary arithmetic and input/output operations.

Trace driven. As discussed in Section 6.4, a trace is a record of the sequence of events that occurred when the system was traced. When a trace is used to drive a discrete-event simulator, this list of events is usually time-ordered. One of the advantages of driving the simulator with a program trace is that the simulator itself does not have to provide all of the functionality needed by the program, as is required in an execution-driven simulation. On the other hand, the trace represents only one possible execution path for the system. Thus, the simulation result will be valid for only that single trace, which need not be representative of the 'typical' workload. To obtain a simulation result for a different set of inputs to the program traced, the program must be reexecuted with the new inputs while a new trace is collected. Additionally, since the trace is fixed at the time it is collected, it can be difficult to accurately simulate events that would affect the order of execution. Providing a dynamic-feedback path from the simulator to the trace-collecting system can sometimes alleviate this problem, though.

Another concern with trace-driven simulation is the difficulty of dealing with the large trace files. The tremendous amount of information generated during the tracing operation typically limits traces to only a few seconds of total system-execution time. Thus, the system being simulated will be evaluated on the basis of its simulated performance during only a few seconds of actual execution time on relatively small benchmark programs. This situation is roughly equivalent to evaluating the performance of a new type of automobile by measuring how quickly it can get out of the drive-way! Because of these limitations, execution driven simulations are becoming more popular than trace-driven simulations in computer-systems performance analysis, in spite of their complexity.

Distribution driven. A distribution driven simulation is similar to a trace-driven simulation, except that the input events are generated by the simulator itself to follow some predefined probabilistic function. For example, sending messages over a communication network could be modeled by using an exponential distribution to determine the amount of time that elapses between each message. That is, sequences of random numbers are generated to model the expected statistical behavior of the inputs to the system being simulated. The simulator then produces an output that would occur if the real system were driven by an application program that produced the same sequence of inputs.

Since there is no assurance that any real application program actually would produce this input sequence, the simulation should be run many times with several different input sequences. The outputs produced then can be averaged in some appropriate fashion to produce a statistical view of the performance of the system being simulated.

This type of probabilistic (or *stochastic*) simulation is often used when actual application programs are not available to drive the simulator. It is also useful in evaluating the behavior of the system over a wider range of input conditions than could be generated by the application programs available. One important concern with this stochastic simulation is, of course, how accurately the selected probability distributions model the actual system's behavior.

Comments. To summarize, an execution-driven simulation actually executes an input application program and produces the same output result that the application would produce if it were executed on a real system. One of the main advantages of execution-driven simulation is that, since the simulator executes the application program as it simulates the desired system, it provides a level of control of the timing between events, and the timing of each individual event, that is not possible with the other types of simulation.

The primary disadvantage of an execution-driven simulation is that the simulator itself must have the capability of executing every type of instruction that may appear in the application programs it is to execute. A trace-driven simulation, on the other hand, captures the events produced by a single execution of an application when it is executed on some real system capable of recording the desired trace. This trace is then later played back as the input to the simulator. One of the primary shortcomings of this trace-based simulation is that, since the trace has already been recorded and is therefore fixed, it is difficult for the simulator to reorder the input events on the basis of changes that may occur as the simulation progresses. That is, it is very difficult to provide a feedback path that allows the simulator to alter the input trace.

A distribution-driven simulation is similar to a trace-driven simulation, except that the input to the distribution-driven simulation is a sequence of artificially generated random numbers. Because the inputs to this type of simulation are random, the outputs produced are but a single statistical sample of the system's potential behavior. Thus, the simulation must be repeated numerous times with different sequences of random values (that still follow the same statistical distribution, however) to determine the system's average behavior. The primary advantage of this distribution-driven simulation is that, by changing the parameters of the input distributions, it is easy to study a wide variety of situations for which the experimenter may not have appropriate test programs available.

10.2.3.5 Recording and summarization of data

In addition to maintaining the state variables necessary for simulating the system, the simulator must also maintain appropriate event counts and time measurements. These values will be used at the end of the simulation to calculate appropriate statistics to summarize the simulation results. For example, if a memory system is being modeled, the simulator would probably count the total number of memory references and the number of those references that result in cache misses. At the end of the simulation, these values can be used to calculate the overall cache-miss ratio. Similarly, a simulation of a communications network would likely maintain a count of the number of messages sent and a running total of the number of bytes sent in each message. These values can then be used at the end of the simulation to calculate the average number of bytes sent per message.

10.2.3.6 The simulation algorithm

Given these basic components, the overall processing done by a discrete-event simulator can be summarized in the following steps.

```
Initial global state variables.
Initialize the global time to 0.
Obtain the first input event.
while((no more events) AND (time < maximum simulation time limit))
        {
        Advance the global time.
        Remove the next event from the pending-event list.
        Process the event.
            {
            Perform event-specific operations.
```

```
                    Update global variables.
                    Update simulation statistics.
                    Generate new events triggered by this event.
                    }
            }
Print the simulation results.
```

Of course, the specifics of each simulator will depend on the system being simulated.

10.3   Random-number generation

Random numbers are the life-blood of probabilistic simulations, such as distribution-driven discrete-event simulations and Monte Carlo simulations, since an
essentially unlimited supply of random numbers is necessary for driving these
types of simulators. This section explains how a deterministic algorithm can be
used to generate sequences of numbers that *appear* to be random. First, we
discuss how to generate a random sequence of numbers that appear to be uniformly distributed. We then present techniques for transforming this uniformly
distributed sequence into sequences that appear to be from any desired distribution. Section 10.4.4 then discusses statistical techniques used for testing the
'quality' of the random sequences generated.

10.3.1   Uniformly distributed sequences

Sequences of random numbers are necessary to drive stochastic simulators.
However, generating random-number sequences is not as easy it might seem at
first glance. For instance, there would seem to be an inherent contradiction in
using a deterministic algorithm to generate a sequence of numbers that is, by
definition, nondeterministic. In fact, to allow us to exactly repeat a simulation
(for testing, for example), we do not really want truly random numbers. Instead,
a variety of techniques to generate *pseudorandom*-number sequences has been
developed.

Unlike truly random numbers, pseudorandom numbers only appear to be
random while, in fact, they are generated by a completely deterministic algorithm. With a truly random sequence of numbers, knowing what values have
come so far will not help us in any way to predict what value will come next.
With a pseudorandom sequence, though, we know the exact sequence of values
that will be produced. From a statistical point of view, and, perhaps more

importantly, from the point of view of the probabilistic simulator, a pseudorandom sequence can appear to be a sufficiently random sequence.

The first step in generating a sequence of random numbers that appears to come from any type of distribution is to be able to generate a sequence that appears to be uniformly distributed on the interval [0, 1). That is, the probability of obtaining any value within this interval is constant. A good pseudorandom-number generator should have the following properties.

- It should be *efficient*. Since a typical simulation will require a large number of random values, the generator should be easy to compute efficiently.
- It should have a *long period*. The sequence of random values generated by a finite algorithm must necessarily be finite. That is, the sequence will repeat with some period k, such that $x_{n+k} = x_n$, $x_{n+k+1} = x_{n+1}$, $x_{n+k+2} = x_{n+2}$, ... To make the sequence appear as random as possible, we would like the period k to be as large as possible.
- Its values should be *independent and uniformly distributed*. The values produced should appear to be uniformly distributed in the interval [0, 1). That is, every value should have the same likelihood of appearing in the sequence. Furthermore, the *order* in which the values occur should appear to be independent in a statistical sense. (More about this independence property will be said in Section 10.4.4.)
- It should be *repeatable*. To facilitate testing of our simulator, and to allow the direct comparison of different simulation configurations being driven by the same sequence of random values, we would like the generator to be able to reproduce exactly the same sequence as that it produced at some previous time.

A *linear-congruential generator* (LCG) is one of the simplest generators that exhibits the above desirable properties. The basic form of the LCG is the equation

$$z_i = (az_{i-1} + c) \bmod m \tag{10.1}$$

where a, c, and m are constants carefully chosen to ensure that the LCG satisfies the desired properties and the z_i values are the desired sequence of random values. If the constants are chosen correctly, this generator can be made to produce the complete sequence of integers from the set $\{0, 1, 2, \ldots, m-1\}$ in some permuted order. Since $0 \le z_i < m$, the sequence of values $u_i = z_i/m$ will appear to be uniformly distributed on the interval [0, 1).

There are a few interesting characteristics of this type of generator that make the sequence of values it generates somewhat different than a truly random sequence. For instance, each of the m values produced by this generator appears exactly once in the sequence. Thus, the probability of obtaining any particular value is $1/m$, which satisfies our uniformity requirement. However, since z_i is calculated using z_{i-1}, when a value repeats, the entire sequence will begin all over again. As a result, unlike a truly random sequence, it is impossible for the same value to appear twice in a row in the sequence of values generated.

Furthermore, since we use $u_i = z_i/m$ to approximate the values distributed on the interval $[0, 1)$, the smallest difference between any two values is $1/m$. This type of *quantization error* would also not appear in a truly random sequence. Nevertheless, even with these limitations, this type of LCG can produce samples that *appear*, in a statistical sense, to be from the desired distribution.

10.3.1.1 Choosing the constants

The constants a, c, and m in the LCG must be carefully chosen to ensure that the generator has the desired properties described above. Since it is guaranteed that the period of the generator can be no larger than m, this constant should be chosen to be as large as possible, within the limits of the arithmetic precision of the system on which the generator will be executed. It also is convenient to make m a power-of-two value; that is, choose $m = 2^j$, where j is a positive integer. Then the modulo operation can be performed with a simple truncation of the result to j bits.

In addition to these constraints on m that are related to the efficiency of calculating the sequence, it has been shown that, if $c \neq 0$, the maximum period will be obtained if and only if

1. the constants m and c are relatively prime,
2. every prime that is a factor of m is also a factor of $a - 1$, and
3. if 4 divides m, then $a - 1$ must be a multiple of 4.

These constraints are all true if the constants are chosen such that $m = 2^j$, $a = 4d + 1$, and c is odd, where j and d are positive integers.

As an example, various implementations of the UNIX operating system often provide the following LCG:

$$z_i = (1{,}103{,}515{,}245 z_{i-1} + 12{,}345) \bmod 2^{32}. \tag{10.2}$$

Since these constants satisfy the above constraints, this generator has a complete period of 2^{32} values. Also, the modulo operation can be performed simply by truncating the final value to 32 bits.

Some LCGs use $c = 0$. This choice for c eliminates the need to perform the addition, which, thereby, simplifies the overall calculation and improves the efficiency of the random-number-generation process. These types of generators are called *multiplicative LCGs*. If m is chosen as a power of 2 in a multiplicative LCG, though, the period is reduced by a factor of 4 to 2^{j-2}. Choosing m to be a prime number, along with an appropriate value of a, can produce a generator with a period of $2^m - 1$. Note that the period is not 2^m since a multiplicative LCG can never produce the value 0. A reasonably good multiplicative LCG is

$$z_i = (16,807z_{i-1}) \bmod (2^{31} - 1).$$ (10.3)

10.3.1.2 Cautions and suggestions

Looking at the above formulas for the LCG and the multiplicative LCG may leave the reader with the impression that producing a good random-number generator is rather simple. However, it turns out that there are many subtleties that can strongly and adversely affect the quality of the final random-number sequence generated. For instance, the properties of an LCG, such as the length of its period, are maintained only if all computations are done precisely with no round-off error. Thus, the computations should use only integer arithmetic instead of floating-point operations. Note also that the multiplication operation in the az_{i-1} step could easily exceed the number of bits in the standard integer data type since multiplying two m-bit numbers can produce a $2m$-bit result. Thus, the intermediate calculations all need to be performed with extended-precision arithmetic operations.

A related caution is that subsets of an m-bit generator need not exhibit the same randomness characteristics as those of the complete generator. If you want only a single bit that is randomly 0 or 1 with equal probabilities, for instance, you should not simply look at the least-significant bit of the m-bit value. Multiplicative LCGs where m is a power of 2 actually exhibit short-period cycles in their low-order bits. Thus, looking only at the least-significant bit would produce a sequence with very high autocorrelation. A better solution, which is discussed more completely in Section 10.3.2, is to compare the $u_i = z_i/m$ value with 0.5, returning 0 if $u_i < 0.5$ and 1 otherwise.

In addition to these calculation difficulties, it is important not to confuse complexity with randomness. A long, complex sequence of operations will not necessarily produce a good sequence of random values. A better generator is one that consists of a relatively simple sequence of operations whose properties can be proven analytically, such as a LCG. Furthermore, recognize that pseudorandom numbers are *not* unpredictable. They are actually perfectly predictable once the algorithm used to generate the values is known. This characteristic of predictability is good for simulations, however, since it allows the repetition of an experiment with the identical input conditions. What we want from a random-number generator is statistical randomness, not 'perfect' randomness.

The LCG is not the only type of random-number generator. Other types include linear-feedback-shift registers, extended Fibonacci generators, and generators that combine several other generators to further randomize the resulting sequence. Given the numerous subtleties involved in producing a good random-number generator, though, it is much better to use a generator that has been proven robust through extensive analysis and use than trying to develop one yourself. To paraphrase a popular saying, 'Don't try this at home.' Leave the development of a good *unif* (0, 1) pseudorandom-number generator to the experts.

10.3.2 Nonuniformly distributed random numbers

Many of the processes in a computer system that we may wish to include in a simulation can often be reasonably modeled using a sequence of random numbers that appears to be from some nonuniform distribution. For example, the time that elapses between the sending of two messages on an interprocessor communications network can often be modeled using an exponential distribution. That is, if we were to measure the times that elapse between the messages sent on a real system, and plotted them as the histogram shown in Figure 10.2, we may find that the times appear to roughly follow an exponential distribution parameterized with some mean value. We may then decide that we could simulate the times that messages are sent by using a sequence of random values that we generate. Each of the values would be the simulated time that must elapse after one simulated message is sent before the next can be sent. To perform this

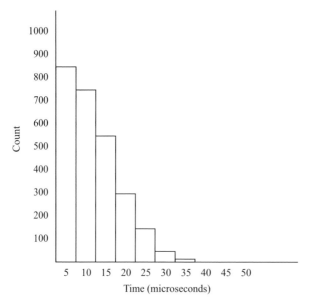

Figure 10.2 A histogram of the distribution of the times measured between two successive send operations for some interprocessor communication network. The horizontal axis shows the subranges of times measured, and the vertical axis is the number of occurrences of times in each subrange.

type of nonuniform-distribution-driven simulation, we need some way to generate a sequence of random values that *appears* to follow an exponential distribution with the desired mean.

Generating these nonuniform distributions is a two-step process. The first step is to generate a sequence of values that appears to be uniformly distributed between 0 and 1 by using one of the techniques discussed in Section 10.3.1. This type of sequence is denoted *unif* (0, 1). The second step then is to transform this sequence into a sequence from the desired distribution. Several different techniques for performing these transformations are discussed in the following sections. Several distributions that are commonly used in computer simulations are described in Appendix B.

10.3.2.1 Inverse transformation

Let $f(x)$ be the probability density function of the distribution we wish to generate. Then the cumulative distribution function is

$$F(x) = \int_{-\infty}^{x} f(x) \, dx. \tag{10.4}$$

Notice that

$$\int_{-\infty}^{+\infty} f(x) \, dx = 1 \tag{10.5}$$

so that $0 \le F(x) \le 1$ for all values of x. Furthermore, it can be shown that $F(x)$ is uniformly distributed between 0 and 1. As shown in Figure 10.3, this characteristic of a cumulative distribution function allows us to randomly select a value y of the cumulative distribution function $y = F(x)$ using a random value $u = \mathit{unif}(0, 1)$. Then, using the inverse of the cumulative distribution function, we find the desired sample value $x = F^{-1}(y)|_{y=u}$.

So the procedure for generating a random sample using this inverse transformation method is to first generate a random value $u = \mathit{unif}(0, 1)$, and then plug this value into the inverse of the cumulative distribution function of the desired distribution. The calculated value x is then one sample of a sequence of values that will appear to be distributed according to the probability density function $f(x)$. Of course, this method works only if the cumulative distribution function of $f(x)$, i.e. $F(x)$, is invertible.

Example. The exponential distribution is commonly used to model the time that elapses between two events, such as the time between access requests to some input/output device. The probability density function of this distribution is

$$f(x) = \frac{1}{\beta} e^{-x/\beta}, \qquad x \ge 0 \tag{10.6}$$

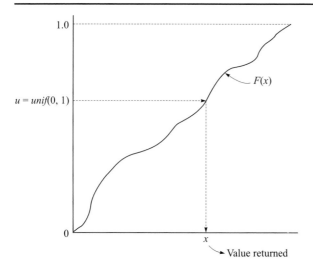

Figure 10.3 The inverse-transformation method for generating a sequence of nonuniformly distributed random values begins by generating a random value $u = unif(0, 1)$. The transformed value that should be returned is then $x = F^{-1}(y)|_{y=u}$, where $F(x)$ is the cumulative distribution function of the desired probability density function $f(x)$.

where β is the mean value. The cumulative distribution for this density function is then easily found to be

$$F(x) = 1 - e^{-x/\beta}, \qquad x \geq 0. \tag{10.7}$$

Letting $y = F(x)$, we find that

$$x = F^{-1}(y) = -\beta \ln(1 - y), \qquad 0 \leq y \leq 1. \tag{10.8}$$

To use this expression to generate a value of x, we first need to generate a value $y = unif(0, 1)$. Note, however, that, if $y = unif(0, 1)$, then $1 - y = unif(0, 1)$, also. Thus, we can simplify the above expression to give

$$x = -\beta \ln(y) \tag{10.9}$$

where $y = unif(0, 1)$.   ◇

Example. The inverse-transformation method is quite useful also for generating a sequence of values that is uniformly distributed over any arbitrary interval. Consider transforming a $unif(0, 1)$ sequence into a sequence that is $unif(a, b)$. The probability density function for a value $x = unif(a, b)$ is

$$f(x) = \begin{cases} \dfrac{1}{b - a} & \text{for } a \leq x \leq b \\ 0 & \text{otherwise.} \end{cases} \tag{10.10}$$

The corresponding cumulative distribution function is

$$F(x) = \begin{cases} 0 & x < a \\ \dfrac{x-a}{b-a} & \text{for } a \le x \le b \\ 1 & x > b \end{cases} \qquad (10.11)$$

which is shown graphically in Figure 10.4. Finding the inverse of $F(x)$, we have

$$x = F^{-1}(y) = a + (b-a)y. \qquad (10.12)$$

Then, if $y = unif(0, 1)$, the values of x will be $unif(a, b)$. ◇

10.3.2.2 The alias method

The alias method is useful for generating nonuniformly distributed random values that appear to be from an arbitrary discrete probability density function with a finite range. It uses a uniformly distributed random value to index into a table to find the appropriate value of x to return. To see how this technique works, consider an experiment in which each of the possible outcomes occurs with a probability that is a multiple of $1/k$, where k is a positive integer. That is, the probability of obtaining the outcome i is $\Pr(i) = f(i) = k_i/k$, where k_i is the number of times that outcome i can occur. Note that $k = \sum_{\forall i} k_i$ for all possible outcomes i.

Before the simulation begins, a table with k entries in total must be initialized for all possible outcomes such that k_i entries contain outcome value i. To generate a value from this distribution, a random value y that is $unif(1, k)$ is first generated. This value is used to index into the table. The value previously stored in the table entry at this location is then returned as the desired sample value x. Although this procedure may sound rather complicated, it is actually quite straightforward, as shown in the following example.

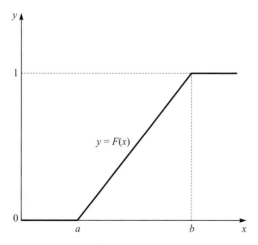

$y = F(x)$

Figure 10.4 The cumulative distribution function $F(x) = (x-a)/(b-a)$.

Table 10.1. The possible outcomes that can occur when flipping three coins

Configuration	Number of heads (outcome x)
HHH	3
HHT	2
HTH	2
HTT	1
THH	2
THT	1
TTH	1
TTT	0

Example. The distribution we wish to model is the number of 'heads' that occur when three coins are flipped simultaneously. That is, each time this function is invoked, it should return a value from the set $\{0, 1, 2, 3\}$, where the value returned corresponds to the number of heads that occurred.

To produce this function, we first enumerate all possible outcomes for the experiment, as shown in Table 10.1. From this enumeration, we see that the outcomes with three heads and no heads each occur exactly once, while three outcomes produce two heads and another three outcomes produce only one head. Since there are $k = 8$ outcomes in total, we find the probabilities shown in Table 10.2 for each of the possible outcomes.

Since $k = \sum_{\forall i} k_i = 8$, we need a table with eight entries. One of the entries in the table should be initialized with 0, three should be initialized with 1, three more should be initialized with 2, and the remaining one should be initialized with 3. These values correspond to the outcomes of no head, one head, two heads, and three heads, respectively. To generate a value for x, a random index into the table is generated using $i = \lceil unif(1, 8) \rceil$. The ceiling operator ensures that the index into the table is an integer value. If the previously initialized table is the array x[.], then the value to be returned is simply x[i]. ◇

10.3.2.3 Decomposition

Decomposition is used when the desired distribution function can be expressed as two or more other distributions that are easier to generate than the original distribution. One $unif(0, 1)$ random value is used to select one of these other distributions with the appropriate probability. Then one or more additional $unif(0, 1)$ values are used to generate a value from the selected distribution.

Table 10.2. The probabilities associated with each of the outcomes shown in Table 10.1

Number of heads (outcome x)	Number of occurrences (k_i)	Probability $(f(i) = k_i/k)$
0	1	$\frac{1}{8}$
1	3	$\frac{3}{8}$
2	3	$\frac{3}{8}$
3	1	$\frac{1}{8}$

More precisely, say that the desired probability density function, $f(x)$, can be expressed as the weighted sum of n other density functions, $f_i(x)$. Thus, $f(x)$ can be written

$$f(x) = \sum_{i=1}^{n} p_i f_i(x) \tag{10.13}$$

where p_i is is the fraction of $f(x)$ that decomposes into $f_i(x)$. The first $unif(0, 1)$ random value is used to select the appropriate density function $f_i(x)$ according to the corresponding weight p_i. A random value is then generated to follow the $f_i(x)$ distribution using whatever method is appropriate for that distribution.

Example. We would like to generate random values for a probability density function in which two-thirds of the time the value is uniformly distributed between 0 and 5 and one-third of the time it is uniformly distributed between 5 and 10. That is,

$$\Pr(x < 0) = 0$$
$$\Pr(0 \leq x \leq 5) = \frac{2}{3}$$
$$\Pr(5 < x \leq 10) = \frac{1}{3} \tag{10.14}$$
$$\Pr(x > 10) = 0.$$

We first generate a random value $u_1 = unif(0, 1)$. If $u_1 \leq \frac{2}{3}$, then we need to return a value that is $unif(0, 5)$. This is easily accomplished using the inverse transform method, giving $x = 5u_2$, where $u_2 = unif(0, 1)$. If $u_1 > \frac{2}{3}$, however, we need to return a value that is $unif(5, 10)$. This is again easily accomplished using an inverse transform, giving $x = 5 + 5u_2$.   ◇

This decomposition technique is particularly useful when one is generating empirical distributions that are derived from actual measured values. For instance, say you measure the size of messages sent on a communications network and find that the resulting distribution does not appear to fit any standard analytical distribution. Instead of trying to force the observed distribution into some standard distribution, you could decompose your observations into several other distributions. You would then choose, on the basis of the observed probabilities of these distributions, which of these other distributions to use for generating the next sample.

10.3.2.4 Special characterization

Many probability distributions have special relationships to other distributions. We can often take advantage of these relationships to develop algorithms for generating random sequences that appear to be from the desired distribution. There are no standard strategies to follow with this technique. Rather, you must notice that the special relationship exists, and then produce a specific algorithm to exploit it. The following examples demonstrate the idea of special characterization for a few common distributions.

Example. The Poisson distribution is a discrete distribution that is often used to model the number of events that occur within a specified interval. The probability of exactly x events occurring is

$$f(x) = \frac{\lambda^x e^{-\lambda}}{x!}, x = 0, 1, 2, \ldots \tag{10.15}$$

where λ is the mean number of events that occur within the specified interval. It is closely related to the exponential distribution in that, if the time between events follows an exponential distribution, the number of events that occur within a given interval follows a Poisson distribution.

We can take advantage of this relationship between the two distributions to generate Poisson-distributed values. In particular, one sample from a Poisson distribution would be the count of how many samples from an exponential distribution with mean $\beta = 1$ must be added together to exceed the mean value λ. A sample from an exponential distribution with mean $\beta = 1$ can be computed simply by using the inverse-transform method, giving $z = -\ln(y)$, where y is distributed $unif(0, 1)$. A simple algorithm for a Poisson sample is then:

```
sum = 0,  i = -1
while (sum <= lambda)
        y = unif(0,1)
        z = - ln (y)
        sum = sum + z
        i = i + 1
endwhile
return(i)
```

◇

Example. A *Bernoulli* distribution has two possible outcomes, 0 and 1. These outcomes are typically assumed to mean either success or failure in one trial, such as the flipping of a coin. If the probability of obtaining 1 is p, then $1 - p$ is the probability of obtaining 0. A *binomial* distribution with parameters n and p is the probability of obtaining x successes out of n trials where the probability of a success in a single trial is p. The binomial distribution is the sum of n independent Bernoulli distributions. Thus, to generate a *binomial*(n, p) sample, simply count the number of *unif* $(0, 1)$ samples out of n that are less than or equal to p. This is essentially simulating n Bernoulli experiments that comprise the binomial experiment each time a value for the binomially distributed sequence of random values is needed.   ◇

10.3.2.5 The accept–reject method

The *accept–reject* method is a general technique for generating random sequences. The basic idea behind this technique can be explained with a simple geometric argument. First, draw the probability density function for the desired distribution, $f(x)$, as shown in the shaded region in Figure 10.5. If we could throw a dart at this figure so that it has an equal probability of hitting anywhere in the area under $f(x)$, the corresponding value of x where the dart hit would be one sample from the desired distribution. It should be easy to see that the sequence of x values generated through multiple dart throws will follow the distribution defined by $f(x)$.

Owing to the complexity of evaluating the corresponding inverse function, however, it may be difficult, or impossible, to ensure that the random point selected (i.e. where the dart hits) is always uniformly distributed in two dimensions while remaining below $f(x)$. Instead, we choose a simpler function, $g(x)$, for which we already know how to calculate appropriate random values. We then

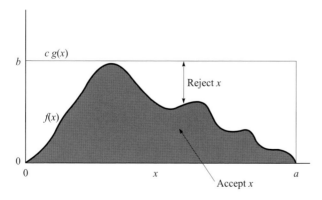

Figure 10.5 Generating samples from the distribution $f(x)$ using the accept–reject method.

scale $g(x)$ with the constant c so that $f(x) \leq cg(x)$, as shown in Figure 10.5. We now generate a random point that is within the area bounded by $cg(x)$ using whatever technique is appropriate for $g(x)$. That is, we again throw a dart at the larger target defined by $cg(x)$. If this randomly selected point is within the area bounded by the desired distribution $f(x)$, we accept the corresponding value of x as a good sample from this distribution. If it is in the area between $f(x)$ and $cg(x)$, though, we must reject it and repeat the entire process by generating a new random point. Eventually, a dart will hit within the area bounded by $f(x)$ giving us our desired sample value, x.

Note that the probability of any particular point being accepted as a good sample for $f(x)$ is the ratio of the area under $f(x)$ to the area under $cg(x)$. Thus, the efficiency of this technique depends on how close the bounding function $cg(x)$ is to the desired distribution $f(x)$. There is a trade-off here, though. While it may be easier to generate samples from looser bounding functions for $g(x)$, these samples are more likely to be rejected. On the other hand, functions that more closely follow $f(x)$, and so produce fewer rejections, may be correspondingly more computationally expensive to calculate.

This accept–reject algorithm is summarized as follows.

1. Find a function $g(x)$ and a constant c such that $f(x) \leq cg(x)$ for all values of x where $f(x)$ is defined. Furthermore, $g(x)$ should be chosen so that it is easy to generate samples from this distribution.
2. Generate a sample x from the distribution described by $g(x)$. This x could potentially be returned as a value from the desired distribution $f(x)$.
3. Calculate $Y = cg(x)$. Then generate a second random sample, y, that is uniformly distributed on the interval $[0, Y]$.
4. If $y \leq f(x)$, the randomly selected point (x, y) falls under the distribution $f(x)$. The value x then should be accepted as a sample from the desired distribution $f(x)$. If $y > f(x)$, however, then x should be rejected and the process repeated beginning at step 2.

Example. To generate random values that follow the arbitrary distribution $f(x)$ shown in Figure 10.5, we perform the following steps. First, we must find a function that completely bounds $f(x)$. Owing to the complex shape of $f(x)$, the simplest bounding function is the rectangle shown in the figure. Random points within this box can be easily generated by selecting a random value x that is uniformly distributed on the interval $[0, a]$ and a value y that is uniformly distributed on $[0, b]$. Then, if $y \leq f(x)$, we accept x as a sample from the desired distribution. Otherwise, we reject x and repeat the process, beginning with the generation of new values for x and y.   ◇

10.4   Verification and validation of simulations

The quality of the results obtained from any simulation of a system is fundamentally limited by the quality of the assumptions made in developing the simulation model, and the correctness of the actual implementation. Throughout the
development of the simulator, you should bear in mind how your assumptions
impact the reasonableness of your simulation model. You should also rigorously
follow good programming practices to reduce the number of bugs that creep into
your simulator, and to simplify its implementation.

The *validation* process attempts to ensure that your simulator accurately models the desired system. That is, validation attempts to determine how close the
results of the simulation are to what would be produced by an actual system.
Verification, on the other hand, is the process of determining that your simulator
actually implements the desired model. Verification is not concerned with
whether the model is correct, but, rather, whether the given model is implemented correctly. It is essentially a software-debugging problem, although there are a
few additional things that must be verified beyond simple programming errors.
These include the 'randomness' of any probabilistic distributions that may be
used in the simulation, for instance. The following subsections discuss the validation and verification issues in more detail.

10.4.1   Validation

The goal in validating a simulation model is to determine how accurately it
reflects the actual system being simulated. The types of questions that need to
be addressed in this process include the following.

- Is this a good model?
- Are the assumptions reasonable?
- Are the input distributions a good representation of what would be seen in
  practice?
- Are the output results reasonable?
- Are the results explainable?

While there is no foolproof method for addressing these questions, there are at
least three approaches that can be used to help validate a simulation model.
These are

- comparisons with a real system,
- comparisons with an analytical model, and
- engineering judgement.

10.4.1.1 Comparisons with real systems

In many situations, a simulation model is used to study a system that does not yet exist. This obviously makes it difficult to determine whether the simulation results match the output of the real system! However, it may be possible to at least partially validate a simulation by comparing some of its outputs with those produced by a similar system. Consider a simulation of a processor, for example, in which we wish to study the effect of varying the number of pipeline stages. While an actual system with the identical pipeline configuration most likely does not exist, we may be able to set the simulation parameters to match those of some existing processor. Comparing the simulation results obtained when running a collection of benchmarks with the results obtained on the real processor may help in validating that, at least in that particular configuration, the simulation output closely approximates the output of the real system.

As another example, we might develop a simulator for studying how the size of input/output requests affects the bandwidths that can be obtained for different types of disk-array systems. To partially validate our simulator, we could first measure the disk bandwidth of some existing system. We next set the parameters of our simulator to match those of this existing system, and execute the simulation using the same sequence of requests. Finally, we compare these simulated results with the results from the real system. Although this does not validate that the simulator produces accurate results for all possible parameter configurations, it at least validates the output results for one specific design point.

Measurements of real systems can also be used to estimate the characteristics of certain system inputs. For instance, the size and interarrival time of messages received on a communication network can be measured on an existing system. These measurements then can be used to develop a probabilistic distribution for generating an event trace to drive the simulator. Although these comparisons with real systems are incomplete and imperfect, they are infinitely better than no validation at all.

10.4.1.2 Analytical results

If comparisons with an actual system are impossible or impractical, it may be feasible to develop a simplified analytical model of the system. This simple mathematical model can then be used to validate some specific results from the simulator. Or, the model may be useful in validating overall performance trends. For example, the delay observed when sending a message on some communications network can be approximated with the following equation:

$$t_{\text{send}} = t_{\text{o}} + n/b. \tag{10.16}$$

In this approximation, t_o is the overhead required to initiate the sending of any message, such as the time required to perform the appropriate system call, set up appropriate buffers and pointers, and so forth, n is the number of bits to be sent, b is the bandwidth of the network in bits transmitted per second, and t_{send} is the total time required to send a message of n bits.

Comparing the simulated time required to send a message with the time calculated using this simple model can provide some insights into the validity of the simulation. More importantly, perhaps, the shape of the curve defined by this simple model could be compared against the simulation output as the number of bits sent is varied. Although it is unlikely that the values produced by the simulator will exactly match the values produced by this model, the trends that are observed can be helpful in validating the overall behavior of the simulator. A detailed analytical model can be very complex and time-consuming to develop. Nevertheless, even simple 'back-of-the-envelope' calculations can often provide surprising insights into the validity of a simulation. It is good practice to always develop at least a crude model to help reassure yourself that the simulation output is not unreasonable. Some additional analytical modeling techniques are presented in Chapter 11.

10.4.1.3 Engineering judgement

Finally, you should never underestimate the power of solid engineering judgement in helping validate a simulator. Through years of experience, systems designers and performance analysts can often develop an uncanny ability to determine whether a simulation result 'looks right.' Oftentimes they are not even aware of how they know that a simulation result appears to be suspect. However, they have learned to trust their instincts. If a result just does not appear to 'feel' right, determine why. If you cannot explain why the simulator produces an unusual result in a specific situation, it is difficult to trust any of its results. If you can't explain it, don't believe it.

10.4.2 Verification

The verification process attempts to ensure that the simulator is implemented correctly and that it accurately reflects the chosen model. All simulators require some *deterministic* verification in which all aspects of the simulator that are not dependent on a probabilistic distribution are checked. Stochastic simulators also require some additional checks to verify that the random-number distributions are being generated correctly, for instance. Techniques that have been proven useful for performing both types of verifications are described in the following.

10.4.3 Deterministic verification

The most basic form of deterministic verification is to follow good software-engineering practices. These may include such techniques as an emphasis on structured programming, top-down modular design, detailed code walk-throughs in which the simulator's operation is explained to someone else, and standard internal-error checking, such as checks for accessing arrays out of bounds and common memory leaks. Beyond these basics of good programming, the simulator writer should carefully verify the operation of the simulator by simulating a simple case for which the expected output can be determined by hand. It can also be useful to follow a trace of the simulator's execution to verify that it proceeds through the desired states and transitions as expected.

It can also be quite helpful to build consistency checks into the program's logic. These consistency checks are carefully designed to ensure that different values produced by the simulator are self-consistent. If any discrepancy is found during a simulation, the simulator should abort and report the error. For example, in a simulation of a processor's memory system, the simulator should maintain a count of the total number of memory references generated, the number of references that cause cache hits, and the number of references that cause cache misses. At the end of each simulation run, the simulator should then verify that the sum of the number of hits and misses is equal to the total number of references. Other types of consistency checks are likely to become apparent as the simulator is written and debugged.

Another form of verification that can expose subtle programming errors is to simulate the system for all of the special cases, often called the *corner conditions*. These are the degenerate cases that can cause buffer overflows or underflows and other unexpected conditions. In a simulation of a large multiprocessor computer system, for instance, verify that the simulation works correctly with only a single processor. Or ensure that all memory references produce cache misses if the cache size is set to zero. As another example, verify what happens in a network simulator when the send memory buffer is smaller than the message being sent. Even though it might not seem important to verify many of these cases since they are not likely to happen in a real system, verifying these corner cases often exposes programming errors that do in fact cause the wrong result to be produced by the simulator even in 'normal' situations. These cases often turn out to be the most enlightening ones.

10.4.4 Stochastic verification

Simulations that include components driven by sequences of pseudorandom numbers pose an interesting verification challenge since, by definition, the random components are supposed to be unpredictable. In particular, how do we verify that a sequence of pseudorandom numbers is indeed 'random enough?' We can never say with 100% certainty that a sequence of values is indeed random. Instead, we apply appropriate statistical tests to verify that the random values generated *appear* to be random in a statistical sense. Or, more precisely, that we have no reason to think that they do not appear to be random.

We divide the problem of verifying a random-number stream into two components. First, we use statistical *goodness-of-fit* tests to determine whether the *shape* of the generated sequence is statistically 'close enough' to the expected distribution. We then use extensions of these standard tests, plus some additional tests, to verify that the *order* of the samples occurs in such a way as to make each sample appear to be statistically independent of the other samples. These two components of random-number testing are described further in the following subsections.

10.4.4.1 Goodness-of-fit testing

Goodness-of-fit testing is a general technique used to compare a collection of generated or measured values with an ideal or expected distribution. That is, we wish to determine how close the observed (or measured) values are to the expected values for a given distribution. The goodness-of-fit test quantifies the deviation of the observed values from the expected values. An appropriate statistical test is then performed on this calculated measure of deviation to determine the likelihood that the calculated deviation would occur by chance if the sampled values did in fact come from a distribution of the expected type.

For example, suppose that we have a simulation in which we generate values that appear to be from a binomial distribution with $n = 5$ and $p = 0.2$. (See Appendix B for an explanation of how to generate these values.) This particular distribution is defined by the density function

$$f(x) = \binom{n}{x} p^x (1 - p)^{n-x} \tag{10.17}$$

where $0 < p < 1$, n is a positive integer, and $x = 0, 1, 2, \ldots, n$.

To determine whether the values generated actually appear to follow this desired distribution, we generate 100 samples and count how many of each of the six possible outcomes occur, where $x \in \{0, 1, 2, 3, 4, 5\}$. The results of our measurements are shown as the *observed* values in Table 10.3. Next, we must calculate how many of each of the values we would expect to occur if the distribution were actually binomial. The predicted number of times that $x = 0$ is the outcome is found by evaluating $f(0) = \binom{5}{0}(0.2)^0(1 - 0.2)^5 = 0.328$. Since we have 100 samples in total, we must scale this probability by 100. This gives the predicted number of times $x = 0$ occurs as the outcome to be 32.8. We perform a

Table 10.3. A histogram of the values observed from a generated sequence of pseudorandom values compared with the values that would be expected if the distribution were binomial with $n = 5$ and $p = 0.2$

	Outcome values					
	0	1	2	3	4	5
Observed (O_i)	36	40	18	6	0	0
Predicted (P_i)	32.8	40.9	20.5	5.1	0.7	≈ 0

similar calculation for $f(1), f(2), \ldots, f(5)$ to obtain the *predicted* values for this specific binomial distribution shown in Table 10.3.

We see that the predicted and observed values for each outcome in Table 10.3 are not the same. In fact, since the observed values are supposed to approximate a random sequence, we should not be surprised that they are different. Indeed, we would be quite surprised if they were exactly the same! The question now is, given that we expect some difference between the observed and predicted values, how likely is it that we would see this amount of variation due to normal random fluctuations?

To begin to answer this question, we need some way to quantify the deviation between the predicted and observed values. One obvious idea is to take the maximum difference as our measure of deviation. That is,

$$dev = \max_{\forall i} |O_i - P_i|. \tag{10.18}$$

A problem with this simple absolute deviation, however, is that it overemphasizes histogram cells with large predicted values. For example, if the predicted value for a cell is 1,000 and the observed value is 900, the absolute deviation is 100. If another cell had a predicted value of 15 and an observed value of 10, its absolute difference would be only 5. Thus, we would have 100 as our measure of deviation when using Equation (10.18).

However, the deviation relative to the predicted value is only 10% $((1,000 - 900)/1,000)$ for the first cell, while it is 33.3% $((15 - 10)/15)$ for the second cell. It seems reasonable to expect that this larger relative deviation is more important in comparing the observed and predicted values. Consequently, a better measure of the deviation between the observed and predicted values may be the maximum relative deviation:

$$dev = \max_{\forall i} \frac{|O_i - P_i|}{P_i}. \tag{10.19}$$

The problem with using only the maximum value as the measure of deviation is that we do not take advantage of all of the information available.

A better measure, then, may be to take the sum of the relative differences, giving

$$dev = \sum_{i=1}^{m} \frac{|O_i - P_i|}{P_i},$$
(10.20)

where m is the total number of histogram cells. Although this measure does take into account all of the available information, that is, the deviations in each histogram cell, we have no way of knowing how large this value can become before we decide that it is too large to have occurred strictly by chance fluctuations in the observed values.

Fortunately, we end up being saved by some smart statisticians. The *chi-squared* statistic for a given set of observed values is calculated as

$$\chi^2_{m-1} = \sum_{i=1}^{m} \frac{(O_i - P_i)^2}{P_i}.$$
(10.21)

By relying on the central-limit theorem, our smart statisticians have determined that the statistic χ^2_{m-1} calculated as shown in Equation (10.21) follows a chi-squared distribution with $m-1$ degrees of freedom, where m is the number of histogram cells used in making our observations. Critical values for this distribution have been tabulated in Appendix C.3. These critical values can be used to determine whether the deviations between the observed and the predicted values are likely to have been caused by chance fluctuations. If not, then we must conclude that it is unlikely that the observed values follow the expected distribution.

One word of caution is appropriate here. Since knowing the distribution of the chi-squared statistic χ^2_{m-1} relies on the central-limit theorem, it is necessary for each histogram to have a 'large enough' number of predicted values. In practice, it is usually adequate to ensure that $P_i > 5$ or 6. If this requirement is not satisfied for the given histogram, adjacent cells must be combined until the predicted value for the combined cell is large enough to satisfy this normalization assumption.

Example. For the observed and predicted values in Table 10.3, we see that outcomes 4 and 5 occur too infrequently to satisfy the chi-squared approximation. Consequently, we add together outcomes 3, 4, and 5 to produce a single cell with a predicted value of 5.8 and an observed value of 6. The corresponding chi-squared statistic for these values is found to be

$$\chi^2_{4-1} = \frac{(36 - 32.8)^2}{32.8} + \ldots + \frac{(6 - 5.8)^2}{5.8} = 0.6438.$$
(10.22)

The critical values in the table in Appendix C.3 show the probability that the tabulated value of the chi-squared statistic will occur due to random fluctuations, with the given number of degrees of freedom. In our current situation, we have $m - 1 = 3$ degrees of freedom. From the table, we find that there is a 95% chance that the chi-squared statistic will be as large as 7.815 with this many degrees of freedom. Since our calculated statistic, $\chi_3^2 = 0.6438$, is smaller than this critical value, we conclude with 95% confidence that there is no reason to suspect that the observed values do not come from the expected distribution.

Note that we cannot say that the observed values actually do come from the expected distribution. The best we can say is that there is no evidence to lead us to believe otherwise.   ◇

This example concerned a histogram that corresponded to the natural structure of the distribution being tested. That is, each cell corresponded to a single outcome value, except for the last cell which was aggregated to make the predicted number of outcomes in that cell large enough for the chi-squared approximation to hold. However, each term in Equation (10.21) is normalized with respect to the predicted value P_i. Thus, cells with small values of P_i will tend to have a greater influence on the value of the calculated statistic than will cells with comparatively larger values of P_i. To reduce this bias, it is best to combine adjacent cells in the histogram to make the P_i values for each cell approximately the same. This aggregating of values potentially decreases the information available, but it tends to make the chi-squared test work better in practice.

There are other types of goodness-of-fit tests that are appropriate for specific situations. The Kolmogorov–Smirnov test, for example, is specifically designed to compare a small number observations with an expected continuous distribution. This is in contrast to the chi-squared test, which assumes a discrete distribution with a large number of samples. It is possible to 'discretize' a continuous distribution and still apply a chi-squared test to obtain an approximate result, though. Consequently, for most of the applications you are likely to encounter, the chi-squared test is usually adequate.

10.4.4.2 Tests of independence

The fact that a sequence of values passes a goodness-of-fit test is no guarantee that the sequence is actually random. For example, the sequence $(0, 1, 2, 3, \ldots, 19, 0, 1, 2, 3, \ldots, 19, \ldots)$ will appear to follow a perfect $unif(0, 19)$ distribution with any goodness-of-fit test. However, it is obviously not a random sequence at all. A goodness-of-fit test quantifies whether the number of unique values in the sequence, that is, the histogram of all of the samples that occurred, is not too far away from the expected number for each. It says nothing about the *order* in which those values occurred, though. Determining whether the order of the values appears to be appropriately random is the goal of an *independence* test.

Typically, we apply an independence test only to the sequence of *unif*(0, 1) samples that we use as the inputs to the other functions that actually produce the values following the desired distributions. *Theoretical tests* analyze the properties of the specific algorithm used to generate the *unif*(0, 1) samples to verify that its mathematical properties will ensure the generation of apparently independent sample sequences. For example, theoretical tests of the LCG described in Section 10.3.1 ensure that this type of generator will produce independent samples. These theoretical tests do not ensure that the algorithm is actually implemented correctly, however. For this type of verification, we must rely on a statistical test of the actual values produced.

The *serial test* attempts to verify the uniformity of a sequence of *unif*(0, 1) values in k dimensions. The basic idea in two dimensions is to plot points in a two-dimensional plane using nonoverlapping pairs of values from the generated sequence as the (x, y) coordinates of the points. After these points have been plotted on the plane, the uniformity of the resulting distribution is tested. For example, given the sequence $(z_1, z_2, z_3, \ldots)$, the coordinates of successive points are $(z_1, z_2), (z_3, z_4), (z_5, z_6), \ldots$.

The first step in verifying uniformity is a simple visual inspection. Do the points appear to be uniformly distributed when they are plotted? If the values in the sequence are not independent, the points will tend to form lines, or they will cluster into groups. Next, the plane can be divided into a grid of $a \times a$ cells, as shown in Figure 10.6. If the distribution were completely uniform, each cell would be expected to contain $n/(2a^2)$ points, where n is the total of points plotted. A chi-squared test with $a^2 - 1$ degrees of freedom can be used to gauge the uniformity of the distribution more precisely than by a simple visual test.

The serial test can be extended to k dimensions by using k successive values from the sequence to form the nonoverlapping k-tuple representing the coordinates for each point. If the values at these higher dimensions are not independent, planes and hyperplanes will tend to appear. Again, a chi-squared test with an appropriate number of degrees of freedom can be used to check the uniformity of the resulting distribution of points in the k-dimensional space.

Other tests for independence include the *serial-correlation* test, which uses the autocovariance function, the *spectral* test, which measures the maximum distance between hyperplanes using either overlapping or nonoverlapping k-tuples, and the *runs-up* test, which measures the lengths of subsequences that are monotonically increasing. All of these various tests measure a necessary condition for independence. That is, if the sequence of values exhibits statistical independence, these tests will produce a 'true' answer. However, the converse is not necessarily true. A test that produces the result expected for independence is not sufficient to prove independence.

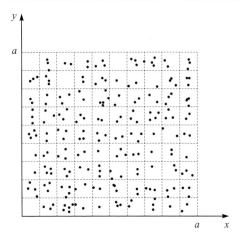

Figure 10.6 In the serial test for independence, the uniformly distributed random values $(z_1, z_2, z_3, \ldots)$ are paired to form the coordinates of points, $(z_1, z_2), (z_3, z_4), (z_5, z_6), \ldots$, to be plotted on the (x, y) plane. If the values in the sequence are not independent, the points will tend to form lines or clusters on the plane. After a visual inspection to determine whether the points appear to be uniformly distributed across the plane, a chi-squared test can be applied to the area $a \times a$.

The goal of this discussion is not to make you an expert in testing the independence properties of random-number generators. Instead, it is to expose you to the basic ideas of this testing so that you know what problems may arise. Since independence tests are verifying the quality of the $unif(0, 1)$ random generator that underlies all of your random-number generation tasks, you are best off following the advice from Section 10.3.1. That is, your best option is to use a $unif(0, 1)$ generator that has been demonstrated to be robust and reliable by experts in the field and through extensive use by others. Testing for independence is a subtle task that is best left to someone who really knows what they are doing.

10.5   Summary

Simulation is a commonly used tool for estimating the performance of computer systems. Simulations are particularly useful for predicting the performance of computer systems that do not yet exist, for instance. They are also commonly used to investigate some aspect of a system's performance that would be difficult or impossible to measure directly. An emulation is a simulation program that is intended to make some existing system appear to a user to be something else. Monte Carlo simulations are typically used to evaluate probabilistic systems and to model physical phenomena. Simulations of computer systems and their various constituent components, on the other hand, typically use a discrete-event approach. These discrete-event simulations can be driven by previously collected traces, by the direct execution of a test program, or by a sequence of random numbers that have been generated to follow a desired distribution.

Generating these sequences of random numbers is a two-step process. First, a *pseudorandom-number generator*, such as the linear-congruential generator, is used to generate a sequence of values that appears, in a statistical sense, to be uniformly distributed on the interval [0, 1). Then one of several different techniques can be used to transform this uniformly distributed sequence into a sequence that follows any desired distribution.

Finally, no simulation result should be taken at face value. You should not carelessly believe that the output of any simulator is correct without first validating the simulated result against the result produced by some other means. In the best case, this validation compares the simulation outputs with the results measured on an actual system. Since this is often not feasible, or in many cases even possible, however, you should instead (or in addition) try to validate a few critical design points or overall trends using some sort of analytical model. Verifying the statistical properties of any random-number sequences that are generated for the simulation is an important component of this verification and validation process. Regardless of how a simulation is validated, you should always maintain a healthy skepticism towards the results it produces and you should always be sure to critically apply your engineering judgement and good old common sense.

10.6 For further reading

- Chapter 7 of the following text provides some ready-to-run programs written in the C programming language for generating a variety of random numbers. It also provides an extensive discussion and several examples of Monte Carlo simulation used for numerical integration.

  William H. Press, Saul A. Teukolsky, William T. Vetterling, and Brian P. Flannery, *Numerical Recipes in C* (Second Edition), Cambridge University Press, New York, 1992.

  Additional discussions of random number generation can be found in the following:

  Donald E. Knuth, *The Art of Computer Programming, Volume 2: Seminumerical Algorithms* (Second Edition), Addison-Wesley, Reading, MA, 1981,

S. K. Park and K. W. Miller, 'Random Number Generators: Good Ones Are Hard to Find,' *Communications of the ACM*, Vol. 31, No. 10, October 1988, pp. 1192–1201.

George Marsaglia, 'Technical Correspondence: Remarks on Choosing and Implementing Random Number Generators,' *Communications of the ACM*, Vol. 36, No. 7, July 1993, pp. 105–110, and

L. Devroye, *Non-Uniform Random Variate Generation*, Springer-Verlag, New York, 1986.

- This text discusses techniques for generating random numbers that can be implemented directly in hardware:
  Christian Ronse, *Feedback Shift Registers*, Springer-Verlag, New York, 1984.
- Some good texts on general simulation topics include:
  P. Bratley, B. L. Fox, and E. L. Schrage, *A Guide to Simulation*, Springer-Verlag, New York, 1983, and

  A. M. Law and W. D. Kelton, *Simulation Modeling and Analysis*, McGraw-Hill, New York, 1982.
- This text describes the popular DLX processor simulator:
  Philip M. Sailer and David R. Kaeli, *The DLX Instruction Set Architecture Handbook*, Morgan Kaufmann Publishers, San Mateo, CA, 1996.
- Finally, there are numerous simulators available on the Web. A little judicious searching can uncover a wealth of information about various types of simulators and simulation software packages.

10.7   Exercises

1. A simulation experiment may be considered a 'failure' because a bug in the program causes it to produce incorrect results. What are other ways in which a simulation may fail? (For instance, consider the analysis of the results, the time required to complete a simulation, and so forth.)
2. Why is a more detailed simulation not always better than one with less detail?
3. What are the key differences among emulation, Monte Carlo simulation, and discrete-event simulation?
4. What are the key differences between stochastic and deterministic simulations?
5. Use a Monte Carlo simulation to calculate the integral $\int_0^1 (1-x)/(1+x)\,dx$.
6. One technique that can be used to help verify the correctness of a simulator is to perform consistency checks whenever possible. For instance, a memory simulator could verify that the number of cache misses plus the number of

hits is always equal to the total number of memory references. What other consistency checks could be performed?

7. What types of system-level checks can be performed to verify a simulator? (For example, compare the results of a simulation with the results obtained on an equivalent real system.)

8. How many results are required when using a probabilistic simulation? *Hint*: think about the number of data samples required to produce a confidence interval.

9. If a trace-driven simulation always produces the same result for a given input trace, how general are the conclusions that can be drawn from the simulation? How can this be improved?

10. A trace-driven simulation terminates when the end of the trace input is encountered. Similarly, an execution-driven simulation terminates when the benchmark program it is executing terminates. What causes a probabilistic simulation to terminate? How long must a probabilistic simulation be run to ensure a valid result?

11. One criticism of trace-driven simulation is that any trace of manageable size represents only a very small interval of actual run-time. What techniques could be used to allow the simulation of longer representative run-times using traces?

12. If a LCG with a period of $m = 2^n$ is used to generate a sequence that is *unif*(0, 1), what is the largest value that could appear in this sequence? What is the smallest value? What is the smallest interval between successive values?

13. Can the same value ever appear more than once within the period of a LCG?

14. What do your answers to the previous two questions imply about the randomness of sequences produced with a LCG?

15. What are the similarities and differences between complexity and randomness?

16. What are the problems with using a random seed in a random-number generator?

17. What is the difference between 'statistical' randomness and 'perfect' randomness? Are they mutually exclusive?

18. It is important to test the randomness of any random-number generator before using it, but are these tests sufficient to ensure randomness?

19. What is the difference between a theoretical test of randomness and an empirical test? Which is stronger?

20. Why does a higher confidence level allow a larger error statistic in a goodness-of-fit test? This seems counter-intuitive.

21. Several different techniques can be used to generate numbers that appear to come from a normal (Gaussian) distribution. Compare the two techniques described in Appendix B for generating a normal distribution with a mean of

100 and a standard deviation of 45. Measure the average execution time per sample for each method (be sure to include an appropriate confidence interval) and use the chi-squared test to determine whether both methods generate samples that appear to actually come from the desired distribution.

22. Test the uniformity of the random-number generator available on your system using the chi-squared test with $c = 10$ and 100 equal-width cells.

23. Test the independence of the random-number generator available on your system using a two-dimensional version of the serial test.

11 Queueing analysis

'It is very difficult to make an accurate prediction, especially about the future.'

Niels Bohr

At the beginning of our study of computer-systems performance analysis, it was pointed out that there are three fundamental techniques that can be used to find the desired solution to a performance-analysis problem. We have so far examined *measurement* and *simulation* techniques. The third and final fundamental solution technique is *analytical modeling*.

In the memory-performance example in Section 1.3, we developed a very simple analytical model to estimate the memory delay observed by an application program. This equation required only a few pieces of information, specifically, the times required to service a cache hit and a cache miss, and the miss ratio of the application program. Even though this analytical model was a tremendous over-simplification of the performance of a complex memory hierarchy, it can help us develop some insight into the performance trade-offs that are made in a memory subsystem. In this chapter, we extend our view of analytical modeling to provide greater insights into the performance of a computer system than are possible when using only this simple type of intuitive model.

Queueing analysis is an important analytical modeling technique for computer systems. There is a very large body of literature on this topic, and hundreds of new research papers and books are being published every year. This chapter will only scratch the surface of queueing analysis by focusing on a few of the fundamental results that form the basis of the more complex analytical modeling techniques. Fortunately, these fundamental results are often sufficient for answering many of the basic questions you are likely to have about a computer system. The goal is to provide you with some simple analytical tools allowing quick estimates of a system's behavior. These models can be used to compare against the results of a simulation or a measurement experiment to help validate the results, for example. Analysis of more complex systems, taking into account the interactions of networks of queues, has been an area of intensive research for many years. See some of the references cited in the 'further reading' section at the end of this chapter for more information on these advanced techniques.

11.1   Queueing-network models

The basic notion behind queueing analysis is to think of all the *jobs* that must be executed in a computer system as *customers* to be serviced by the system's individual subsystems, such as the memory, the processor, the input/output devices, and so forth. Each of these resources, often called *service centers*, or simply *servers*, can process only one job at a time. Other jobs wanting to use a busy resource must wait in a *queue* until the current job has been serviced completely. The various servers and queues are interconnected with a series of arcs showing how jobs can flow between the servers in the system.

There are two different types of these *queueing-network models*. In an *open* network model, such as that shown in Figure 11.1, jobs arrive in the system from some external source. In Figure 11.1, requests enter the system from the left and are first processed by the CPU. This processing may initiate one or more disk accesses, which would cause requests to flow from the CPU to the appropriate disk servers. After processing the requests, the disk subsystems will respond back to the CPU by sending a job across the arc connecting the disks to the CPU. The CPU may generate additional disk requests based on these responses, or it may complete its processing of the job by routing it to the exit arc.

While all of the jobs that enter this open system will eventually depart, an unbounded number of jobs could be in the system at any given time. A *closed-network* model, in contrast, has a fixed number of jobs that circulate among the various queues and servers in the system. For example, in the previous open-network example shown in Figure 11.1, the requests coming into the system are

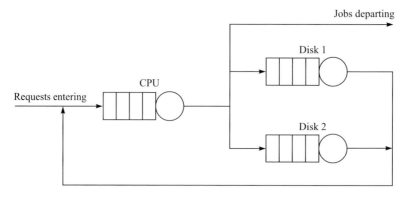

Figure 11.1 An open-queueing-network model of a simple Web server.

most likely generated by some users working at remotely connected terminals. After a user makes a request, he or she most likely will make no more requests until the first request completes. Then, after some period of 'thinking' time, the user may make another request. Thus, when a command is issued by a user, a job moves into the CPU. When it finally finishes its processing within the CPU and the disks, it completes by returning to the user's terminal. This type of situation is more accurately modeled as a *closed*-network model in which the total number of jobs in the system is constant. Figure 11.2 adds a network-interface node to convert the model of Figure 11.1 into a closed system.

Open-queueing models assume that an essentially unlimited number of jobs are continuously flowing into and out of the system. However, real systems have hard physical-resource limitations. For instance, queues in a real system would have to be constructed out of some sort of physical memory device that would buffer the pending requests. Since a system cannot have an infinite amount of memory, the number of jobs that could queue up at a particular server will be limited by these physical constraints. Thus, closed-queueing models are often assumed to more accurately model real systems than do open models. Unfortunately, obtaining mathematical solutions for closed models is typically much more difficult than obtaining solutions for open models.

The remainder of this chapter focuses on solutions for open models of single-queue systems. This type of single-queue system could be a component or sub-system within a larger computer system, such as a disk drive or network inter-face, for instance. It also could be used to model the overall system itself. In that case, we ignore the internal details of the system's operation, and instead focus on its overall behavior as observed through its inputs and output responses.

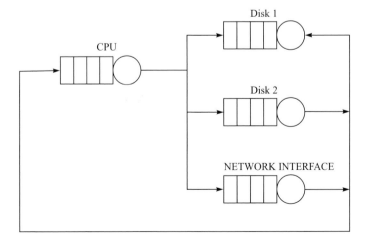

Figure 11.2 A network-interface node is added to the queueing-network model of Figure 11.1 to make it a closed-queueing-network model.

It is important to bear in mind that these open-single-queue models only approximate the characteristics of a real system. Consequently, the solutions we obtain are necessarily only approximations of the behavior we would expect to see in a real system. This analysis describes the average, or steady-state, behavior of a system and cannot be used to analyze the behavior of an individual job.

11.2   Basic assumptions and notation

Before we move any deeper into this queueing analysis, it is helpful to describe the assumptions we make about the queueing system in order to apply this type of analysis. It is also helpful to define all of the notation that will be used. The basic assumptions are summarized below.

- **Job-flow balance.** The number of jobs arriving at a server within a sufficiently large observation interval must be equal to the number of jobs that depart from the server. That is, no jobs are lost within the server or its queue. Furthermore, the server cannot spontaneously generate new jobs. Notice that this job-flow balance does not hold over shorter intervals since jobs must wait in the queue while the server is busy. However, over the long term, the number of jobs going into a server must match the number of jobs that complete service.

- **One-step behavior.** At any instant of time, only a single job can enter or leave a server so that the system's state changes only incrementally. This assumption specifically disallows jobs from moving simultaneously between servers within the system. It also disallows the coupling of arrivals and departures of jobs.

- **Homogeneity.** Homogeneity means that the average job-arrival rate and the average service rate are independent of the system's state. Furthermore, the probability of moving between two servers is independent of the numbers of jobs both at the source and at the destination servers.

- **Exclusivity.** A job can be present in only a single server, either waiting in the queue or receiving service. Thus, a single job cannot make a request of two servers simultaneously. Similarly, when a job is receiving service, it has exclusive use of the server so that all other jobs wanting to use the server must wait in its queue.

- **Non-blocking.** The service provided by a server cannot be controlled by any other device in the system. When a job appears at the head of a queue, the server must begin serving it immediately.

- **Independence.** Jobs are not allowed to interact in any way, except for sharing space in a queue. Specifically, jobs are not allowed to synchronize.

The following notation will be used throughout the remaining discussion of the analysis of these single-queue models.

- s is the average time required to service a job.
- $\mu = 1/s$ is the average service rate measured in jobs completed per unit time.
- λ is the average arrival rate; that is, the total number of jobs that arrive in time T divided by T.
- $\rho = \lambda/\mu$ is the *traffic intensity*.
- r is the average response time. This is the average time a job spends in the system, including both the time spent waiting in the queue and the time being serviced.
- w is the average time a job spends waiting in the queue.
- q is the average number of jobs in the queue.
- n is the number of jobs in the system, including both those in the queue and those being serviced.
- U is the utilization of the system, which is the average fraction of the total time that it is busy.
- a is the number of arrivals that occur within the fixed observation interval T.
- d is the number of departures that occur in the fixed observation interval T.

Given these basic assumptions and this notation, we now develop several laws relating the various system parameters and arrivals of jobs. We first look at a general technique called *operational analysis*. The following section then focuses on *stochastic analysis*.

11.3   Operational analysis

Operational analysis views the system being studied as a black box in which jobs arrive at one end, are processed for some period of time, and then depart at the other end. This view, which is summarized in Figure 11.3, allows us to analyze a queueing model while making no assumptions about the distribution of the times between arrivals of jobs and the times required to service these jobs. Instead, we directly measure the operational characteristics of the system being studied. We can then apply some simple laws to determine the system's overall, or average, behavior.

11.3.1   The utilization law

Suppose that we observe the system for a fixed period of time, T, while recording the number of jobs that arrive at the system and how long it takes to service each

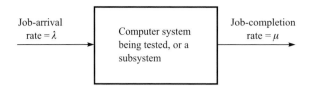

Figure 11.3 Operational analysis views the system being studied as a black box in which jobs enter the system from the left, are processed for some period of time, and finally depart from the system on the right.

job. Then the average *arrival rate* of jobs is simply the total number of arrivals, a, divided by T. This mean arrival rate is denoted λ so that

$$\lambda = \frac{a}{T}. \tag{11.1}$$

Since λ is the reciprocal of the mean time between jobs, it is measured in units of jobs arriving per time. A typical value of λ may be 240 requests per second, for instance. The mean job-completion rate, also called the mean *service rate*, is denoted μ. It is simply the reciprocal of the average time required to service a job, and so is measured in units of the number of jobs completed per time.

The average *utilization* of the system is the fraction of the total time that it is busy servicing jobs. If we observe the system for a time interval T and find that it is busy for b time units during that interval, the average utilization of the device is

$$U = \frac{b}{T}. \tag{11.2}$$

We can factor this ratio into two components to give

$$U = \frac{b}{T} = \frac{b}{d} \times \frac{d}{T} \tag{11.3}$$

where d is the number of departures from the system during the interval. That is, d is the number of jobs that are serviced by this device in the interval T.

Notice that the ratio b/d is the average amount of time the device is busy servicing each of the d jobs. This is simply the definition of the average service time per job, $s = b/d$. Furthermore, d/T is the average rate at which jobs depart from this device. If the device is job-flow balanced, the number of departures in the interval T must be equal to the number of arrivals in the same interval. Therefore, the average rate of arrival at the device must equal the average rate of departure, so $\lambda = d/T$. On substituting these expressions for s and λ into Equation (11.3), we find that the average utilization of a device, defined as the average fraction of the total time that the device is busy, is the product of its average arrival rate and its average service time:

$$U = \lambda s. \tag{11.4}$$

This simple result is called the *utilization law*.

Example. Consider an input/output subsystem that consists of a single disk and the associated controller hardware and software. If the average time required to service each request to this disk subsystem is 600 µs, what is the maximum possible request rate it can tolerate?

The maximum capacity of the disk subsystem occurs when it is at 100% utilization, or $U = 1$. Since $U = \lambda s$, we find that the maximum request rate is $\lambda_{max} = U/s = 1/(600 \times 10^{-6}) = 1{,}667$ requests per second. ◇

Traffic intensity. Since the average service rate is related to the average service time by $\mu = 1/s$, Equation (11.4) for the utilization can also be written as

$$U = \frac{\lambda}{\mu}. \tag{11.5}$$

The ratio λ/μ is called the *traffic intensity*. Owing to its importance in queueing systems, it is given its own symbol, $\rho = \lambda/\mu$.

A value of $\rho > 1$ implies that $\lambda > \mu$. Thus, the arrival rate of jobs is greater than the rate at which jobs are being serviced. Intuitively, this situation means that jobs are arriving at the system faster than they can be processed. As a result, the number of the jobs in the queue will increase without bound, which will lead to infinite waiting times. Obviously, then, to maintain a stable system, the average arrival rate must be less than the service rate. That is, on the average, jobs must be serviced more quickly than they arrive at the system. Thus, in a stable system, we must have $\rho < 1$. Stated more simply, the utilization of any device can never exceed 100%.

11.3.2 Little's law

If we observe the black-box system shown in Figure 11.3 for some long time period T, we will see a jobs arrive. If the total amount of delay experienced by all of the jobs is D, then the average time each job waits in the queue, w, is

$$w = \frac{D}{a}. \tag{11.6}$$

Also, the average arrival rate is $\lambda = a/T$. On substituting this into Equation (11.6) and rearranging, we then have

$$D = w\lambda T. \tag{11.7}$$

We can also find another expression for the total delay experienced by the jobs by observing that the jobs are waiting only while they are in the queue. Therefore, the total amount of delay experienced by all of the jobs is the average number of jobs queued multiplied by the total observation time. If there are on average q jobs waiting in the queue during the observation period T, we have

$$D = qT. \tag{11.8}$$

By equating Equations (11.7) and (11.8), we obtain

$$qT = w\lambda T. \tag{11.9}$$

The observation interval, T, drops out of this equation to give

$$q = \lambda w. \tag{11.10}$$

This expression, which is known as *Little's law*, says that the average number of jobs that will be seen in the system's queue is the product of the average time spent waiting in the queue and the average arrival rate.

Little's law is actually very general and can be applied to any system, or to any component within the system, for which the job-flow-balance criterion is satisfied. To use Little's law, you can think about drawing a box around any portion of the system, or around the system as a whole, as shown in Figure 11.4. Little's law then can be applied to the portion of the system surrounded by the box if the number of jobs that enter the box is equal to the number of jobs that depart from the box. Thus, by drawing the appropriate box, Little's law can be formulated in several different ways. Here are some examples.

- The derivation of Little's law above implicitly drew a box around the queue at the input to the server. The inputs to the box are the arriving jobs that are placed in the queue. The outputs from the box are the jobs that leave the queue to enter the server. Little's law then says that the average number of

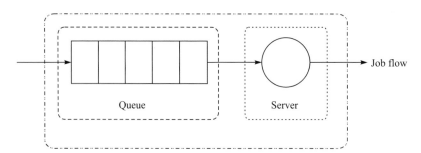

Figure 11.4 Little's law can be applied to any system, or any portion of the system, by drawing a conceptual box around the portion of the system of interest. The only requirement is that the number of jobs that enter the box must equal the number of jobs that depart from the box. Drawing the box around the queue itself leads to the relation $q = \lambda w$, whereas drawing the box around the entire system produces $n = \lambda r$. Analyzing the server in isolation leads to another derivation of the utilization law, $U = \lambda s$.

jobs in the queue equals the average arrival rate times the average time jobs spend waiting in the queue; that is, $q = \lambda w$.

- If we draw the box around the entire system to include both the queue and the server, we have the black-box view of the system shown previously in Figure 11.3. We then find that the average number of jobs in the system equals the average arrival rate times the average response time of the system; that is, $n = \lambda r$.

- Finally, if we draw the box around only the server itself, excluding the queue, we have that the average number of jobs being serviced equals the average arrival rate times the average service time. Recall that the assumption of exclusivity means that the server can service only a single job at a time. Consequently, the average number of jobs being serviced is the same as the utilization of the server. Little's law then provides another way to derive the utilization law, $U = \lambda s$.

Example. The average response time of a Web server is measured to be 11 ms when the request rate is 450 requests per second. What is the average number of requests that are buffered in the system?

From the system-level formulation of Little's law, we have $n = \lambda r$ with $\lambda = 450$ requests per second and $r = 11 \times 10^{-3}$ s. Thus, there are $n = 450 \times (11 \times 10^{-3})$ $= 4.95$ requests in the system. $\Diamond$

It is important to point out that this value of n is only an average value. The peak number of requests that must be buffered in the server could be substantially higher. Consequently, this average value cannot be used to determine how much memory space must be allocated in the server to queue incoming requests. Determining this value requires more information (or assumptions) about the characteristics of the incoming requests. This is exactly where the stochastic analysis presented in the following section becomes useful.

11.4   Stochastic analysis

Examining the behavior of a system with operational analysis requires no assumptions about the distribution of the times between arriving jobs and the distribution of times required to service jobs at each resource. The Utilization law and Little's law provide a high-level view of the flow of jobs through a system by abstracting away the low-level details of what goes on within the system. If we assume that the times between the arrivals of new jobs, and the times required to service these jobs, follow certain probabilistic (stochastic) distributions, however, we can often provide more detailed answers than is possible using only operational analysis.

The fundamental stochastic queueing model consists of one or more servers processing jobs taken from a single queue, as shown in Figure 11.5. In this model, the time between successive jobs arriving at the queue for service (the *interarrival time*) is a stochastic (random) process described by some appropriate probability distribution function. Similarly, the time required to service each job is also modeled as a stochastic process. Jobs enter the system at times determined by the *arrival process*. If a server is available, the job can be serviced immediately. Otherwise, it must wait in the queue until one of the jobs currently being serviced completes. The time required to service each job also follows some assumed stochastic distribution.

Given this basic model, the queueing analysis described in the subsequent sections allows us to determine such important performance parameters as the average time a job spends in the queue, the average number of jobs in the queue, the probability of having a given number of jobs in the queue, and the average response time.

11.4.1 Kendall's notation

The basic stochastic queueing model can be completely specified using six parameters. *Kendall's notation* is a shorthand method for specifying these six parameters in the form $A/S/c/B/N/D$.

- The A term in this notation specifies the *arrival process*. This stochastic process describes *when* jobs arrive at the queue. What is actually more useful, though, is knowing the times *between* arrivals of jobs. Thus, if jobs arrive at times $T_0, T_1, \ldots, T_i, \ldots,$ the times $t_1 = T_1 - T_0, t_2 = T_2 - T_1, \ldots, t_i = T_i - T_{i-1}, \ldots$ are called the *interarrival times*. It is typically assumed that

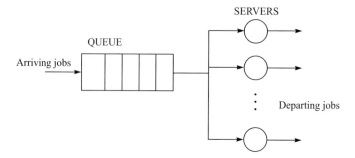

SERVERS

QUEUE

Arriving jobs

Departing jobs

Figure 11.5 A single-queue model of a system consists of one or more servers that process jobs entering the system. A single queue temporarily stores (buffers) jobs that must wait to be processed while jobs that arrived earlier are being processed.

these interarrival times follow a specified probabilistic distribution function. The most common arrival process used in queueing analysis is the Poisson process. A Poisson process is one in which the interarrival times appear to follow an exponential distribution. As discussed in Appendix B.7, the exponential distribution has some nice mathematical properties, specifically the property of *memorylessness*. This property allows extensive analysis of a single-queue system. Fortunately, many real arrival processes in computer systems also seem to be reasonably well described by a Poisson arrival process. An exponential distribution is denoted by M in Kendall's notation to emphasize the property of memorylessness. Other distributions sometimes used to describe an arrival process include the Erlang distribution (denoted by E in Kendall's notation), the hyperexponential distribution (denoted by H), a deterministic distribution (denoted by D), and a general random distribution (denoted by G).

- The S term in this notation specifies the distribution of times required to service a job when it leaves the queue and enters one of the servers. The notation for the service-time distribution follows the same form as that of the interarrival time distributions, with a Poisson service process again being the most commonly used distribution.

- The number of servers in the system is specified by the value c. All of the subsequent analysis of this queueing system assumes that all c servers are identical so that each has the same distribution of service times. A system in which all the servers are not identical must be broken up into separate queueing systems before it can be analyzed using these techniques.

- The total number of jobs that can be in the system, including both those in the queue and those being served, is specified by the parameter B. Most real systems have finite maximum queue sizes due to their having limited amounts of buffer memory. However, a single-queue system is easier to analyze if the queue size is assumed to be infinite. Consequently, if the buffers that comprise the queue in a system are sufficiently large, it is common to assume that the total system capacity is approximately infinite.

- The parameter N specifies the total number of jobs that could ever enter the system. Just like with the system-capacity parameter, B, the analysis is greatly simplified if this parameter is assumed to be infinite.

- The final parameter, D, specifies the order in which jobs are removed from the queue and passed to a server. This is referred to as the *service discipline*. The most common service order is first come, first served (FCFS). Many other service orders are possible, however, including last come, first served (LCFS), and a variety of orders that allow preemption of a job being serviced, such as round robin (RR).

For analyzing most single-queue systems, both the queue size and the population are assumed to be infinite, and the service discipline is assumed to be FCFS,
unless they are explicitly specified to be some other value. Thus, it is common to
not even write the last three parameters when describing a queueing system in
Kendall's notation. The notation M/M/c, for instance, specifies a single-queue
model with exponential interarrival times of jobs, exponential service times, and
c servers. Because it can be thoroughly analyzed mathematically, this type of
queue is probably the most common type used in performance analysis. It also
forms the basis for more complex analyses. Consequently, we now examine this
single-queue system beginning with the single-server M/M/1 case.

11.4.2 The single-queue, single-server (M/M/1) system

We begin our analysis of a single-queue system by assuming that all jobs arrive at
the queue one at a time. This assumption specifically says that groups of jobs
cannot arrive as a single batch all at the same time. With this assumption, we can
describe the state of the entire system using a single integer n, which is the total
number of jobs in the system. Note that n includes both jobs in the queue and
jobs being serviced.

The arrival of a new job into the system is called a *birth*. This arrival causes the
system to transition from state n to state $n + 1$. Similarly, when a server completes a job, the system transitions from state n to state $n - 1$. The completion of
a job is known as a *death*. This type of queueing process, which is called a *birth–
death* process, can be represented by the state-transition diagram shown in
Figure 11.6.

One of the basic assumptions in this analysis is that the next state depends only
on the current state. That is, the next state is independent of the sequence of
states through which the system passed to arrive at the current state. The next
state also is independent of how long the system has been in the current state.
This assumption is valid only if the interarrival and service times follow an

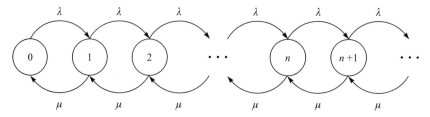

Figure 11.6 The state of a system described by a *birth–death* process is the number of jobs
in the system, n. A *birth* occurs when a job enters the system and increases n by 1. The
departure of a job from the system is called a *death*, and causes n to decrease by 1.

exponential distribution and so are memoryless. Finally, only a single birth or death can occur at any instant of time. Thus, the system can transition only between adjacent states. A discrete-state process that follows these assumptions is called a *Markov chain*.

In the steady state, the average rate at which the system enters state n must be equal to the average rate at which the system moves out of state n. Another way to think of this requirement for steady-state behavior is that the average *flow* across the vertical line drawn between states $n-1$ and n in Figure 11.7 must be the same in both directions. That is, the rate at which the system's state flows to the right across the line must be equal to the rate at which it flows back to the left of the line. If this were not true, then the number of jobs in the system would grow without bound. This steady-state behavior is often referred to as the *conservation of flow*.

We can now write *balance equations*, which are also called *flow equations*, directly from this state-transition diagram to describe this steady state-behavior. The flow across the line to the right is the probability of being in state $n-1$ times the rate at which the system transitions from state $n-1$ to state n. As shown, this rate of flow to the right is simply the average arrival rate, λ. Thus, the flow from state $n-1$ to state n is λP_{n-1}, where P_{n-1} is the probability of being in state $n-1$. Similarly, the flow across the line to the left is the probability of being in state n times the average service rate, μ, which gives μP_n. Since in the steady state these two flows must be equal, we have

$$\lambda P_{n-1} = \mu P_n. \tag{11.11}$$

By rearranging this balance equation we obtain the recurrence equation

$$P_n = \frac{\lambda}{\mu} P_{n-1} = \rho P_{n-1}. \tag{11.12}$$

Recall that $\rho = \lambda/\mu$ is the traffic intensity. From this recurrence equation, we have $P_1 = \rho P_0$, $P_2 = \rho P_1 = \rho^2 P_0$, $P_3 = \rho P_2 = \rho^3 P_0, \ldots$. In general, we obtain

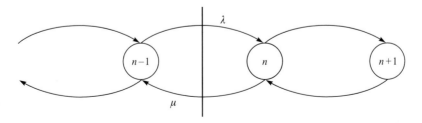

Figure 11.7 When a birth–death process is in a steady state, the average number of births will equal the average number of deaths. Thus, the average flow from state $n-1$ to state n across the vertical line must equal the average flow from state n to state $n-1$.

the following expression for P_n, the probability of having exactly n jobs in the system:

$$P_n = \rho^n P_0.$$ (11.13)

We now wish to find a closed-form expression for P_n. We begin by noticing that the sum of all of these probabilities must be 1. That is,

$$\sum_{n=0}^{\infty} P_n = \sum_{n=0}^{\infty} \rho^n P_0 = 1.$$ (11.14)

Expanding this equation, we have

$$\rho^0 P_0 + \rho^1 P_0 + \rho^2 P_0 + \ldots = 1$$ (11.15)

which can be solved for P_0 to give

$$P_0 = \frac{1}{\rho^0 + \rho^1 + \rho^2 + \cdots + \rho^{\infty}} = \sum_{n=0}^{\infty} \frac{1}{\rho^n}.$$ (11.16)

With $\rho < 1$, it can be shown that this infinite sum converges to the value $1 - \rho$. Thus, on substituting this value for P_0 into Equation (11.13), we find that the probability of having n jobs in the system is

$$P_n = (1 - \rho)\rho^n, n = 0, 1, 2, \ldots.$$ (11.17)

Given this expression for P_n, we can now derive many other performance parameters for M/M/1 queueing systems. For example, the average number of jobs in the system is found by computing the expected value of n. From the definition of the expected value, we have

$$E[n] = \sum_{n=0}^{\infty} nP_n = \sum_{n=0}^{\infty} n(1 - \rho)\rho^n = \frac{\rho}{1 - \rho}.$$ (11.18)

The corresponding variance of the number of jobs in the system is

$$\mathrm{Var}[n] = E[(n - E[n])^2] = E[n^2] - (E[n])^2$$

$$= \sum_{n=0}^{\infty} n^2(1 - \rho)\rho^n - \left(\sum_{n=0}^{\infty} n(1 - \rho)\rho^n\right)^2 = \frac{\rho}{(1 - \rho)^2}.$$ (11.19)

From Little's law, we know that the average number of jobs in the system is the product of the average response time of the system and the average arrival rate. This gives the average response time

$$r = \frac{E[n]}{\lambda} = \left(\frac{\rho}{1 - \rho}\right)\left(\frac{1}{\lambda}\right) = \frac{1}{\mu(1 - \rho)} = \frac{1}{\mu - \lambda}.$$ (11.20)

Since there is at most a single job being serviced at any time, the average number of jobs waiting in the queue can be found by calculating

$$q = \sum_{n=1}^{\infty}(n-1)P_n = E[n] - \rho = \frac{\rho^2}{1-\rho}. \tag{11.21}$$

The corresponding average time a job spends waiting in the queue can be found by recognizing that the average time a job spends in the system is simply the average response time, r. Then the average time a job spends waiting in the queue must be this total time in the system minus the average time the job is being serviced, which is $1/\mu$. Therefore, the average time spent waiting in the queue is

$$w = r - \frac{1}{\mu} = \frac{\rho}{\mu(1-\rho)}. \tag{11.22}$$

Finally, the probability of finding k or more jobs in the system can be found by summing the probabilities $P_k, P_{k+1}, P_{k+2}, \ldots$. This gives

$$\Pr(K \geq k) = \sum_{n=k}^{\infty} P_n = \sum_{n=k}^{\infty}(1-\rho)\rho^n = \rho^k \tag{11.23}$$

where K is the total number of jobs in the system.

Using these results, we can now make some general comments about the performance of any single-queue system. First, notice that the server is busy whenever one or more jobs are in the system. So the average utilization of the server, or, equivalently, its average load, is the probability of finding one or more jobs in the system. This is simply one minus the probability of finding no jobs in the system, giving

$$U = 1 - P_0 = 1 - (1-\rho) = \rho. \tag{11.24}$$

Notice that this result is the same as that which we derived in Equation (11.4) for the utilization law.

Figure 11.8 shows how the average number of jobs waiting in the queue (Equation (11.21)) changes as a function of the server utilization. The queue length increases slowly at first as the server utilization is increased. When the utilization reaches about 80% ($\rho = 0.8$), however, the queue length begins to increase sharply. As the server utilization continues to increase, the number of jobs waiting in the queue grows without bound. As can be seen from Equation (11.20), the response time will also become unbounded as the server utilization approaches 100%. To provide a good average response time, then, it is necessary to ensure that the server does not become loaded beyond about 70% of its maximum capacity.

Example. The time between requests to a Web server is measured and found to approximately follow an exponential distribution with a mean time between

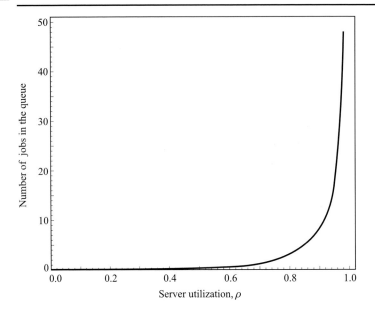

Figure 11.8 The average number of jobs waiting in the queue of an M/M/1 system increases nonlinearly as the server utilization, ρ, increases.

requests of 8 ms. The time required by the server to process each request was also found to roughly follow an exponential distribution with an average service time of approximately 5 ms.

(a) What is the average response time observed by the users making requests on this server?

The average request rate is one request per 8 ms, giving $\lambda = 0.125$ requests per millisecond. Each request requires 5 ms of processing time, so the average service rate is $\mu = 0.2$ jobs per millisecond. The server utilization is then found to be $\rho = 0.125/0.20 = 0.625$. Stated another way, the server is operating at an average of 62.5% of its maximum capacity. The average response time then is $R = 1/[\mu(1 - \rho)] = 1/[0.20(1 - 0.625)] = 13.33$ ms.

(b) How much faster must the server process requests to halve this average response time?

Assuming that the request rate remains constant, we wish to reduce the average response time to $13.33/2 = 6.67$ ms. We know that

$$R = \frac{1}{\mu(1 - \rho)} = \frac{1}{\mu - \lambda}. \tag{11.25}$$

By rearranging this expression, we find that we need an average service rate of $\mu = 1/R + \lambda = 1/6.67 + 0.125 = 0.275$ jobs per millisecond. This is $[(0.275 - 0.2)/0.2] \times 100\% = 37.5\%$ faster than the existing server. Thus, by increasing the performance of the server by 37.5%, we can cut the average response time in half.

(c) Approximately how many queue entries are necessary to buffer requests so that, on average, no more than one request per billion is lost?

We need to choose a value k such that the probability of finding k or more jobs in the system is no more than 10^{-9}. Using Equation (11.23), we have $\rho^k \leq 10^{-9}$. Solving for k with $\rho = 0.625$, we find

$$k \geq \frac{\ln 10^{-9}}{\ln 0.625} = 44.09. \qquad (11.26)$$

Thus, we need sufficient buffer space to store 45 or more requests waiting to be serviced. ◇

It is important to point out that the last result is only an approximation. We actually should use a slightly refined analysis that takes into account the effect of a finite queue size. However, the number of queue entries needed is substantially larger than the average queue size. Furthermore, the service times and the times between requests are only approximated by an exponential distribution, making the entire analysis only approximate. Even with these approximations, though, this estimate should be adequate for most purposes.

11.4.3 The single-queue, multiple-server (M/M/c) system

The generalization of the single-server M/M/1 model is a system consisting of c identical servers removing jobs from a single queue. This type of system would correspond to a symmetric multiprocessor system with c processors in which the processors obtain their work from a common task queue, for example. Just like in the single-server case, we assume that the job-arrival rate is λ and that there are n jobs in total in the system. This value of n again includes both jobs being processed by one of the servers and jobs waiting in the queue. We further assume that the service rate *for each server* is μ.

If all c servers are busy, the mean service rate for the overall system will be $c\mu$. That is, the system's service rate will be c times faster than that of a single server since all of the servers are identical. Note that this analysis implicitly assumes that there is no cost in determining which server will process the next job waiting at the head of the queue. If there are fewer than c jobs in the system, though, some of the servers will be idle. The system's average service rate then will be $n\mu$ where $n < c$ is the number of jobs in the system. The state-transition diagram corresponding to this situation is shown in Figure 11.9.

By writing the same type of balance equations as those we used in the previous section for the M/M/1 queue, it is straightforward to show that the probability of finding n jobs in the system is

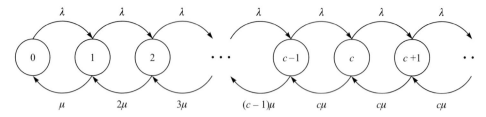

Figure 11.9 The state-transition diagram for an M/M/c queueing model.

$$P_n = \begin{cases} \dfrac{(c\rho)^n}{n!} P_0, & n = 1, 2, ..., c \\[2ex] \dfrac{(c\rho)^n}{c!c^{n-c}} P_0, & n > c. \end{cases} \qquad (11.27)$$

The total traffic intensity in this multiple-server environment is $\rho = \lambda/(c\mu)$ since each of the c servers can service requests at the rate μ. As before, ρ can also be interpreted as the utilization *of each server*.

Also as before, we can find P_0 by observing that the sum of all of the probabilities must be 1. That is,

$$\sum_{n=0}^{\infty} P_n = \sum_{n=0}^{c-1} \frac{(c\rho)^n}{n!} P_0 + \sum_{n=c}^{\infty} \frac{(c\rho)^n}{c!c^{n-c}} P_0 = 1. \qquad (11.28)$$

Solving for P_0 and simplifying the infinite sum, we obtain

$$P_0 = \frac{1}{\displaystyle\sum_{n=0}^{c-1} \frac{(c\rho)^n}{n!} + \frac{(c\rho)^c}{c!(1-\rho)}}. \qquad (11.29)$$

A newly arriving job will have to wait in the queue when all of the servers are busy. The probability of all servers being busy is simply the probability that there are c or more jobs in the system, which we denote $\Pr(K \geq c)$. This leads us to the following expression, which is known as *Erlang's C formula*:

$$\kappa = \Pr(K \geq c) = \sum_{n=c}^{\infty} P_n = P_0 \frac{(c\rho)^c}{c!} \sum_{n=c}^{\infty} \rho^{n-c} = \frac{(c\rho)^c}{c!(1-\rho)} P_0. \qquad (11.30)$$

The average total number of jobs in the system can again be found by computing the expected value of n, giving

$$E[n] = \sum_{n=0}^{\infty} n P_n = \frac{(c\rho)^c \rho P_0}{c!(1-\rho)^2} + c\rho = c\rho + \frac{\rho\kappa}{1-\rho}. \qquad (11.31)$$

Similarly, the average number of jobs waiting in the queue is

$$q = \sum_{n=c+1}^{\infty} (n-c)P_n = P_0 \frac{(c\rho)^c}{c!} \sum_{n=c+1}^{\infty} (n-c)\rho^{n-c} = \frac{\rho(c\rho)^c}{c!(1-\rho)^2} P_0 = \frac{\rho\kappa}{1-\rho}. \qquad (11.32)$$

Little's law again gives us the response time:

$$r = \frac{E[n]}{\lambda} = \frac{1}{\mu} + \frac{\kappa}{c\mu(1-\rho)}. \qquad (11.33)$$

It also can be used to find the average time jobs wait in the queue:

$$w = \frac{q}{\lambda} = \left(\frac{\rho\kappa}{1-\rho}\right)\left(\frac{1}{\lambda}\right) = \left(\frac{\kappa}{1-\rho}\right)\left(\frac{\lambda}{c\mu}\right)\left(\frac{1}{\lambda}\right) = \frac{\kappa}{c\mu(1-\rho)}. \qquad (11.34)$$

Example. How does the response time in the previous M/M/1 example change if the number of servers in the system is increased to four?

This new system can be modeled as an M/M/4 queueing system. With $\lambda = 0.125$ requests per millisecond and $\mu = 0.2$ jobs per millisecond, we calculate

$$\rho = \frac{\lambda}{c\mu} = \frac{0.125}{4 \times 0.2} = 0.1563. \qquad (11.35)$$

The probability of the system being idle is then found to be

$$P_0 = \frac{1}{\dfrac{(4 \times 0.1563)^0}{0!} + \dfrac{(4 \times 0.1563)^1}{1!} + \dfrac{(4 \times 0.1563)^2}{2!} + \dfrac{(4 \times 0.1563)^3}{3!} + \dfrac{(4 \times 0.1563)^4}{4!(1-0.1563)}}$$

$$= 0.5352. \qquad (11.36)$$

Erlang's C formula is used to find

$$\kappa = \frac{(4 \times 0.1563)^4}{4!(1-0.1563)}(0.5352) = 0.0040326. \qquad (11.37)$$

which leads to an average response time of

$$r = \frac{1}{\mu} + \frac{0.0040326}{4(0.2)(1-0.1563)} = 5.01 \text{ ms.} \qquad (11.38)$$

We can conclude, then, that increasing the number of servers by a factor of four will reduce the average response time by approximately 62% (from 13.33 to 5.01 ms).   ◇

11.5   Summary

The type of queueing analysis presented in this chapter is quite attractive to many computer-systems performance analysts. The analysis is built on a solid mathematical foundation, which gives it a sense of robustness and authority that is often felt to be lacking in a simulation or measurement-based analysis, for instance. The noise and uncertainty inherent in measurements of real systems, and the extensive assumptions necessary to make a simulation model tractable, can make conclusions based on these techniques seem somewhat tentative and 'soft.' Additionally, if you repeat a measurement experiment several times, you will most likely obtain different numerical values each time. This inconsistency can lead one to question the usefulness of the results. The results of a queueing analysis, though, are perfectly repeatable.

It is important to bear in mind, however, that the conclusions drawn from a queueing analysis must eventually be applied to a real system if they are to be of any use. The results of this analysis will be accurate only insofar as the assumptions made in the analysis match the system's characteristics. This means that, if the characteristics of the actual system only approximate some of the assumptions made in the queueing analysis, then the conclusions drawn from the analysis will (at best) only approximate what will happen in the actual system.

For example, the stochastic queueing analysis presented above assumes that both job arrivals and service times are Poisson processes. That is, both the interarrival times and the service times must be exponentially distributed. It is likely, however, that these times will be only approximated by an exponential distribution for an actual system. Furthermore, the analysis assumes that all job arrivals and service times are independent. However, it would not be unusual for jobs arriving at a system to be dependent on some dynamically varying system characteristic, such as the load on the servers. Users trying to access a Web server, for instance, will likely give up if the response time begins to increase beyond a certain threshold. This behavior will then cause the average queue length to decrease, which will subsequently cause an improvement in the average response time. This type of feedback is not considered in the queueing analysis presented here, though. Another assumption is that jobs always arrive one at a time. That is, they cannot arrive in batches. However, it is not at all unlikely that, in a real system, jobs will arrive in batches.

All of this is not to say that queueing analysis is a worthless tool, however. In fact, queueing analysis does provide a very flexible means for quickly obtaining useful insights into a system's overall behavior. It is important to be careful not to exceed its inherent limitations, though.

This chapter has focused on analyzing single-queue systems with infinite buffers (open systems), for which the interarrival and service times are assumed to be exponentially distributed and the service discipline was first come, first served. Beyond these fundamental results, there is an extensive body of literature presenting techniques for solving cases of interconnected networks of queues with a wide variety of arrival and service processes and service disciplines. These include such techniques as mean-value analysis, decomposition, convolution, and generating functions for analyzing resource contention in queueing networks. Petri nets are another analytical tool for taking into account synchronization between jobs. The reader interested in these more advanced techniques is referred to the following texts.

11.6   For further reading

- The classic texts in queueing analysis are
  L. Kleinrock, *Queueing Systems, Volume 1: Theory*, John Wiley, New York, 1975, and
  L. Kleinrock, *Queueing Systems, Volume 2: Computer Applications*, John Wiley, New York, 1976.
- Another good introductory text is
  E. D. Lazowska, J. Zahorjan, G. S. Graham, and K. C. Sivcik, *Quantitative System Performance – Computer System Analysis Using Queueing Network Models*, Prentice-Hall, Englewood Cliffs, NJ, 1984.
- The following texts provide more in-depth mathematical developments of some advanced topics in queueing analysis:
  S. M. Ross, *Stochastic Processes*, John Wiley, New York, 1983,
  E. Gelenbe and I. Mitrani, *Analysis and Synthesis of Computer Systems*, Academic Press, New York, 1980,
  K. Kant, *Introduction to Computer System Performance Evaluation*, McGraw-Hill, New York, 1992,
  S. S. Lavenberg (ed.), *Computer Performance Modeling Handbook*, Academic Press, New York, 1983, and
  Gunter Bolch, Stefan Greiner, Hermann de Meer, and Kishor S. Trivedi, *Queuing Networks and Markov Chains: Modeling and Performance Evaluation with Computer Science Applications*, John Wiley, New York, 1998.

11.7   Exercises

1. If the average time required to service each request to a network interface is 250 μs, what is the maximum possible request rate it can handle?
2. What is the utilization of the network interface in the previous problem if the request rate is one-half of the maximum rate calculated in the previous problem?

3. If the average response time of a time-shared system is 60 ms, what is the maximum average arrival rate that can be tolerated to ensure that no more than 100 jobs on average are in the system at any time?

4. Determine whether it is better on average to maintain a separate queue for each of several identical servers, or whether it is better to maintain a single queue that is shared among all of the servers. *Hint:* if the single-queue, multiple-server (M/M/c) configuration has an arrival rate of λ, the multiple-separate-queue configuration can be modeled as c M/M/1 queues that each have an arrival rate of λ/c.

5. Compare a computer system with a single powerful processor with a multi-processor system with c processors, each of which can service jobs at $1/c$ the rate of the single-processor system.

6. Determine the average response time of a single-server system in which the mean time between arrivals of jobs is 230 µs and the mean time required to service a job is 52 µs.

7. How many additional identical servers would have to be added to the system in the previous problem to reduce its average response time by a factor of ten?

8. If five additional servers are added to the system in the previous problem, how many additional job requests can be handled while still maintaining the same average response time as that of the single-server configuration?

Appendix A Glossary

"What is another word for thesaurus?"

Unknown

Accuracy. The absolute difference between a measured value and the corresponding reference value.

Analysis of variance (ANOVA). A general statistical technique used to separate the total variation observed in a set of measurements into the variation due to measurement error within each alternative and the variation across alternatives.

Basic block. A sequence of instructions in a program that has no branches into or out of the sequence. Thus, it is ensured that the sequence will execute as an indivisible unit.

Benchmark program. Any program that is used to measure the performance of a computer system.

Coefficient of determination. A value between 0 and 1 that indicates the fraction of the total variation explained by a linear-regression model. It is the square of the correlation coefficient.

Coefficient of variation (COV). The ratio of the sample's standard deviation to the corresponding mean of the sample. It provides a dimensionless value that compares the relative size of the variation in a set of measurements with the mean value of those measurements.

Confidence level. The probability that a confidence interval actually contains the real mean.

Contrast. A linear combination of the effects, α_j, of the alternatives: $c = \sum_{j=1}^{k} w_j \alpha_j$. The weights in this linear combination must be chosen such that $\sum_{j=1}^{k} w_j = 0$. A contrast is typically used to separate the effects of two alternatives.

Correlation coefficient. A value between -1 and $+1$ that indicates the nature of the linear relationship between the input and output variables in a linear-regression model. It is the square root of the coefficient of determination, although the sign must be determined through a separate calculation.

Density function. The derivative of the distribution function.

Distribution function. A function that provides the probability that a random variable will be less than or equal to a given value x.

Emulator. A program that makes a computer system appear to be a different type of system.

Factors. The input variables of an experiment that can be controlled or changed by the experimenter.

Interaction. When the effect of one factor depends on the level of another factor.

Levels. The specific values to which the factors of an experiment may be set.

Mean square. The sum of squares of a component term (i.e. the total variation of the component term) divided by the number of degrees of freedom of that component term.

Mean-square error. The sum of squares of the error term divided by the corresponding number of degrees of freedom.

Median. The middle value in a set of measurements. If there is an even number of values, the median is the mean of the middle two values.

Mode. The value that occurs most frequently.

Normalize. To convert values to a common basis for comparison.

Operational analysis. Uses direct measurements of the characteristics of a system being studied.

Outlier. A measured value that is significantly different than the other values in a set of measurements.

Perturbation. The changes in a system's behavior caused by measuring some aspect of its performance.

Precision. The amount of scatter in a set of measurements. Corresponds to the repeatability of the measurements.

Profile. An aggregate characterization of the overall behavior of an application program or of an entire system.

Quantization error. A random error introduced into a measurement due to the finite resolution of the measuring tool.

Random errors. Errors in measurements that are completely unpredictable, nondeterministic, and perhaps not controllable. They are unbiased in that a random error has an equal probability of either increasing or decreasing a measurement.

Range. The difference between the largest and smallest values in a set of measurements.

Regression. A mathematical model derived from measured values.

Replication. A complete repetition of an experiment performed with exactly the same experimental configuration as that in a previous run of the experiment.

Resolution. The smallest incremental change that can be detected and displayed by a measuring tool.

Response time. The time measured from when a request is submitted until the system has returned a response.

Response variable. The output value of a system that is measured as the input values are changed. A common response variable is the total execution time.

Service discipline. The order in which jobs are removed from the queue and passed to a server.

Significance level. The probability, typically denoted α, that a confidence interval does *not* contain the actual mean.

Simulator. A program that models the internal operation of a system in order to allow its performance to be studied.

Standard deviation. The square root of the variance.

Stochastic. Involving a random or unpredictable element.

Systematic error. Errors in measurements that are the result of some experimental "mistake," such as a change in the experimental environment or an incorrect procedure, that introduces a constant or slowly changing bias into the measurements.

Throughput. The rate at which a system can process a given computation. Typically measured in instructions executed per second, jobs completed per second, etc.

Trace. A time-ordered sequence of events.

Utilization. A number between 0 and 1 showing the average fraction of the total time that a system is busy.

Validation. Determining how close the results of a simulation are to what would be produced by an actual system.

Variance. A common index of dispersion for a set of measurements.

Verification. Determining whether a simulation model is implemented correctly.

Appendix B Some useful probability distributions

Several different distributions are commonly encountered in computer-systems performance analysis. These distributions may be used for generating a sequence of random values to drive a simulator, for instance. It also is not unusual to try to determine whether a set of measured values appears to come from one of these standard distributions. This comparison of measured values with a given distribution is commonly performed using a chi-squared test, as described in Section 10.4.4.

In addition to providing the typical information about each distribution, including the density function, $f(x)$, the mean, μ, and the variance, σ^2, some intuition about the distribution is also given. When it is appropriate, this intuition is based around an example random process in which we have a barrel containing an effectively infinite number of links of a chain. Some fraction p of these links are good, while $1 - p$ of them are defective. A brief description of how to generate a sequence of random values that appears to follow the distribution is also given.

B.1 The Bernoulli distribution

Intuition. The possible outcomes of a Bernoulli distribution are 0 and 1. In our example process, a Bernoulli distribution corresponds to the probability of a randomly selected link from the barrel being good. Or, equivalently, it is the number of good links in a sample size of 1.

Density function.

$$f(x) = p^x (1-p)^{1-x}, \qquad x = 0, 1. \tag{B.1}$$

Mean. $\mu = p$.

Variance. $\sigma^2 = p(1 - p)$.

Random-number generation. Generate $u = unif(0, 1)$. If $u \le p$ return 1. Otherwise, return 0.

B.2   The binomial distribution

Intuition. The binomial distribution has two parameters, n and p. The probability of success in a single trial is p, with $0 < p < 1$, and $n = 1, 2, 3, \ldots$ is the number of trials. The outcome x corresponds to the number of successes out of n trials. In our example process, the number of successes is the number of good links out of n selected from the barrel.

Density function.

$$f(x) = \binom{n}{x} p^x (1 - p)^{n-x}, \qquad x = 0, 1, 2, \ldots, n; \qquad 0 < p < 1. \tag{B.2}$$

Mean. $\mu = np$.

Variance. $\sigma^2 = np(1 - p)$.

Random-number generation. As can be seen in the density function $f(x)$, the binomial distribution is the sum of n independent Bernoulli distributions. Thus, to generate a $binomial(n, p)$ sample, simply count the number of $unif(0, 1)$ samples out of n that are less than or equal to p.

B.3   The geometric distribution

Intuition. If the probability of success in a single trial is p, the outcome x of a geometric distribution with parameter p is the number of trials that are successful, up to and including the first failure. In our example process, this corresponds to the number of links removed from the barrel that are good, up to and including the first bad link. Since an infinite number of links could be good, $x = 1, 2, 3, \ldots$. In the following density function, note that p^{x-1} is the probability of drawing x good links in a row, while $1 - p$ is the probability that link x is bad.

Density function.

$$f(x) = p^{x-1}(1 - p), \qquad x = 1, 2, 3, \ldots \tag{B.3}$$

Mean. $\mu = 1/(1 - p)$.

Variance. $\sigma^2 = p/(1 - p)^2$.

Random-number generation. The simplest method of generating geometric samples uses the inverse-transform method. First, generate $u = unif(0, 1)$. Then return the value $x = \lceil \ln u / \ln(1 - p) \rceil$. Of course, the value $\ln(1 - p)$ needs to be calculated only once and stored in a temporary variable for use in subsequent computations.

B.4 The discrete uniform distribution

Intuition. If n good links are removed from the barrel and exactly one of them is bad, the outcome x of the discrete uniform distribution is the location of the bad link. All outcomes (i.e. locations) are equally likely, so the probability of any given location being bad is $1/n$.

Density function. Given a range of possible outcomes $[a, b]$,

$$f(x) = \frac{1}{b-a+1}, \qquad x = a, a+1, a+2, \ldots, b. \tag{B.4}$$

Mean. $\mu = (b+a)/2$.

Variance. $\sigma^2 = (b-a+1)^2/12 - 1$.

Random-number generation. Generate $u = unif(0, 1)$. Then, using the inverse-transformation method, return $x = a + \lfloor(b-a+1)u\rfloor$.

B.5 The continuous uniform distribution

Intuition. This is the continuous equivalent of the discrete uniform distribution. It is often used when no information about the distribution is known, other than its bounds and the fact that it is continuous.

Density function.

$$f(x) = \frac{1}{b-a}, \qquad a \le x \le b. \tag{B.5}$$

Mean. $\mu = (b+a)/2$.

Variance. $\sigma^2 = (b-a)^2/12$.

Random-number generation. We again can use the inverse-transformation method to generate a sample from this distribution. First, generate $u = unif(0, 1)$. Then return $x = a + (b-a)u$.

B.6 The Poisson distribution

Intuition. The Poisson distribution is the limiting form of the binomial distribution as n becomes very large with np fixed. It is often used to model the number of events that occur within a given interval. It is closely related to the exponential distribution in that, if the time between events follows an exponential distribution, the number of events that occur within a given interval follows a Poisson distribution.

Density function. The probability of exactly x events occurring is

$$f(x) = \frac{\lambda^x e^{-\lambda}}{x!}, \qquad x = 0, 1, 2, \ldots \tag{B.6}$$

where λ is the mean number of events that occur within the specified interval.

Mean. $\mu = \lambda$.

Variance. $\sigma^2 = \lambda$.

Random-number generation. One sample from a Poisson distribution is the number of samples from an exponential distribution with mean $\beta = 1$ that must be added together to exceed the value λ. This gives the following algorithm:

```
sum = 0, i = -1
while (sum <= lambda)
      y = unif(0,1)
      z = - ln (y)
      sum = sum + z
      i = i + 1
endwhile
return(i)
```

B.7   The exponential distribution

Intuition. The exponential distribution is the continuous approximation of the geometric distribution. The continuous analog using our example process occurs as the links in the chain blend into a continuous cable. The outcome x of the exponential distribution then is the distance to the first defect in the cable. The exponential distribution is often used to model the time between successive events, or the time required to service an event.

The Poisson and exponential distributions are related in that, if the times (or distances, or some other appropriate continuous value) between events are independent with an exponential distribution with mean $\mu = \beta$, then the number of events within time T is Poisson distributed with $\mu = \lambda = T/\beta$.

The exponential distribution has the interesting property of being *memoryless*. That is, knowing the time that the last event occurred is in no way helpful in predicting when the next event may occur. For example, assume that the times between events in a system follow an exponential distribution with mean $\mu = \beta$. If it has been β time units since the last event occurred, we may intuitively think that the next event is likely to occur 'soon.' However, even though we know that the last event occurred β time units in the past, the mean time to wait for the next event is still β. In fact, no matter how long we have been waiting, the mean time that we must still wait for the next event is always β! (The proof of this can be found in almost any textbook on probability and statistics.)

This property of memorylessness leads to some useful simplifications in the study of queueing systems, as discussed in Section 11.4. Thus, it is very common to assume that the interarrival times of events in a computer system follow an exponential distribution.

Density function.

$$f(x) = \frac{1}{\beta} e^{-x/\beta}, \qquad x \geq 0 \tag{B.7}$$

Mean. $\mu = \beta$.

Variance. $\sigma^2 = \beta^2$.

Random-number generation. Samples from the exponential distribution can be generated using the inverse-transform method. The value to be returned is simply $x = -\beta \ln u$, where $u = unif(0, 1)$. See Section 10.3.2 for more details.

B.8   The Gaussian (normal) distribution

Intuition. The Gaussian distribution is the classical *bell-shaped curve*. It is symmetric around the mean, μ, and its width is determined by the variance, σ^2. The Gaussian distribution is also called the *normal* distribution. The *standard normal* or *unit normal* distribution is simply a Gaussian distribution with mean $\mu = 0$ and variance $\sigma^2 = 1$.

Density function.

$$f(x) = \frac{1}{\sigma\sqrt{2\pi}} e^{-(x-\mu)^2/(2\sigma^2)}, \qquad -\infty \leq x \leq \infty. \tag{B.8}$$

Mean. μ.

Variance. $\sigma^2 > 0$.

Random-number generation.

Method 1. A generalization of the inverse-transformation method to two dimensions, known as the *Box–Muller* method, allows the generation of two samples at a time from a Gaussian distribution. The procedure begins with the generation of two samples $u_1 = unif(0, 1)$ and $u_2 = unif(0, 1)$. Then the two values to return are

$$x_1 = \mu + \sigma \cos(2\pi u_1)\sqrt{-2 \ln u_2} \tag{B.9}$$

$$x_2 = \mu + \sigma \sin(2\pi u_1)\sqrt{-2 \ln u_2} \tag{B.10}$$

Method 2. The Box–Muller method effectively picks two samples from the unit square. If we instead pick a random point from inside the unit circle using the accept–reject method, we can eliminate the need for the trigonometric functions. This approach essentially converts the problem to be solved into an equivalent representation using polar coordinates. The procedure in this case is to first generate two random samples $u_1 = unif(0, 1)$ and $u_2 = unif(0, 1)$, and then compute $v_1 = 2u_1 - 1$ and $v_2 = 2u_2 - 1$. This generates a point (v_1, v_2) within the square bounded by $-1 \le x \le 1$ and $-1 \le y \le 1$. If $r = v_1^2 + v_2^2 \ge 1$, then the point is outside the unit circle, so reject u_1 and u_2 and begin the process all over again. Otherwise, return the values $x_1 = \mu + \sigma v_1 t$ and $x_2 = \mu + \sigma v_2 t$, where $t = \sqrt{-2 \ln r / r}$. The values x_1 and x_2 are two independent samples from the Gaussian distribution with mean μ and variance σ^2.

B.9 The Erlang distribution

Intuition. The Erlang distribution can be thought of as a generalization of the exponential distribution. For this distribution two parameters have to be specified, namely a, which is called the scale parameter, and m, which is the shape parameter. These parameters are constrained such that $a > 0$ and and m is a positive integer.

Density function.

$$f(x) = \frac{x^{m-1}e^{-x/a}}{(m-1)!a^m}, \qquad 0 \le x \le \infty \tag{B.11}$$

Mean. am.

Variance. $a^2 m$.

Random-number generation. Samples from an Erlang (a, m) distribution are easily generated using the convolution technique. Begin by generating m values, $u_1, u_2, \ldots, u_m$, that are $unif(0, 1)$. Then return the value

$$x = -a \ln(u_1 \times u_2 \times \cdots \times u_m). \tag{B.12}$$

B.10 The Pareto distribution

Intuition. The Pareto distribution is a generalized power function. It has a single shape parameter, a. Given a set of observations $\{x_1, x_2, \ldots, x_n\}$, it can be shown that, if the observations follow a power relationship, the value of this shape parameter that best fits these data is

$$a = \frac{n}{\sum_{i=1}^{n} \ln x_i}.$$ (B.13)

Density function.

$$f(x) = ax^{-(a+1)}.$$ (B.14)

Mean. $a/(a-1)$, for $a > 1$
Variance. $a/[(a-1)^2(a-2)]$, for $a > 2$.
Random-number generation. The inverse-transform method can be used to generate a sample from a Pareto distribution by computing $x = 1/u^{1/a}$, where u is a $unif(0, 1)$ sample.

B.11   For further reading

- If your recollection of basic probability is a little rusty, the following text provides a nice review:

    David Applebaum, *Probability and Information: An Integrated Approach*, Cambridge University Press, Cambridge, 1996.

Appendix C Selected statistical tables

'There are three types of mathematicians. Those who can count, and those who cannot.'

Robert Arthur

C.1 Critical values of Student's *t* distribution

The derivation of the *t* distribution was first published by W. S. Gosset in 1908. Gosset was employed by an Irish brewery that did not allow its employees to publish the results of their research. Gosset instead published his work using the pseudonym 'Student.' Consequently, the *t* distribution is often referred to as *Student's t distribution.*

The *t* distribution is commonly used for calculating confidence intervals. It is bell-shaped and symmetric around a mean of zero, similar to the Gaussian (normal) distribution. The *t* distribution has a higher variance than a Gaussian distribution, making it appear flatter and more spread out. As the number of degrees of freedom in the *t* distribution becomes very large, it is well approximated by a Gaussian distribution with a mean of 0 and a variance of 1, that is, the so-called 'standard normal distribution.' Consequently, the last line in the following table shows the critical values for a standard normal distribution.

The values shown in the following table are the critical values of the *t* distribution. Each $t_{a;n}$ value in the table is the value on the *x* axis for which there is an area of a to the left of $t_{a;n}$, as shown in Figure C.1, where n is the number of degrees of freedom. For example, say you want to find the *t* value necessary to compute a 95% confidence interval with eight degrees of freedom. The corresponding significance level is $\alpha = 1 - 0.95 = 0.05$. Since the distribution is symmetric around zero, but the table shows the area to the left of $t_{a;n}$, we must use $1 - \alpha/2 = 1 - 0.05/2 = 0.975$ as the area a for finding the critical *t* value. The necessary value from the table is then $t_{0.975;8} = 2.306$.

Critical values of the t distribution

n	0.7000	0.8000	0.9000	a 0.9500	0.9750	0.9950	0.9995
1	0.727	1.376	3.078	6.314	12.706	63.657	636.619
2	0.617	1.061	1.886	2.920	4.303	9.925	31.599
3	0.584	0.979	1.638	2.354	3.183	5.841	12.924
4	0.569	0.941	1.533	2.132	2.777	4.604	8.610
5	0.559	0.920	1.476	2.015	2.571	4.032	6.869
6	0.553	0.906	1.440	1.943	2.447	3.708	5.959
7	0.549	0.896	1.415	1.895	2.365	3.500	5.408
8	0.546	0.889	1.397	1.860	2.306	3.356	5.041
9	0.544	0.883	1.383	1.833	2.262	3.250	4.781
10	0.542	0.879	1.372	1.813	2.228	3.169	4.587
11	0.540	0.876	1.363	1.796	2.201	3.106	4.437
12	0.539	0.873	1.356	1.782	2.179	3.055	4.318
13	0.538	0.870	1.350	1.771	2.161	3.012	4.221
14	0.537	0.868	1.345	1.761	2.145	2.977	4.141
15	0.536	0.866	1.341	1.753	2.132	2.947	4.073
16	0.535	0.865	1.337	1.746	2.120	2.921	4.015
17	0.534	0.863	1.333	1.740	2.110	2.898	3.965
18	0.534	0.862	1.330	1.734	2.101	2.879	3.922
19	0.533	0.861	1.328	1.729	2.093	2.861	3.884
20	0.533	0.860	1.325	1.725	2.086	2.845	3.850
21	0.533	0.859	1.323	1.721	2.080	2.832	3.819
22	0.532	0.858	1.321	1.717	2.074	2.819	3.792
23	0.532	0.858	1.320	1.714	2.069	2.807	3.768
24	0.531	0.857	1.318	1.711	2.064	2.797	3.746
25	0.531	0.856	1.316	1.708	2.060	2.788	3.725
26	0.531	0.856	1.315	1.706	2.056	2.779	3.707
27	0.531	0.855	1.314	1.703	2.052	2.771	3.690
28	0.530	0.855	1.313	1.701	2.048	2.763	3.674
29	0.530	0.854	1.311	1.699	2.045	2.757	3.660
30	0.530	0.854	1.310	1.697	2.042	2.750	3.646
40	0.529	0.851	1.303	1.684	2.021	2.705	3.551
50	0.528	0.849	1.299	1.676	2.009	2.678	3.496
60	0.527	0.848	1.296	1.671	2.000	2.660	3.460
70	0.527	0.847	1.294	1.667	1.994	2.648	3.435
80	0.527	0.846	1.292	1.664	1.990	2.639	3.416
90	0.526	0.846	1.291	1.662	1.987	2.632	3.402
100	0.526	0.845	1.290	1.660	1.984	2.626	3.391
110	0.526	0.845	1.289	1.659	1.982	2.621	3.381
120	0.526	0.845	1.289	1.658	1.980	2.618	3.374
130	0.526	0.844	1.288	1.657	1.978	2.614	3.367
140	0.526	0.844	1.288	1.656	1.977	2.612	3.362
150	0.526	0.844	1.287	1.655	1.976	2.609	3.357
∞	0.524	0.842	1.282	1.645	1.960	2.576	3.291

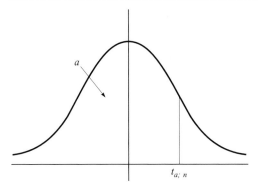

Figure C.1 Each $t_{a;n}$ value in the t table is the value on the x axis for which there is an area of a to the left of $t_{a;n}$.

C.2   Critical values of the *F* distribution

The *F*-test is used to determine whether two variances are significantly different. The *F statistic* is the ratio of the two variances, s_1^2 and s_2^2:

$$F_{\text{calculated}} = \frac{s_1^2}{s_2^2}.$$ (C.1)

where variance s_1^2 has n_1 degrees of freedom and variance s_2^2 has n_2 degrees of freedom. If $F_{\text{calculated}}$ is larger than the critical value obtained from one of the following tables, we can conclude, with the confidence level shown for the table used, that there is a statistically significant difference between the variances.

For example, given $s_1^2 = 23.12$ and $s_2^2 = 3.44$ with $n_1 = 4$ and $n_2 = 20$, we find $F_{\text{calculated}} = 23.12/3.44 = 6.72$. The critical value from the 90% confidence-level F distribution table is $F_{0.90;4,20} = 2.249$. Since $F_{\text{calculated}} > F_{0.90;4,20}$, we conclude with 90% confidence that there is a statistically significant difference between the variances.

Critical values of the F distribution for a 90% confidence level

| | n_1 | | | | | | |
n_2	1	2	3	4	5	6	10
1	39.863	49.500	53.593	55.833	57.240	58.204	60.195
2	8.526	9.000	9.162	9.243	9.293	9.326	9.392
3	5.538	5.462	5.391	5.343	5.309	5.285	5.230
4	4.545	4.325	4.191	4.107	4.051	4.010	3.920
5	4.060	3.780	3.619	3.520	3.453	3.405	3.297
6	3.776	3.463	3.289	3.181	3.108	3.055	2.937
10	3.285	2.924	2.728	2.605	2.522	2.461	2.323
20	2.975	2.589	2.380	2.249	2.158	2.091	1.937
40	2.835	2.440	2.226	2.091	1.997	1.927	1.763
60	2.791	2.393	2.177	2.041	1.946	1.875	1.707
80	2.769	2.370	2.154	2.016	1.921	1.849	1.680
100	2.756	2.356	2.139	2.002	1.906	1.834	1.663
200	2.731	2.329	2.111	1.973	1.876	1.804	1.631
500	2.716	2.313	2.095	1.956	1.859	1.786	1.612

| | n_1 | | | | | | |
n_2	20	40	60	80	100	200	500
1	61.740	62.529	62.794	62.927	63.007	63.167	63.264
2	9.441	9.466	9.475	9.479	9.481	9.486	9.489
3	5.184	5.160	5.151	5.147	5.144	5.139	5.136
4	3.844	3.804	3.790	3.782	3.778	3.769	3.764
5	3.207	3.157	3.140	3.132	3.126	3.116	3.109
6	2.836	2.781	2.762	2.752	2.746	2.734	2.727
10	2.201	2.132	2.107	2.095	2.087	2.071	2.062
20	1.794	1.708	1.677	1.660	1.650	1.629	1.616
40	1.605	1.506	1.467	1.447	1.434	1.406	1.389
60	1.543	1.437	1.395	1.372	1.358	1.326	1.306
80	1.513	1.403	1.358	1.334	1.318	1.284	1.261
100	1.494	1.382	1.336	1.310	1.293	1.257	1.232
200	1.458	1.339	1.289	1.261	1.242	1.199	1.168
500	1.435	1.313	1.260	1.229	1.209	1.160	1.122

Critical values of the F distribution for a 95% confidence level

n_2	n_1						
	1	2	3	4	5	6	10
1	161.448	199.500	215.707	224.583	230.162	233.986	241.882
2	18.513	19.000	19.164	19.247	19.296	19.330	19.396
3	10.128	9.552	9.277	9.117	9.013	8.941	8.786
4	7.709	6.944	6.591	6.388	6.256	6.163	5.964
5	6.608	5.786	5.409	5.192	5.050	4.950	4.735
6	5.987	5.143	4.757	4.534	4.387	4.284	4.060
10	4.965	4.103	3.708	3.478	3.326	3.217	2.978
20	4.351	3.493	3.098	2.866	2.711	2.599	2.348
40	4.085	3.232	2.839	2.606	2.449	2.336	2.077
60	4.001	3.150	2.758	2.525	2.368	2.254	1.993
80	3.960	3.111	2.719	2.486	2.329	2.214	1.951
100	3.936	3.087	2.696	2.463	2.305	2.191	1.927
200	3.888	3.041	2.650	2.417	2.259	2.144	1.878
500	3.860	3.014	2.623	2.390	2.232	2.117	1.850

n_2	n_1						
	20	40	60	80	100	200	500
1	248.013	251.143	252.196	252.724	253.041	253.677	254.059
2	19.446	19.471	19.479	19.483	19.486	19.491	19.494
3	8.660	8.594	8.572	8.561	8.554	8.540	8.532
4	5.803	5.717	5.688	5.673	5.664	5.646	5.635
5	4.558	4.464	4.431	4.415	4.405	4.385	4.373
6	3.874	3.774	3.740	3.722	3.712	3.690	3.678
10	2.774	2.661	2.621	2.601	2.588	2.563	2.548
20	2.124	1.994	1.946	1.922	1.907	1.875	1.856
40	1.839	1.693	1.637	1.608	1.589	1.551	1.526
60	1.748	1.594	1.534	1.502	1.481	1.438	1.409
80	1.703	1.545	1.482	1.448	1.426	1.379	1.347
100	1.676	1.515	1.450	1.415	1.392	1.342	1.308
200	1.623	1.455	1.386	1.346	1.321	1.263	1.221
500	1.592	1.419	1.345	1.303	1.275	1.210	1.159

Critical values of the F distribution for a 99% confidence level

n_2	n_1						
	1	2	3	4	5	6	10
1	4,052.181	4,999.500	5,403.352	5,624.583	5,763.650	5,858.986	6,055.847
2	98.503	99.000	99.166	99.249	99.299	99.333	99.399
3	34.116	30.817	29.457	28.710	28.237	27.911	27.229
4	21.198	18.000	16.694	15.977	15.522	15.207	14.546
5	16.258	13.274	12.060	11.392	10.967	10.672	10.051
6	13.745	10.925	9.780	9.148	8.746	8.466	7.874
10	10.044	7.559	6.552	5.994	5.636	5.386	4.849
20	8.096	5.849	4.938	4.431	4.103	3.871	3.368
40	7.314	5.179	4.313	3.828	3.514	3.291	2.801
60	7.077	4.977	4.126	3.649	3.339	3.119	2.632
80	6.963	4.881	4.036	3.563	3.255	3.036	2.551
100	6.895	4.824	3.984	3.513	3.206	2.988	2.503
200	6.763	4.713	3.881	3.414	3.110	2.893	2.411
500	6.686	4.648	3.821	3.357	3.054	2.838	2.356

n_2	n_1						
	20	40	60	80	100	200	500
1	6,208.730	6,286.782	6,313.030	6,326.197	6,334.110	6,349.967	6,359.501
2	99.449	99.474	99.482	99.487	99.489	99.494	99.497
3	26.690	26.411	26.316	26.269	26.240	26.183	26.148
4	14.020	13.745	13.652	13.605	13.577	13.520	13.486
5	9.553	9.291	9.202	9.157	9.130	9.075	9.042
6	7.396	7.143	7.057	7.013	6.987	6.934	6.902
10	4.405	4.165	4.082	4.039	4.014	3.962	3.930
20	2.938	2.695	2.608	2.563	2.535	2.479	2.445
40	2.369	2.114	2.019	1.969	1.938	1.874	1.833
60	2.198	1.936	1.836	1.783	1.749	1.678	1.633
80	2.115	1.849	1.746	1.690	1.655	1.579	1.530
100	2.067	1.797	1.692	1.634	1.598	1.518	1.466
200	1.971	1.694	1.583	1.521	1.481	1.391	1.328
500	1.915	1.633	1.517	1.452	1.408	1.308	1.232

C.3   Critical values of the chi-squared distribution

The *chi-squared* statistic for a given collection of measurements is calculated as follows:

$$\chi^2_{m-1} = \sum_{i=1}^{m} \frac{(O_i - P_i)^2}{P_i} \tag{C.2}$$

where P_i is the predicted number of outcomes in histogram cell i, O_i is the number actually observed in cell i, and m is the total number of histogram cells.

The critical values in the following table show the probability that a chi-squared statistic with the given number of degrees of freedom could have a value as large as that shown in the table due to random fluctuations. Thus, if the calculated statistic χ^2_{m-1} is smaller than the value obtained from the table, we can conclude, with the given level of confidence, that there is no evidence to lead us to believe that the observed values do not come from the expected distribution.

For example, we calculate the chi-squared statistic for a series of observations with 17 histogram cells to be $\chi^2_{16} = 19.8$. Looking at the 0.90 column in the table, we find the maximum allowed value of the chi-squared statistic with 16 degrees of freedom to be 23.542. Since our calculated value is smaller than this critical value, we conclude with 90% confidence that there is no reason to suspect that the observed values do not come from the expected distribution.

Note that the chi-squared test works best when the size of the cells is adjusted so that the predicted number of outcomes in each cell is approximately the same. Also, for the approximations used in deriving the chi-squared test to hold, the predicted number of outcomes in each cell must be larger than five or six. See Section 10.4.4 for more details.

Critical values of the chi-squared distribution

				a			
n	0.5000	0.7500	0.8000	0.9000	0.9500	0.9900	0.9950
1	0.455	1.323	1.642	2.706	3.842	6.635	7.879
2	1.386	2.773	3.219	4.605	5.992	9.210	10.597
3	2.366	4.108	4.642	6.251	7.815	11.345	12.838
4	3.357	5.385	5.989	7.779	9.488	13.277	14.860
5	4.352	6.626	7.289	9.236	11.071	15.086	16.750
6	5.348	7.841	8.558	10.645	12.592	16.812	18.548
7	6.346	9.037	9.803	12.017	14.067	18.475	20.278
8	7.344	10.219	11.030	13.362	15.507	20.090	21.955
9	8.343	11.389	12.242	14.684	16.919	21.666	23.589
10	9.342	12.549	13.442	15.987	18.307	23.209	25.188
11	10.341	13.701	14.631	17.275	19.675	24.725	26.757
12	11.340	14.845	15.812	18.549	21.026	26.217	28.300
13	12.340	15.984	16.985	19.812	22.362	27.688	29.820
14	13.339	17.117	18.151	21.064	23.685	29.141	31.319
15	14.339	18.245	19.311	22.307	24.996	30.578	32.801
16	15.339	19.369	20.465	23.542	26.296	32.000	34.267
17	16.338	20.489	21.615	24.769	27.587	33.409	35.719
18	17.338	21.605	22.760	25.989	28.869	34.805	37.157
19	18.338	22.718	23.900	27.204	30.144	36.191	38.582
20	19.337	23.828	25.038	28.412	31.410	37.566	39.997
21	20.337	24.935	26.171	29.615	32.671	38.932	41.401
22	21.337	26.039	27.302	30.813	33.925	40.290	42.796
23	22.337	27.141	28.429	32.007	35.173	41.639	44.181
24	23.337	28.241	29.553	33.196	36.415	42.980	45.559
25	24.337	29.339	30.675	34.382	37.653	44.314	46.928
26	25.337	30.435	31.795	35.563	38.885	45.642	48.290
27	26.336	31.528	32.912	36.741	40.113	46.963	49.645
28	27.336	32.621	34.027	37.916	41.337	48.278	50.994
29	28.336	33.711	35.140	39.088	42.557	49.588	52.336
30	29.336	34.800	36.250	40.256	43.773	50.892	53.672
40	39.335	45.616	47.269	51.805	55.759	63.691	66.766
50	49.335	56.334	58.164	63.167	67.505	76.154	79.490
60	59.335	66.982	68.972	74.397	79.082	88.380	91.952
70	69.335	77.577	79.715	85.527	90.531	100.425	104.215
80	79.334	88.130	90.405	96.578	101.880	112.329	116.321
90	89.334	98.650	101.054	107.565	113.145	124.116	128.299
100	99.334	109.141	111.667	118.498	124.342	135.807	140.170
110	109.334	119.609	122.250	129.385	135.480	147.414	151.949
120	119.334	130.055	132.806	140.233	146.568	158.950	163.648
130	129.334	140.483	143.340	151.045	157.610	170.423	175.278
140	139.334	150.894	153.854	161.827	168.613	181.840	186.847
150	149.334	161.291	164.349	172.581	179.581	193.208	198.360

C.4 For further reading

- The tables in this appendix were calculated using extensions of the computer programs described in

  William H. Press, Saul A. Teukolsky, William T. Vetterling, and Brian P. Flannery, *Numerical Recipes in C* (Second Edition), Cambridge University Press, New York, 1992.

Index